CHARLOTTE AND EMILY BRONTË

GARLAND REFERENCE LIBRARY
OF THE HUMANITIES
(VOL. 167)

CHARLOTTE AND EMILY BRONTË

An Annotated Bibliography

Anne Passel
California State College, Bakersfield

GARLAND PUBLISHING, INC. • NEW YORK & LONDON
1979

PR
4168
P37

Library of Congress Cataloging in Publication Data

Passel, Anne.
Charlotte and Emily Brontë, an annotated bibliography.

(Garland reference library of the humanities ; v. 167)
Includes indexes.
1. Brontë, Charlotte, 1816–1855—Bibliography. 2. Brontë,
Emily Jane, 1818–1848—Bibliography. I. Title.
Z8122.P37 [PR4168]   016.823′8   78-68259
ISBN 0-8240-9770-X

Printed on acid-free, 250-year-life paper
Manufactured in the United States of America

PREFACE

Among the many publications on the Brontës there are intelligent scholarly approaches to all the obvious problems of interest to current scholars and students. There are also marvelously strange and *outré* conjectures which may start modern thoughts coursing toward new discoveries, new possibilities of interpretation. The books listed in this volume range in approach from various uses of "Thou" and "You" in *Wuthering Heights* (B272) to serious evaluation of Charlotte Brontë as feminist (A267) to a report on "Little Smith's" day with the Reverend Brontë and Charlotte in 1850 (A434) to mysticism in Emily Brontë's poetry (B407).

The early criticism of the Brontës was concerned with identifying the authors. Once identified, they remained the subject of discussion: their lives, their personalities, their "inspiration," the identification of people and places in their novels. From the beginning, critics compared the works. They wrote of "the Brontës," feeling somehow that to talk about *Wuthering Heights* required one to compare it with *Jane Eyre.* As Charlotte Brontë's work (particularly her first novel) was at first found to be unquestionably superior to Emily's novel, positive and constructive consideration of *Wuthering Heights* did not appear until the beginning of this century. Once the brutality and primitive emotions of the novel became acceptable, *Wuthering Heights* came into its own. Significant in revealing the complexity of this novel was the work done by C. P. Sanger (B290) in 1926. The effort of Miss Fannie E. Ratchford in the 1930s to show the relationship of the juvenilia to the author's mature work also opened a new area for investigation (B391 and C182).

Today we see an obvious interest in scholarship on textual accuracy, on such current issues as feminism and social problems in the novels, on language analysis, and on mysticism and archetypal significance of the works. But there is enough variety in approach and enough eccentricity in scholarship that Brontë research has many directions in which to go.

In an effort to aid this scholarship I have divided the items in this bibliography into four categories. In the first, designated A1 through A442, are items on Charlotte Brontë. In the second, B1 through B512, are those on Emily. In the third section, C1 through C359, items appear which are about other members of the family, or any members of the family considered together. The last section, D1 through D66, lists bibliographies which may be of help for further investigation. In order to make each section an independent unit, some items are listed in more than one section — for example, *The Poems of Currer, Ellis, and Acton Bell* and the related reviews appear in sections A, B, and C.

The first 1846 review of *Poems by Currer, Ellis, and Acton Bell* is the earliest critical item listed, though the primary material written by the Brontës is, of course, of earlier date. The *Brontë Bibliography* by Yablon and Turner, published in October 1978, is probably the most recent publication listed. I have tried to include all the informative items published between those dates, all which have come to my attention. I will, no doubt, have omitted items of interest to particular researchers. I hope they may be minor omissions.

For the most part, the items are annotated. In each case I have tried to give a summary statement of the information contained in the criticism and, wherever possible, a quotation or paraphrase which points to any unusual and significant contribution made by the critic. The longer annotation indicates a work of unusual help in some area of scholarship. The medium-length note indicates a standard valuable work which has been annotated many times in many sources. A short annotation or an item without annotation indicates one of three things: (1) the work seems to me to be of minimal importance, (2) the work is in a foreign language and therefore not of interest to everyone, or (3) the work is difficult to obtain and therefore not of great use to the average reader. I have omitted queries, reviews, and letters to the editor except where discussion touches on questions of scholarly interest today.

I have also omitted catalogues of Brontë belongings and nineteenth-century "visits with the authors," those chatty discussions of personality. The latter are listed in the Yablon and Turner bibliography (D25). I have also left out general texts on literary history which cover the Brontës briefly, repeating well known facts and opinions. Finally, except when they suggest areas for scholarly investigation, I have omitted fictional or dramatic retelling of biography or plots of the novels.

I have been involved in compiling this bibliography over the last twelve years — with varying intensity — and feel rewarded in seeing it today as an organized presentation. It is my hope that the basic arrangement, supplemented by the detailed index, will make the volume useful to scholars and students.

I must acknowledge the help I have received from several valuable publications: the *Brontë Society Transactions,* particularly Professor Cross's annual reading list; the MLA bibliography; and those works listed in this volume by Miriam Allott (C147), Janet Barclay (D5), Jacques Blondel (D6), Jami Parkison (D17), Margot Peters (D19), Jean-Pierre Petit (B461), F. B. Pinion (C179), and Edith M. Weir (C42). Of particular value to me has been the newly published *Brontë Bibliography* by Yablon and Turner (D25).

My thanks go also to the members of the staffs at the libraries in which I have worked: the Haworth Parsonage Museum; the British Museum; the University of the Pacific; the Huntington Library; Stanford University; the University of California at Berkeley; Mt. St. Mary's College in Los Angeles; the C. G. Jung Library of Los Angeles; California State College, Bakersfield and other cooperating California Universities and Colleges. I am particularly indebted to Anne Marino, Paul Passel, Christie Clements, and Janeen Guest for their skilled assistance; Jacki Lawson for her discernment in deciphering and typing; Joan Lewis and her team in Reprographics for their cooperation. My continuing gratitude goes to Ruth Marie Faurot for her energetic intellect and example and to my husband Howard Passel for encouragement and forbearance.

In this bibliography I have done what I can to facilitate research: to that end I have reduced abbreviations to a minimum. The *Brontë Society Transactions,* so often referred to, is listed as *BST* and *Dissertation Abstracts International* becomes *DAI.* Only those other publications commonly called by their initials have been so listed (for example, *PMLA*). I have used arabic numbers throughout – for periodicals I give volume, date, pages. Wherever a question has arisen, I have let the needs of the reader dictate my decision. I hope my endeavors have resulted in a useful, accurate, and comprehensive bibliography.

TABLE OF CONTENTS

A. CHARLOTTE BRONTË

PRIMARY MATERIAL

Novels
Major Editions Listed in Chronological Order

A1   *Jane Eyre, An Autobiography.* Edited by Currer Bell. 3 vols. London: Smith, Elder, 1847.

This was reprinted in 1848 as "by Currer Bell" with a preface and dedication to Thackeray. It has been reprinted many times since with introductions by such critics as C. K. Shorter, 1889; May Sinclair, 1901; W. Robertson Nicoll, 1902; Margaret Ball, 1931; Bonamy Dobrée, 1942; Peter Quennell, 1947; Phyllis Bentley, 1947; Margaret Lane, 1953-57; Mark Schorer, 1959; Q. D. Leavis, 1966; Jane Jack and Margaret Smith, 1968 (see A5); Inga-Stina Ewbank, 1969.

A2   *Shirley, A Tale.* 3 vols. London: Smith, Elder, 1849.

Each of Charlotte Brontë's novels has been reprinted many times.

A3   *Villette.* 3 vols. London: Smith, Elder, 1853. Reprinted many times.

A4   *The Professor, A Tale.* 2 vols. London: Smith, Elder, 1857.

Reprinted in 1860 with "Emma," a fragment of a novel, this novel too has been reprinted many times.

A5   *Jane Eyre.* Eds. Jane Jack and Margaret Smith. Oxford: Clarendon Press, 1969.

The first novel to be published in the scholarly Clarendon Editions of the Brontë novels. It is based on the first edition of Smith Elder, 1847, and not on the copy-text corrected by Charlotte Brontë. The editors have attempted to annotate the variations. (See also A122 and A128.)

A6   *Villette.* Eds. Geoffrey Tillotson and Donald Hawes. Boston: Houghton Mifflin, 1971.

Here is a scholarly edition of this novel of 1853.

Poetry
Listed in Chronological Order

A7   [with Emily and Anne Brontë]. *Poems by Currer, Ellis, and Acton Bell.* London: Aylott and Jones, 1846.

Vol. also listed as B7 and C1.

A8   *Poems by Currer, Ellis, and Acton Bell.* London: Smith, Elder, 1848.

Reissue of the earlier volume.

A9   *The Complete Poems of Charlotte Brontë.* Ed. Clement K. Shorter and C. W. Hatfield. London, 1923.

This book gives insight into the author's style, although the collection is far from "complete."

Other Writings
Listed in Chronological Order

A10   [Pseudo. Currer Bell]. "The Editor's Preface" [to the second edition] in *Wuthering Heights and Agnes Grey: a new edition with a Biographical Notice of the authors, a selection from their literary remains, and a Preface by Currer Bell.* London: Smith, Elder, 1850.

Vol. also listed as B2.

A11   "Emma." *Cornhill Magazine,* 1 (Jan.-June 1860), 485-498.

This fragment (the first two chapters of a novel), preceded by "The Last Sketch" by Thackeray (A432), appeared first in this magazine and was later reprinted with *The Professor* both in England and America.

A12   "Unpublished Letters of Charlotte Brontë." *Hours at Home,* 11 (June 1870), 101-110.

These are some of the author's letters to Ellen Nussey.

4

A13   "Charlotte's Letters." Part two of *The Story of the Brontës: Their Home, Haunts, Friends, and Works.* Bradford: printed but not published, 1889.

A14   "The Adventures of Ernest Alembert, A Fairy Tale" in *Literary Anecdotes of the Nineteenth Century.* Vol. II. Eds. W. Robertson Nicoll and T. J. Wise. London: privately printed, 1896.

A15   *The Moores, An Unpublished Fragment.* Published with *Jane Eyre.* Introduction by W. Robertson Nicoll. London, 1902.

A16   "The Love Letters of Charlotte Brontë to Constantin Heger." Ed. M. H. Spielmann. *London Times,* July 29, 1913. Reprinted in *BST,* 5 (1914), 49-75.

     The letters were given to the British Museum by Heger's son. They had been printed in French. Spielmann's translation here was copyrighted, though Shorter claimed rights to all unpublished material through an arrangement with A. B. Nicholls. T. J. Wise pirated these letters clipped from the *Times* and published in a private edition in 1914. (See also A426.)

A17   *Letters Recounting the Deaths of Emily, Anne and Branwell Brontë by Charlotte Brontë* "To which are added letters signed 'Currer Bell' and 'C. B. Nicholls.'" Ed. T. J. Wise. London: privately printed, 1913.

A18   "Unpublished Essays in Novel Writing." Ed. G. E. MacLean. *BST,* 5 (1916), 137-143.

A19   *The Four Wishes.* Ed. C. K. Shorter. London: privately printed, 1918.

A20   *Napoleon and the Spectre.* Ed. C. K. Shorter. London: privately printed, 1919.

A21   *Thackeray and Charlotte Brontë: Being some hitherto unpublished letters by Charlotte Brontë.* London: privately printed, 1919.

A22   "Unpublished Manuscripts." *BST,* 5 (1919), 265.

A23   "Albion and Marina." *BST,* 6 (1920), 3.

A story from her juvenilia.

A24   *An Early Essay by Charlotte Brontë.* Ed. M. H. Spielmann. Bradford: The Brontë Society, 1924.

A25   *The Twelve Adventurers and Other Stories.* Eds. C. K. Shorter and C. W. Hatfield. "Note" signed C. K. Shorter. London: Hodder and Stoughton, 1925.

Brief excerpts from Charlotte Brontë's juvenilia, including "Search After Hapiness" [sic].

A26   "Charlotte Brontë on her Contemporaries." Ed. Butler Wood. *BST,* 7 (1926), 3-22.

A27   "Miniature Magazines of Charlotte Brontë with Unpublished Poems." Ed. D. Cook. *Bookman,* Dec. 1926.

A28   *The Spell, an Extravaganza* (an unpublished novel). "Introduction" by George Edwin MacLean. London: H. Milford, Oxford University Press, 1931.

Here for the first time a novel selected from Charlotte's juvenilia is published and offered as a single complete work.

A29   "Two Unpublished Manuscripts, Foreshadowing *Villette.*" *BST,* 7 (1931), 277.

These discarded manuscripts are thought to be earlier attempts to begin the novel.

A30   *Legends of Angria.* Eds. Fannie E. Ratchford and William Clyde DeVane. New Haven: Yale University Press, 1933.

These five tales from Charlotte Brontë's juvenilia include "The Green Dwarf" 1833, "Zamorna's Exile" 1836-1837, "Mina Laury" 1838, "Caroline Vernon" 1839, and "Farewell to Angria" (undated).

A31 "A Leaf from an Unopened Volume" in *Derby Day and Other Adventures*. Ed. A. Edward Newton. Boston: Little, Brown and Company, 1934.

A facsimile of this Brontë manuscript and a transcription of it are included in a pocket inside the back cover of Newton's book. Vol. also listed as C285.

A32 *The Miscellaneous and Unpublished Writings of Charlotte Brontë and Patrick Branwell Brontë.* 2 vols. Eds. T. J. Wise and J. A. Symington. Oxford: Shakespeare Head Press, 1936.

Vol. also listed as C6.

A33 "The Story of Willie Ellin: Fragments of an Unfinished Novel." *BST,* 9 (1936), 3-22.

The manuscript is listed in Christian's *Census* and catalogues of Bonnell and General Collections of the Brontë Museums. This unfinished novel has also been called "The Moores" and was probably to be the same novel as "Emma."

A34 *Stories from Angria* in *Brontës.* Heather Edition. Ed. Phyllis Bentley. London: A. Wingate, 1949.

These stories from Emily Brontë's juvenilia include "Albion and Marina," her first love story, 1830 (age 14); "Mina Laury," 1838; and "Farewell to Angria," undated [1838].

A35 "French Essays." *BST,* 12 (1952), 88.

A36 "French Essays." Translated, Margaret Lane. *BST,* 12 (1954), 273.

A37 *Letters of the Brontës.* Ed. Muriel Spark. Norman, Oklahoma: University of Oklahoma, 1954.

This appeared as *The Brontë Letters.* London: Nevill, 1954.

A38 [and Emily Brontë]. "New Brontë Devoirs." Translated, Phyllis Bentley. *BST,* 12 (1955), 361.

7

A39   *The Search After Hapiness.* Illustrated by Carolyn Dinan. London: Harvill Press, 1969.

This story from Charlotte Brontë's juvenilia was first printed in 1925 by Shorter and Hatfield in *The Twelve Adventurers* (A25).

A40   *Five Novelettes: Passing Events, Julia, Mina Laury, Captain Henry Hastings, Caroline Vernon.* Transcribed from the original manuscript and edited by Winifred Gerin. London: Folio Press, 1971.

Novelettes from five separate manuscripts in U.S.A., written between 1836 and 1839 when Charlotte Brontë was 20-23 years old. These are not really juvenilia. The introduction helps place these stories in the context of Charlotte Brontë's life.

A41   "An Interesting Passage in the Lives of Some Eminent Men of the Present Time" in Judith Chernaik. "An Unpublished Tale by Charlotte Brontë," *Times Literary Supplement,* 72 (Nov. 23, 1973), 1453-1454.

A transcription of the tale written in 1830, now at Harvard University. (See also A246.)

A42   Rejected "Preface" to *Shirley. BST,* 16 (1975), 329-337.

A43   *Two Tales by Charlotte Brontë:* "The Secret" and "Lily Hart." Transcribed and edited by William Holtz. Columbia: University of Missouri Press, 1978.

These two stories were found in the papers of the late Mrs. Stuart Symington and given by her son to the University of Missouri in 1975. They are now in print for the first time. The text is reproduced in enlarged facsimile and is then transcribed by the editor.

SECONDARY MATERIAL

Poems by Currer, Ellis, and Acton Bell

Nineteenth-Century Reviews
Listed in Chronological Order

A44   [Dobell, Sydney]. "Poetry of the Million." *Athenaeum,* 975 (July 4, 1846), 682.

One of the first three published reviews which the Brontës read. The critic calls theirs "a family in whom appears to run the instinct of song. It is, however, by the three brothers — as we suppose them to be — in very unequal portions; requiring, in the case of Acton Bell, the indulgences of affection. . . ."

A45   Butler, William Archer. "Evenings with Our Younger Poets." A review of *Poems by Currer, Ellis, and Acton Bell. Dublin University Magazine,* 28 (Oct. 1846).

One of the three published reviews (of the poems) reported to have been read by the Brontës. The reviewer, as Charlotte Brontë says in a letter (see Gaskell A384), "conjectured that the *soi-disant* three personages were in reality but one. . . ."

A46   Anon. A review of *Poems by Currer, Ellis, and Acton Bell. Spectator,* Nov. 11, 1846, pp. 1094-1095.

Noted but not read. Listed in Parkison   (D17).

A47   Anon. A review of *Poems of Currer, Ellis, and Acton Bell. Critic,* 1846.

One of the three published reviews of the poems which the Brontës read, according to T. J. Wise and J. A. Symington, *The Brontës: Their Lives, Friendships and Correspondence.* Vol. 2, p. 102. Oxford: The Shakespeare Head Press, 1932. Listed as C7.
The reviewer comments that "in these compositions" the alert reader will recognize "more genius than it was supposed this utilitarian age had devoted to the loftier exercise of the intellect. . . ."

A48   Anon. A review of *Poems by Acton, Currer, and Ellis Bell. Spectator,*
           Nov. 18, 1848, pp. 1094-1095.

           As Charlotte Brontë reports in a letter to Mr. Williams of Smith,
           Elder (the publisher of the second edition of the poems in Oct. 1848):
           "The *Spectator* consistently maintains the tone it first assumed
           regarding the Bells." (See also A386.)

Jane Eyre – Nineteenth-Century Reviews
Listed in Chronological Order

A49   Anon. A review of *Jane Eyre. Spectator,* Nov. 6, 1847, pp.
           1074-1075.

           A hostile review, of which Charlotte Brontë says to her editor
           (see A48): "The critique . . . gives that view of the book which
           will naturally be taken by a certain class of mind."

A50   Anon. A review of *Jane Eyre. Economist,* 5 (Nov. 27, 1847), 1376.

           Praises the beginning of the novel, not the romance between
           Jane and Mr. Rochester.

A51   Anon. "The Literary Examiner." A review of *Jane Eyre. Examiner,*
           Nov. 27, 1847, pp. 756-757.

           Jane Eyre is deemed to be a "very clever book," one of "decided
           power." The style is judged to be "resolute, straight-forward, and
           to the purpose," though here and there "rude and uncultivated." On
           the whole, a very favorable review.

A52   Anon. "New Books." A review of *Jane Eyre. Douglas Jerrold's Shilling
           Magazine,* 6 (Nov. 1847), 473-474.

           A favorable review comments on the author's artistic sensitivity.

A53   [Lewes, George Henry]. "Recent Novels: French and English." A
           review of *Jane Eyre. Fraser's Magazine,* 36 (Dec. 1847), 690-694.

           This influential literary gentleman finds "deep, significant
           reality" as "the great characteristic of the book." He suggests that

the author writes of "actual suffering and experience." He admits, "We wept over *Jane Eyre*."

A54   Anon. Comments on *Jane Eyre* in a review of *Wuthering Heights* and *Agnes Grey*. *Athenaeum*, Dec. 25, 1847, pp. 1324-1325.

All three novels (*Wuthering Heights, Agnes Grey,* and *Jane Eyre*) were not only thought to be "the work of one hand," but this reviewer says that "the first issued" *Jane Eyre* "remains the best."

A55   Anon. "Some Correspondence. Literary Intelligence." A review of *Jane Eyre. Literary World* (New York), 2 (Jan. 20, 1848), 633.

In *Jane Eyre* the plot is improbable but the tone full of pathos and freshness.

A56   Anon. A review of *Jane Eyre. Westminster Review,* 48 (Jan. 1848), 581-584.

Recognizing the novelist as being a lady, "and a clever one too," the critic (Lewes?) calls *Jane Eyre* "decidedly the best novel of the season." He praises "originality and freshness of its style."

A57   Anon. "Review of New Books." A review of *Jane Eyre. Peterson's Magazine* (Philadelphia), 13 (March 1848), 126.

A favorable comment on the author's "genius."

A58   Anon. "Review of New Books." A review of *Jane Eyre. Graham's Gentlemen's Magazine* (Philadelphia), 32 (May 1848), 299.

A hostile review which points out the "old-maid" qualities of the author.

A59   Anon. "Literary Register." A review of *Jane Eyre. Tait's Edinburgh Review,* n.s. 15 (May 1848), 346-348.

A favorable review, commenting on the reality and "instructive nature" of the plot.

A60   Anon. A review of *Jane Eyre*. *The Christian Remembrancer*, 15 (June 1848), 396-409.

The author is still unknown at the time of this review, but "we, for our part, cannot doubt that the book is written by a female," says this reviewer. "There is an intimate acquaintance with the worst parts of human nature" and "the plot is most extravagantly improbable." But the review admits "all the power is shown and all the interest lies in the characters."

A61   Eliot, George. *The George Eliot Letters.* Edited by Gordon S. Haight. New Haven: Yale University Press, 1954.

In a letter to Charles Bray on June 11, 1848, George Eliot writes: "I have read *Jane Eyre*, mon ami, and shall be glad to know what you admire in it. All self-sacrifice is good — but one would like it to be in somewhat nobler cause than that of a diabolical law which chains a man soul and body to a putrefying carcass. However the book *is* interesting — only I wish the characters would talk a little less like the heroes and heroines of police reports." Vol. also listed as A383.

A62   Whipple, Edwin Percy. A review of *Jane Eyre* (*Wuthering Heights* and *The Tenant of Wildfell Hall*). *North American Review*, 67 (Oct. 1848), 354-357.

Whipple comments on the masculine tone and clarity of style in *Jane Eyre*, but feels that in detail and expression of feeling the novel is feminine. The character of Rochester gives proof that the author is masculine. He admires the "freshness, raciness, and vigor of mind" shown in the novel. But he suggests that the Brontës "confound vulgarity with truth, and awaken too often a feeling of unmitigated disgust."

A63   Forcade, Eugène. A review of *Jane Eyre*. *Revue des Deux Mondes*, 4th s. 24 (Nov. 1, 1848), 470-494.

The critic reports that "*Jane Eyre* is not a tale likely to interest everyone." He praises the characters but finds the plot too intricate.

A64   Rigby, Elizabeth from *"Vanity Fair* – and *Jane Eyre." Quarterly Review,* 84 (Dec. 1848), 153-185.

A savage review, vituperative and devastating in its effect on Charlotte Brontë. The reviewer states "We have no remembrance of another [book] combining such genuine power with such horrid taste." Vol. also listed as B46.

A65   Anon. A review of *Jane Eyre. Dublin University Magazine,* 31 (1848), 608-614.

A66   Chasles, Philarète. A review of *Vanity Fair* and *Jane Eyre. Revue des Deux Mondes,* March 1, 1849, cited by Emile Langlois. *BST,* 16:1 (1971), 11–18 (A81).

He compares the novels, preferring *Vanity Fair,* which he calls a "vast prose epic," to *Jane Eyre,* a "small elegy."

A67   Duran-Forgues, Emile. A review of *Jane Eyre* in *Revue de Paris* (Belgium), April-June, 1849, cited by Emile Langlois. *BST,* 16:1 (1971), 11-18 (A81).

One of the three earliest French reviews by the man who published a French translation of *Jane Eyre* in that issue.

A68   Anon. "Noteworthy Novels." *North British Review,* 11 (August, 1849), 475-493.

A discussion of male and female qualities and preferences, both in relation to writer and reader. The critic concluded that this novel must be by a male writer or an "unsexed" female.

A69   Anon. A review of *Jane Eyre* (and *Shirley*), *Dublin Review,* 28 (March 1850), 209-233.

A discussion of the novels of moral purpose and the novels which tell a tale. The critic remarks on the originality of Charlotte Brontë's work.

A70   Anon. "Female Novelists – No. III." *Colburn's New Monthly Magazine,* 2nd s., 95 (July 1852), 295-305.

13

A discussion of *Jane Eyre*, as well as *Wuthering Heights* and *Shirley*, which proposes that philosophically the authors are "kinswomen."

A71   Anon. "Editor's Easy Chair." *Harper's New Monthly Magazine* (New York), 11 (June 1855), 128.

The critic finds Charlotte Brontë's writing "powerful" and calls *Jane Eyre* "the most searching and prodigious novel ever written by an Englishwoman."

A72   Anon. "Currer Bell's Writings." *Hogg's Instructor*, n.s. 4 (1855), 425-36.

An admirer of Charlotte Brontë's forthright approach to life, the critic suggests that the novelist's message states: "I disapprove everything utopian. Look life in its iron face, stare reality out of its countenance."

A73   Anon. "A Few Words About *Jane Eyre*." *Sharpe's Magazine*, June 1855. Reprinted in *Fraser's Magazine*, May 1857.

Earlier thought to be written by Mrs. Gaskell, this exposé of the Brontë home ambiance is now attributed to Catherine Winkworth, who possibly prepared an article based on the details sent to her in a letter from Mrs. Gaskell (see A419). It was this article which roused Ellen Nussey to urge the Reverend Brontë to have an official biography done by Mrs. Gaskell.

A74   Skelton, John. "Charlotte Brontë." A review of Mrs. Gaskell's biography with comments on *Jane Eyre* and *Wuthering Heights*. *Fraser's Magazine*, 55 (May 1857), 569-582.

The critic approves of the biography but notes that in *Jane Eyre* the love affair between Rochester and Jane is highly improbable.

A75   Dallas, Eneas Sweetland. "Currer Bell." Includes a review of *Jane Eyre* with comments on *Wuthering Heights*. *Blackwood's Edinburgh Magazine*, 82 (July 1857), 77-94.

In discussing Mrs. Gaskell's biography (A386), the critic draws a parallel between the lives the Brontës led and the resulting novels they wrote.

A76   Hobart, V. H. "Thoughts on Modern English Literature." A review of *Jane Eyre. Fraser's Magazine,* 60 (July 1859), 91-110.

In a general review of nineteenth-century novels, *Jane Eyre* is considered the best.

A77   Anon. "The 'Taste' of Charlotte Brontë." *BST,* 14 (1962), 20-23.

This restatement of various contemporary reactions to *Jane Eyre* includes that of Queen Victoria.

A78   de Mouy, Charles. "Romanciers anglais contemporains – Miss Brontë (Currer Bell)." *Revue Européenne* (Paris), 12 (1860), 348-370.

An enthusiastic French supporter discusses the novels of Charlotte Brontë. He believes that "Miss Brontë has fully experienced everything she writes about . . . that she has suffered as her heroes suffer." He comments on her "pure literary qualities . . . the overall melancholy and chill range of her pallette." Cited and translated by David Newton-de Molina (A79).

A79   Newton-de Molina, David. "A Note on an Early French View of Charlotte Brontë: Charles de Mouy's 'Romanciers Anglais Contemporains – Miss Brontë (Currer Bell)' *Revue Européene,* Vol. XII (Paris 1860)." *BST,* 15 (1970), 417-420.

The author writes of "De Mouy's forthright enthusiasm for Charlotte Brontë's work" (see A78) and quotes him copiously in translation.

A80   Montégut, Emile. *Ecrivains Modernes de l'Angleterre,* 1st s. Paris: Hachette, 1885.

A study of Charlotte Brontë, cited by Berrill (A365), is a reprint of his enthusiastic evaluation of *Jane Eyre* in *Revue des Deux Mondes* in two July 1857 issues. In it he claims that *Jane Eyre* is "the most beautiful contemporary novel."

A81   Langlois, Emile. "Early Critics and Translators of *Jane Eyre* in France." *BST,* 16:1 (1971), 11-18.

The history of French reviews and French translations of *Jane Eyre* is clearly presented. The French critics seem to be "more attracted by Charlotte Brontë's life than by her works," according to Langlois.

Shirley — Nineteenth-Century Reviews Listed in Chronological Order

A82   Anon. A review of *Shirley. Athenaeum* (Nov. 3, 1849), 1107-1109.

This hostile review was among the first to appear after the publication of the novel. In it, the critic reminds the readers that *Jane Eyre* lacked artistic merit and states further that *Shirley* is not any better.

This was one of several reviews to come out in November 1849, among them that of the French reviewer Eugène Forcade in the *Revue des Deux Mondes* (Nov. 15, 1849) and anonymous reviews in:
   Atlas, Nov. 3, 1849, pp. 696-697.
   Examiner, Nov. 3, 1849, pp. 692-694.
   Observer, Nov. 4, 1849, p. 7.
   Economist, Nov. 10, 1849, pp. 1251-1253.
   Dublin University Magazine, 34 (1849), 680-689.
In December 1849 reviews appeared in:
   Morning Chronicle, Dec. 25, 1849, p. 7.
   Eclectic Review, 26 (Dec. 1849), 739-749.
   Fraser's Magazine, 40 (Dec. 1849), 692-694.
In 1850 Lewes' attack on *Shirley* came out in the *Edinburgh Review* (see A83), and Sydney Dobell's article "Currer Bell" in *Palladium* (see A84) also mentions the novel. Anonymous reviews appeared in:
   Dublin Review, 28 (March 1850), 209-233.
   Westminster Review, 52 (1850), 418-419.
In 1852 notices appeared in:
   Globe, Dec. 6, 1852, p. 1.
   Bell's Weekly Messenger, Dec. 11, 1852, p. 6.
   Non-Conformist, Dec. 15, 1852, p. 992.
and in 1853 a review in the *Sunday Times,* Jan. 2, 1853, p. 2. (See also D17.)

A83   Lewes, G. H. Review of *Shirley*. *Edinburgh Review*, 91 (Jan. 1850), 158-65.

This venerated reviewer attacks the novel for its lack of structure. He treats Charlotte Brontë as woman writer, not just a writer. He continues: "But in *Shirley* all unity . . . is wanting. There is no passionate link: nor is there any artistic fusion, or intergrowth, by which one part evolves itself from another. Hence its falling-off in interest, coherent movement and life." He concludes by saying, "The various scenes are gathered up into three volumes — they have not grown into a work."

Villette — Nineteenth-Century Reviews
Listed in Chronological Order

A84   Dobell, Sydney. "Currer Bell." *Palladium*, 1 (Sept. 1850), 161-175.

Dobell considers all the Brontë novels "as the works of one author under sundry disguises." He devotes most of his article to an analysis of *Wuthering Heights*. Of Currer Bell he says: she "is a woman. Every word she utters is female. Not feminine, but female. There is a sex about it which cannot be mistaken, even in its manliest attire."

A85   Dobell, Sydney. "Currer Bell" in Jolly, Emily. *The Life and Letters of Sydney Dobell*. London: Smith, Elder, 1878.

The critic's article "Currer Bell," which appeared first in *The Palladium*, Sept. 1850 (A84), is included as well as a chapter on "Correspondence with Miss Brontë, 1851."

A86   Martineau, Harriet. A review of *Villette*. *Daily News* (Feb. 3, 1853), 2.

The novelist Martineau reviews Charlotte Brontë's third novel and calls it "the strangest, the most astonishing, though not the best." She is reached by the pain in the work, saying that "Currer Bell here afflicts us with an amount of subjective misery," allowing the reader "no respite." Her reaction: an "atmosphere of pain hangs about the whole." In her most discerning observation she reveals the motivation of the protagonist in this novel and Charlotte Brontë's other novels: the need to be loved.

A87   Anon. A review of *Villette. Examiner* (Feb. 5, 1853), 84-85.

One of the first reviews published, it recommends *Villette* as being as good as Charlotte Brontë's first two novels for characters and plot, but warns of the gloomy tone.
In addition to this review, many other anonymous reviews appeared in 1853, among them:
Morning Advertiser, Feb. 4, 1853, p. 6.
Globe, Feb. 7, 1853, p. 1.
Atlas, Feb. 12, 1853, p. 106.
Athenaeum, Feb. 12, 1853, pp. 186-188.
Weekly News and Chronicle, Feb. 12, 1853, pp. 105-106.
Ball's Weekly Messenger, Feb. 17, 1853, p. 6.
Magnet, Feb. 28, 1853, p. 6.
Sunday Times, March 13, 1853, p. 2.
Nonconformist, March 16, 1853, p. 224.
Eclectic Review, 5th s., 5 (March 1853), 305-320.
Christian Remembrancer, n.s. 25 (April 1853), 401-443.
Edinburgh Review, 97 (April 1853), 380-390.
New Quarterly Review, 2 (1853), 237-240.
Putnam's Monthly Magazine, 1 (1853), 535-539.
Eugène Forcade reviewed the novel in *Revue des Deux Mondes,* March 15, 1853. Another anonymous review appeared in the *Sun,* Nov. 9, 1855, p. 3. (See also D17.)

A88   Arnold, Matthew. *Letters to Arthur Hugh Clough.* Vol. I. Ed. Howard Lowery. London: Oxford University Press, 1932.

Of *Villette* he wrote on March 21, 1853: "Miss Brontë has written a hideous, undelightful, convulsed, constricted novel . . . one of the most utterly disagreeable books I ever read."

A89   Lewes, George H. "*Ruth* and *Villette.*" *Westminster Review,* 59 (1853), 474-491.

Lewes, who had wounded Charlotte Brontë with his review of *Shirley* which attacked her as a woman writer — not just a writer — now reviews Mrs. Gaskell's *Ruth* and *Villette* in the same article.

A90   Anon. "Reading Raids, Currer, Ellis, and Acton Bell." *Tait's Edinburgh Magazine,* 2nd ser., 22 (July 1855), 416-423.

A general look at the three Brontës, with the conclusion that Charlotte Brontë showed changes from her first two novels to her last two, becoming more pessimistic and disenchanted as she grew older. The critic bases this conclusion on a comparison between *The Professor* and *Villette.*

A91   Waring, Susan M. "Charlotte Brontë's Lucy Snowe." *Harper's New Monthly Magazine,* 32 (Feb. 1866), 368-371.

One of those reviews which finds *Villette* "great" and praises everything.

The Professor – Nineteenth-Century Reviews
Listed in Chronological Order

A92   Anon. A review of *The Professor. Examiner,* June 20, 1857, p. 388.

The critic compares this early work with the previously published *Villette* to show that the early gloom has been changed to optimism as the author matured.

A93   Anon. A review of *The Professor. Economist,* 15 (June 27, 1857), 701-702.

A hostile review finds the characters unreal and the plot uncontrolled.

A94   Anon. A review of *The Professor. Dublin University Magazine,* 50 (1857), 88-100.

Criticism of *Jane Eyre*

A95   Adams, Maurianne. *"Jane Eyre*: Woman's Estate" in *The Authority of Experience.* Eds. Arlyn Diamond and Lee R. Edwards. Amherst: University of Massachusetts Press, 1977.

In tracing Jane's "transition from poor orphan into secure woman," the critic points out the parallel between psychic and status motifs which Charlotte Brontë uses, but concludes that "questions of estate and position, status, integrity and equality are resolved in the romantic mode," one in which there are "fortuitous interventions which enable events and the world to conform to the shape of wish and desire."

A96   Beaty, Jerome. *"Jane Eyre* and Genre." *Genre,* 10 (Winter 1977), 619-654.

The critic identifies *Jane Eyre* as a governess novel and finds its pattern traditional. He sees the sources of *Jane Eyre* as: *Pamela, Ellen the Teacher,* and *Caroline Mordaunt.*

A97   Benvenuto, Richard. "The Child of Nature, the Child of Grace, and the Unresolved Conflict of *Jane Eyre." English Literary History,* 39 (Dec. 1972), 620-638.

Charlotte Brontë has attempted a reconciliation of two conflicting forces, a conflict which remains unresolved. *Jane Eyre* strives for the harmony of these two opposing forces: personal fulfillment and conformation to the pressures of society. Jane is a "child of nature" (individual choice) and a "child of grace" (adaptation to society).

A98   Blackburn, Ruth. *"Thornycroft Hall:* A Rebuttal to *Jane Eyre." BST,* 16 (1975), 353-360.

Emma Jane Warboise wrote a partly autobiographical novel, *Thornycroft Hall,* in answer to *Jane Eyre.* Like Charlotte Brontë, Miss Warboise had been a pupil at the Cowan Bridge School but her reaction was totally different. She admired the headmaster, William Carus Wilson, and found him "thoroughly sincere and understandingly generous." He was involved in "works of love and mercy." To vindicate him, this former pupil wrote a novel in imitation of *Jane Eyre*, with similarities of situation but a very different conclusion.

A99   Blom, M. A. *"Jane Eyre:* Mind as Law Unto Itself." *Criticism,* 15 (Fall 1973), 350-364.

In 1848 Elizabeth Rigby (A64) asserted that *Jane Eyre* is "pre-eminently an anti-Christian composition," and Dr. Blom concurs. Death is indeed the doorway to a fathomless abyss in which "the sentient self is extinguished." It is with this understanding that Jane turns inward into herself for a life of "fire and feeling." She has chosen a self-willed existence in this world rather than the promise of the world to come.

A100   Buckley, Jerome Hamilton. *The Victorian Temper.* Cambridge: Harvard University Press, 1951.

In discussing "The Pattern of Conversion," the author suggests the link in *Jane Eyre* to the *flammestod* in Goethe's metaphysical lyrics. He states that in *Jane Eyre* "an actual fire provided the visible means of purgation whereby the Byronic Mr. Rochester might attain the humility of nobler self."

A101   Burkhart, Charles. "Another Key Word for *Jane Eyre." Nineteenth Century Fiction,* 16 (Sept. 1961), 177-179.

The author suggests that "nature" is the word — referring to the conflict between reason and judgment.

102   Burns, Wayne. "Critical Relevance of Freudianism." *Western Review,* 20 (1956), 310-314.

A Freudian reading assumes that a "passionate physicality" is at the base of the novel, only thinly covered by Victorian melodrama and Methodist morality. In a scene "crucial to the entire meaning of the novel" St. John Rivers presses Jane for marriage, and a series of sexual connotations and unconscious uses of expressions can be detected by the Freudian critic.

A103 Bushnell, Nelson S. "Artistic Economy in *Jane Eyre*: A Contrast with *The Old Manor House.*" *English Language Notes,* 5 (March 1968), 197-202.

Bushnell compares the scene in which Jane first encounters Rochester — the natural setting, folkloric overtones, magic, and menace — with a similar scene in Charlotte Smith's Gothic tale with its decaying mansion, dark woods, and frightening wind.

A104 Coveney, Peter James. *Poor Monkey: The Child in Literature.* London: Rockliff, 1957.

Jane Eyre is briefly mentioned in this study of the position of children as revealed by literature.

A105 Craig, G. Armour. "The Unpoetic Compromise: On the Relation Between Private Vision and Social Order in Nineteenth Century English Fiction" in *Self and Society in the Novel.* Ed. Mark Schorer. New York: Columbia University Press, 1956.

Here is an interpretation which follows Jane on her fantasized journey of aggression, asserting herself over the men she encounters. The sexual symbols are "frequent and crude," according to Craig, and they reach their strongest image in the castration of Rochester. Jane is said to fit the pattern of protagonist in this kind of novel. "The beholder of lights, shadows, and distant regions is almost invariably an orphan, is usually a young woman, and is always on the brink of a new social relation."

A106 Crothers, George Dunlap, ed. *Invitation to Learning: English and American Novels.* New York and London: Basic Books, 1966.

One of two roundtable discussions of the Brontë novels, originally presented on CBS: *Jane Eyre* is discussed by John W. Alrich, Margaret Webster, and Lyman Bryson. Vol. also listed as B118.

A107 Day, Martin S. "Central Concepts of *Jane Eyre.*" *The Personalist,* 41 (1960), 495-505.

Here another psychological reading points out the devices: Rochester is the father figure, Jane is the mother figure. Rochester's

23

blinding and maiming is symbolic emasculation and serves to reduce the dominant male to a dependent child. "Jane Eyre dismisses the loveless but otherwise compatible Rivers for the loving but otherwise incompatible Rochester." Their attraction is based on the sultan-slave relationship. Jane's motivation is apparent to the analyst.

A108　Deming, Barbara. "Two Perspectives on Women's Struggle." *Liberation*, 17 (June 1973), 30-37.

Jane's refusal of Rochester has as its basis her rejection of a non-liberated life: his "playful" condescending lovemaking, his dressing her like a doll, and his assumption that in the future she will teach Adele and devote herself to him. The ultimate relationship which they achieve is radical and daring in concept: Charlotte Brontë has Jane say, "I am my husband's life as he is mine."

A109　Downing, Janay. "Fire and Ice Imagery in *Jane Eyre*." *Paunch*, 26 (Oct. 1966), 68-72.

The dichotomy of fire and ice sets the tone for the imagery in this novel. Such extremes are in keeping with the aim of the author to shock and astound.

A110　Dry, Florence (Swinton). *The Sources of Jane Eyre*. Part II of *The Brontë Sources*. Cambridge: W. Heffner, 1940.

A study of material which may have contributed to the genesis of *Jane Eyre*. Dry suggests: Dickens' *Nicholas Nickleby* and *Oliver Twist* and Scott's *Waverley*, *Guy Mannering*, *The Heart of Mid-Lothian*, and *A Legend of Montrose*.

A111　Dunn, Richard. "Preface" in Charlotte Brontë. *Jane Eyre: An Authoritative Text, Backgrounds, Criticism*. New York: W. W. Norton, 1971.

The brief introductory remarks touch on the variety of critical responses, a biography of the author, and notes on the publication of the novel.

A112   Duthie, Enid L. "Henry James's *The Turn of the Screw* and Mrs. Gaskell's *The Old Nurse's Story." BST*, 17 (1977), 133-137.

Duthie sets up a parallel implying that these two stories and *Jane Eyre* have a close interrelationship (see A185).

A113   Ericksen, Donald H. "Imagery as Structure in *Jane Eyre." Victorian Newsletter*, 30 (Fall 1966), 18-22.

Another psychological reading in which *Jane Eyre* is examined for its apparent sexual connotations.

A114   Gates, B. "Visionary Woe and Its Revision: Another Look at Jane Eyre's Pictures." *Ariel: A Review of International English Literature*, 7 (Oct. 1976), 36-49.

This critic sees a basic relationship between the three paintings and the three main places to have influenced Jane as an adult. He sees the first picture as symbolic of Thornfield Hall, the second representing her time on the moors, and the third her time spent with St. John Rivers.

A115   Greene, Mildred Sarah Epstein. "Love and Duty: The Character of the Princesse de Cleves as Reflected in Certain Later English and American Novels." Unpublished doctoral dissertation, University of New Mexico, 1965. *DAI*, 28:230.

Jane Eyre is studied along with Richardson's *Clarissa Harlowe*, Jane Austen's *Sense and Sensibility* and *Persuasion*, George Eliot's *Middlemarch*, and Henry James' *The Wings of the Dove* and *The Portrait of a Lady*.

A116   Gribble, Jennifer. "Jane Eyre's Imagination." *Nineteenth Century Fiction*, 23 (1968), 279-293.

A study of the power and patterning of Jane's imagination and its function as mediator between opposites: between the inner world of the mind and the outer world of society. The examination of creativity also connects the life lived by Jane Eyre and that of Charlotte Brontë.

A117   Grudin, Peter. "Jane and the Other Mrs. Rochester: Excess and Restraint in *Jane Eyre.*" *Novel,* 10 (Winter 1977), 145-157.

The problem posed by the existence of Bertha, Rochester's first wife, is examined in this article in an attempt to balance the excesses and restraints envisioned by Charlotte Brontë in her contrast of Bertha and Jane. Bertha becomes the cause of Jane's behavior, and understanding her position in the novel leads to an understanding of Jane's actions.

A118   Hagan, John. "Enemies of Freedom in *Jane Eyre.*" *Criticism,* 13 (Fall 1971), 351-376.

Jane's quest for freedom is blocked by a series of "enemies" which the protagonist must overcome. The major conflict results when St. John Rivers serves as the major obstacle between Jane and her ultimate marriage to Rochester. The critic traces the history of this quest for freedom.

A119   Halperin, John. *Egoism and Self-Discovery in the Victorian Novel.* New York: Burt Franklin, 1974.

In chapter two, "Thackeray, Charlotte Brontë and Trollope," Halperin discusses the kind of egoism which Rochester has, and is able to subdue, and the kind St. John Rivers has, which he cannot overcome.

A120   Hardy, Barbara. "Dogmatic Form: Defoe, Charlotte Brontë, Thomas Hardy, and E. M. Forster" in *The Appropriate Form: An Essay on the Novel.* London: Athlone Press of University of London, 1964.

This article presents the role of Providence in *Jane Eyre.* Professor Hardy explains that in Charlotte Brontë's novel, as in *Robinson Crusoe,* "The action and characters are shaped by the dogmatism of a special belief, the belief in Providence." Such a traditional "belief in divine intercession" dramatizes "the workings of a heavenly power and grace."

A121   Hardy, Barbara. *Jane Eyre* in Notes on English Literature series. Oxford: Blackwell, 1964.

Here is a close textual examination of plot, character and symbolism, prepared for student use.

A122   Harkness, B. A review of the Oxford edition of *Jane Eyre. Nineteenth Century Fiction,* 25 (Dec. 1970), 355-369.

This critic feels that there are two weaknesses in the then new edition of *Jane Eyre* (see A5): (1) the copy-text should have been the manuscript and (2) editorial emendations should have been supported. (See Ian Jack's reply, A128.)

A123   Hárte, Bret. "Miss Mix." *Sensation Novels Condensed,* (1871).

This parody of *Jane Eyre* by the American humorist is mentioned in Archibald Bolling Shepperson's *The Novel in Motley.* Cambridge: Harvard University Press, 1936.

A124   Higashi, Samiko. "*Jane Eyre*: Charlotte Brontë versus the Hollywood Myth of Romance." *Journal of Popular Film,* 6 (1977), 13-31.

The filming of *Jane Eyre* in 1944 missed the chance of becoming a major artistic statement by adapting the story to fit the Hollywood pattern of the time concerning the heroine's revolt against Victorian convention.

A125   Holloway, Julia Bolton. "*Aurora Leigh* and *Jane Eyre.*" *BST,* 17 (1977), 126-132.

Elizabeth Barrett Browning reacted strongly to Charlotte Brontë's novels. Of *Jane Eyre* she said the qualities were "half savage and half free thinking." *Shirley* she thought "not equal to *Jane Eyre* in spontaneousness and earnestness." *Villette* caused her to remark, "I think it is a strong book." In *Aurora Leigh* the hero is blinded before his reunion with the heroine: Mrs. Browning denied the similarity to Rochester's plight. Actually, the critic tells us, the books are similar in that "in both the women win. In both the men are rendered blind and helpless."

A126   Howells, William Dean. "Thackeray's Ethel Newcome and Charlotte Brontë's Jane Eyre." *Heroines of Fiction.* New York and London: Harper and Bros., 1901.

This article, first published in *Harper's Bazaar,* Dec. 1900, compares the two contemporaneous heroines as to action and motivation.

A127   Hughes, R. A. "Jane Eyre: The Unbaptised Dionysos." *Nineteenth Century Fiction,* 18 (March 1964), 347-364.

The critic finds *Jane Eyre* not a Christian narrative, in spite of Charlotte Brontë's representation of Helen Burns, Rochester, and St. John Rivers. He feels that "the Christianity of the novel is an overlay on the primary pattern, which predates Christianity." He sees Rochester as Dionysiac and St. John Rivers as Apollonian. The novel is structured around this principle. "Romantic, ostensibly Christian veneer" covers the Nietzschean polarities. He also comments on the successful use of imagery: "the window-mirror figure is used with extreme effect" to demonstrate the transparent membrane separating the rational from the irrational.

A128   Jack, I. and Margaret Smith. "The Clarendon *Jane Eyre:* A Rejoinder." *Nineteenth Century Fiction,* 26 (1971), 370-376.

The editors of the scholarly *Jane Eyre* (A5) reply to Harkness (A122), supporting the editorial principles which underlie this edition.

A129   James, David L. "Charades at Thornfield Hall and Gaunt House." *BST,* 17:1 (1976), 35-41.

In comparing the parlor game played in Thornfield Hall with the same entertainment in Thackeray's *Vanity Fair,* the critic indicates two interesting areas of investigation. First, he suggests that the games are Oriental not French in tone — each is a Turkish scene. Second, he discusses the date of publication of the two works, pointing out that Charlotte Brontë completed *Jane Eyre* before she read *Vanity Fair;* that the first edition of *Jane Eyre* was sent to Thackeray in October 1847 and *Vanity Fair,* Part XV with the charade scene was not published until March 1848. Was Thackeray influenced by Charlotte Brontë?

A130 Keyworth, T. "Morton Village in *Jane Eyre.*" *BST,* 1 (1896), 7-20.

An early effort to find the actual village which served as a model for the fictional one.

A131 Knies, Earl A. "The 'I' of *Jane Eyre.*" *College English,* 27 (April 1966), 546-556.

In studying Charlotte Brontë's use of the first person in *Jane Eyre,* the author suggests that the protagonist's ability to re-create a scene brings about a novel which is not wholly subjective.

A132 Kramer, Dale. "Thematic Structure in *Jane Eyre.*" *Papers on Language and Literature,* 4 (1968), 288-298.

The critic discusses revolt and submission in Jane Eyre's career.

A133 Kühnelt, H. H. "Charlotte Brontë: *Jane Eyre*" in *Der englische Roman im 19. Jahrhundert: Interpretation.* Eds. P. Goetsch, H. Kosok, and K. Otten. Berlin: E. Schmidt, 1973. Vol. also listed as B328.

A134 Langford, Thomas. "Prophetic Imagination and the Unity of *Jane Eyre.*" *Studies in the Novel,* 6 (Summer 1974), 228-235.

". . . The novel contains a quality of imagination and insight which borders on the visionary and prophetic. . . ." The critic discusses the importance of Jane's pictures as dream-visions and comments on the descriptions of the paintings and the significance of each one.

A135 Langford, Thomas. "The Three Pictures of *Jane Eyre.*" *Victorian Newsletter,* 31 (Spring 1967), 47-48.

Each of the three pictures painted by Jane is a symbolic representation of one of the major periods of her life, according to Langford. The first picture represents Lowood, the second Thornfield, and the third Marsh End.

A136 Leavis, Q. D. "Dating *Jane Eyre.*" *Times Literary Supplement,* 27 (May 1965), 436.

The critic points to contradictory internal evidence as to the time of the action of the novel. Such discrepancies in dress style and trends in Evangelism indicate that the novel is essentially fantasy.

A137 Leavis, Q. D. "Introduction" in Charlotte Brontë. *Jane Eyre.* Harmondsworth, Middlesex: Penguin, 1966.

The introduction points out the mixture of styles in the novel. But the critic comments that something "personal and morally impressive" integrates them. She compares Charlotte Brontë to D. H. Lawrence, Dickens, and George Eliot.

A138 Lester, John A., Jr. "The Consolations of Ecstasy." *English Literature in Transition,* 6 (1963), 200-211.

In an interesting study of the use of ecstasy in fiction, the critic shows that the escape scene in *Jane Eyre* is an ecstatic experience.

A139 Lodge, David. "Fire and Eyre: Charlotte Brontë's War of Earthly Elements" in *Language of Fiction: Essays in Criticism and Verbal Analysis of the English Novel.* London: Routledge and Kegan Paul, 1966.

In a careful and ambitious study, Lodge reports that he has located 150 literal and figurative usages of the fire image as symbolic passion. He disagrees with Heilman (A292) on the significance of the moon, saying that the moon must be viewed "in the context of a larger system of elemental imagery and reference."

A140 Lubbock, Percy. *The Craft of Fiction.* New York: Viking Press, 1921.

A very brief reference to Charlotte Brontë's *Jane Eyre.*

A141 McCullough, Bruce. *Representative English Novelists: Defoe to Conrad.* New York: Harper Brothers, 1946.

In a chapter called "The Subjective Novel," the author deals in character analysis of the protagonist in *Jane Eyre* and omits the other Brontë novels entirely. The critic explains the unique qualities of the novel, saying that *Jane Eyre* represents a new kind of fictional treatment; never before was: (1) a central character so all-important;

(2) reality conveyed so insistently as the experience of one consciousness; and (3) conflict revealed as between allegiance to nature or one's own integrity. The subjective voice is not Charlotte Brontë's real voice. The novel shows a woman's view of love.

A142   McElrath, Joseph. *"Jane Eyre's* 'Brocklehurst': Names, Sign and Symbol." *C.E.A. Critic,* 32 (Jan. 1971), 23.

This article suggests that in *Jane Eyre* the names have meanings. Brocklehurst, for example, means "the place of a dirty or stinking fellow."

A143   McLaughlin, M. B. "Past or Future Mindscapes: Pictures in *Jane Eyre.*" *Victorian Newsletter,* 41 (Spring 1972), 22-24.

Contrary to Langford's suggestion (A134 and A135) concerning the function of Jane's paintings in the novel, McLaughlin believes that each painting depicts one of the major losses which she had suffered: first, the death of her guardian, Mr. Reed; second, the death of Helen Burns; and third, the marriage of Miss Temple. (See also A148.)

A144   Marshall, William H. "New Introduction" in Charlotte Brontë. *Jane Eyre.* New York: Collier-Macmillan, 1962.

In this short introduction, Marshall speaks of *Jane Eyre*'s concern with individualism, with human consciousness and the problem of identity. *Jane Eyre* is not a biography: Charlotte Brontë has created a narrator separated from author: "art must remain distinct from life."

A145   Marshall, William H. "The Self, the World, and the Structure of *Jane Eyre.*" *Revue des langues vivantes,* 27 (1961), 416-425.

Jane Eyre is neither biographical nor allegorical, Marshall tells us, but is "a protracted dramatic monologue, in which the recurring apostrophe to the reader, found at those points in the narrative of heightened tension, is emotionally revealing and structurally functional rather than merely decorative."

A146   Martin, Robert K. "*Jane Eyre* and the World of Faery." *Mosaic: A Journal for the Comparative Study of Literature and Ideas,* 10 (Summer 1977), 85-95.

Martin shows Jane's relationship to the world "in fairy tale terms." Charlotte Brontë uses various fairytales to delineate her protagonist as "first a childhood Cinderella, then a Sleeping Beauty, a wife in Bluebeard's castle, and finally Beauty wed to Beast, Rapunzel healing the prince." He further explains, "Although Brontë could never have seen these tales in their psychosexual dimensions . . . she nonetheless chose among her traditional material *unconsciously* and made a choice which is peculiarly apt."

A147   Millgate, Jane. "Jane Eyre's Progress." *English Studies Supplement,* 1969, pp. 21-29.

Jane is on a moral journey like that of Christian in *Pilgrim's Progress,* according to this critic. Jane withstands her trials and becomes stronger in her integrity. Ultimately she finds her "safe haven."

A148   Millgate, Jane. "Narrative Distance in *Jane Eyre:* The Relevance of Pictures." *Modern Language Review,* 63 (1968), 315-319.

Another critic speaks on the subject of the pictures. Millgate explains how they represent Jane's development.

A149   Monod, Sylvestre. "L'Imprécision dans *Jane Eyre.*" *Etudes Anglaises,* 17 (Jan.-March 1964), 21-29.

Monod believes that the inaccuracies, contradictions, and misquotations in *Jane Eyre* were caused by the rush and impetus with which Charlotte Brontë wrote.

A150   Monod, Sylvestre. "The Thirty 'Readers' of *Jane Eyre*" in Charlotte Brontë. *Jane Eyre.* Norton Critical Edition. New York: Norton, 1971.

The critic comments on the thirty examples of direct address to "Reader" in *Jane Eyre.* Monod feels that they reveal "the narrator's superiority and the reader's nullity." He feels that Charlotte Brontë demonstrates her "sterling character" and "indomitable courage" but that she disdains males, novel readers, and Frenchmen – and he is all three.

A151   Moser, Lawrence E. "From Portrait to Person: A Note on the Surrealistic in *Jane Eyre.*" *Nineteenth Century Fiction,* 20 (Dec. 1965), 275-281.

A brief note suggests that the surrealistic qualities of Jane's drawings reveal the personality of the author. The paintings show "the internal, the external, and the actual." Through Jane we are able to see the author.

A152   Nissl, Notburga. "Die Charaktere und die Technik ihrer Darstellung in den Romanen Charlotte Brontës (studiert an *Jane Eyre*)." Unpublished doctoral dissertation, University of Innsbruck, 1937.

Another German dissertation discusses the methods Charlotte Brontë used in creating the characters in her most popular novel.

A153   Oldfield, Jennifer. "'The Homely Web of Truth': Dress as the Mirror of Personality in *Jane Eyre* and *Villette.*" *BST,* 16 (1973), 177-184.

We read in *Jane Eyre* that "Externals have a great effect on the young," and in the novel costumes set the person. This critic mentions that Charlotte Brontë felt her own deficiency, felt that she was a "queer, quizzical looking" being, especially with her spectacles. She hated extravagance in clothing. In the novels, dress becomes "a realisation of the illusion versus reality opposition; the duality of the world."

A154   Osborne, Marianne M. "The Hero and Heroine in the British Bildungsroman: *David Copperfield,* and *A Portrait of the Artist as a Young Man, Jane Eyre* and *The Rainbow.*" Unpublished doctoral dissertation, Tulane University, 1972. *DAI,* 32:4013.

The author observes that by ". . . tracing the quests of two heroines, Jane Eyre and Ursula Brangwen, and two heroes, David

Copperfield and Stephen Dedalus, the reader finds that the stories of these quests share the same basic pattern. Each protagonist moves through a trial upon false goals, and through a severe disillusionment marked in the novels by a wilderness experience."

A155   Paden, William D. "Introduction" in *Jane Eyre*. New York: Random House, 1950.

Declaring that "few novels which have survived the test of time contain so many defects as *Jane Eyre*," the editor speaks of the destruction of the "illusion of vital reality" by contrived plot and structure.

A156   Passel, Anne W. *Jane Eyre by Charlotte Brontë*. Book Note Series. New York: Barnes and Noble, 1969.

A study-guide for students reading the novel as a work of literary craftsmanship. Emphasis is placed on the balanced structure of the novel.

A157   Pell, Nancy. "Resistance, Rebellion, and Marriage: The Economics of *Jane Eyre*." *Nineteenth Century Fiction*, 31 (March, 1977), 397-420.

Romanticism with its emphasis on the free feelings of the individual is balanced in *Jane Eyre* by the author's attack on middleclass "patriarchal authority," according to Pell. This attitude of Charlotte Brontë's finds full expression in contrasting Jane's marriage with that of the traditional dowry-marriage of Bertha and Rochester.

A158   Peterson, M. Jeanne. "The Victorian Governess: Status Incongruence in Family and Society" in *Suffer and Be Still: Women in the Victorian Age*. Ed. Martha Vicinus. Bloomington: Indiana University Press, 1972.

The writer uses the example of Jane Eyre's position as governess to introduce the discussion of social conditions.

A159   Peterson, W. S. "Henry James on *Jane Eyre*." *Times Literary Supplement*, July 30, 1971, pp. 919-920.

Peterson comments that Henry James objected to *Jane Eyre* because it confuses art and life. He believed that the public's sentimental reaction to the life of the author gave *Jane Eyre* its long popularity (see C227).

A160   Porter, D. O. "Heroines and Victims." *Massachusetts Review,* 17 (Autumn 1976), 540-542.

In a discussion of Jean Rhys' four novels as views of the alienated woman, the critic talks about *Wide Sargasso Sea* (A162). We are told that the "facts are taken straight out of *Jane Eyre*" in presenting the culture of the Englishman in the colony. The novel serves as a critical essay on *Jane Eyre*, Porter says, as *Wide Sargasso Sea* "illuminates and is illuminated by *Jane Eyre.*"

A161   Prescott, Joseph. "*Jane Eyre:* A Romantic Exemplum with a Difference" in *Twelve Original Essays on Great English Novels.* Ed. Charles Shapiro. Detroit: Wayne State University Press, 1960.

Here the sexual repressions of Charlotte Brontë are discussed as being unintentionally revealed by the erotic imagery in *Jane Eyre*, "which grows more and more pronounced as the narrative unfolds." The article considers the romantic, didactic, and erotic elements in *Jane Eyre,* concluding that it is "a rousing dream of passion."

A162   Rhys, Jean. *Wide Sargasso Sea.* London: Andre Deutsch; New York: W. W. Norton, 1966.

This popular novel tells about Bertha Mason in the Indies, in the days before the Rochesters moved to England. (See also A160.)

A163   Rich, Adrienne. "*Jane Eyre*: The Temptations of a Motherless Woman." *Ms.,* 11 (Oct. 1973), 68.

Rich claims Charlotte Brontë's message in *Jane Eyre* is a feminist manifesto: "It is vain to say human beings ought to be satisfied with tranquility." The protagonist goes on to say, "Women are supposed to be very calm generally, but women feel just as men feel. . . ." The novel, moreover, is one in which "we see women in real and supportive relationship to each other," as the critic points out.

35

A164   Riley, M. "Gothic Melodrama and Spiritual Romance: Vision and Fidelity in Two Versions of *Jane Eyre.*" *Literature/Film Quarterly,* 3 (1975), 145-159.

As many young people know *Jane Eyre* through the films, it is of interest to note one of the better reviews of two film versions of the story.

A165   Robinson, Dennis. "Elizabeth Gaskell and 'A Few Words About Jane Eyre.'" *Notes and Queries,* 23 (1976), 396-398.

He suggests that "A Few Words About *Jane Eyre*" in *Sharpe's London Magazine* (see A73) was not written by Mrs. Gaskell, as suggested by J. G. Sharps in *Mrs. Gaskell's Observation and Invention: A Study of Her Non-biographical Works* (Fontwell, 1970). Robinson puts forward the name of Catherine Winkworth as author. Because of the personal nature of this attack, the item is also listed as A419.

A166   Ronald, Margaret A. "Functions of Setting in the Novel: From Mrs. Radcliffe to Charles Dickens." Unpublished doctoral dissertation, Northwestern University, 1971. *DAI,* 31:5373.

"Within the confines of a novel, setting operates in a number of ways, although in its simplest form it serves merely as a background. But between the end of the eighteenth and the middle of the nineteenth centuries, novelists learned to employ setting in increasingly complex roles. This study examines that development." (Charlotte Brontë's *Jane Eyre* is included in this study.)

A167   Scargill, M. H. "All Passion Spent: A Revaluation of *Jane Eyre.*" *University of Toronto Quarterly,* 19 (Jan. 1950), 120-125.

A further investigation of the struggle between passion and reason reveals the emotional content of the novel. Scargill points out that while *Jane Eyre* is improbable on the surface, it is authentic in its basic poetic truth.

A168   Schorer, Mark. "Introduction" in Charlotte Brontë. *Jane Eyre.* Cambridge, Mass.: Houghton, Mifflin, 1959. Reprinted as *"Jane Eyre"* in *The World We Imagine: Selected Essays.* New York: Farrar, Straus and Giroux, 1968.

A general survey of the novel, this essay touches on biography and juvenilia but is primarily concerned with the symbolic organization of the novel. Emphasizing the nature symbols (of the tree, etc.), the novel uses Freudian and pre-Freudian symbolism. "The basic organizing principle is like that of dramatic poetry rather than like that of conventionally realistic fiction."

A169   Schwartz, Roberta. "Art as Ethic: A Study of *Jane Eyre.*" *North Dakota Quarterly,* 44 (Winter 1976), 20-30.

    Jane Eyre shows Charlotte Brontë as a moral guide, this critic feels. Charlotte Brontë's novels are created to superimpose an aesthetic order on daily existence. She believes that emotion can guide one toward responsible action when it is controlled.

A170   Shannon, Edgar F., Jr. "The Present Tense in *Jane Eyre.*" *Nineteenth Century Fiction,* 10 (Sept. 1955), 141-145.

    A study made in 1955 shows the stylistic complexity of the novel with particular attention to the lapses into the present tense. The critic sees these shifts as indicative of the structural divisions of the novel. The present tense is also used as a device for dramatic immediacy.

A171   Shapiro, Arnold. "In Defense of *Jane Eyre.*" *Studies in English Literature,* 8 (1968), 681-698.

    This article points out that Jane's quest for freedom sets the theme and challenge of the plot and organizes the structure. The triumph of the protagonist becomes the triumph of the human heart.

A172   Showalter, Elaine. *A Literature of Their Own: British Women Novelists from Brontë to Lessing.* Princeton, New Jersey: Princeton University Press, 1977.

    In this feminist book Charlotte Brontë is admired. "In *Jane Eyre,* Brontë attempts to depict a complete female identity." Showalter further states that "Brontë's most profound innovation, however, is the division of the Victorian female psyche into its extreme components of mind and body." Not only in the behavior of the protagonist do we see this dichotomy, but it is externalized in the extremes of Helen Burns and Bertha Mason. This book (written by the director of Women's Studies, Douglass College, Rutgers University) is forthright in attitude.

A173   Siebenschuh, William R. "The Image of the Child and the Plot of *Jane Eyre.*" *Studies in the Novel,* 8 (Fall 1976), 304-317.

The reader is given an early clue to the meaning of the child in Jane's dream in the central dream sequence. Before the dream occurs, Jane explains a bit of folklore, that "to dream of children" is "a sure sign of trouble." The child can be read as a "dream-distorted reminder" of her position as governess, of her as a potential Céline Varens, of her new-born love for Rochester, or of herself seeking comfort and love.

A174   Siefert, Susan E. *The Dilemma of the Talented Woman: A Study in Nineteenth-Century Fiction.* St. Albans, Vt.: Eden Press Women's Publications, 1978. First appearing as unpublished doctoral dissertation, Marquette University, 1974. *DAI,* 36:285.

The author observes that ". . . nineteenth century women are all too often regarded without exception, as creatures who were kind, gentle, unaspiring, unassertive, and intellectually feeble. This study explores the limitation of this stereotype by focusing upon five atypical heroines of nineteenth century fiction: Elizabeth Bennet of *Pride and Prejudice,* Emma Woodhouse of *Emma,* Dorothea Brook of *Middlemarch,* Maggie Tulliver of *The Mill on the Floss,* and Charlotte Brontë's Jane Eyre."

A175   Sloman, J. "Jane Eyre's Childhood and Popular Children's Literature" in *Children's Literature: the Great Excluded,* Vol. 3. Eds., F. Butler and B. A. Brockman. Storrs, Conn.: Children's Literature Association, 1974.

A176   Smith, David. "Incest Patterns in Two Victorian Novels." *Literature and Psychology,* 15 (Summer 1965), 135-162.

The author deals with what he considers incest patterns in *Jane Eyre* and *The Mill on the Floss.* He sees a perverted father-daughter relationship between Jane and Rochester. The novel is said to be patterned on the Freudian "swing of Jane's psyche between the incest wish and the incest taboo." This is Jane's central conflict throughout the novel.

A177   Smith, Margaret. "Introduction," in Charlotte Brontë. *Jane Eyre.* London: Oxford University Press, 1972.

In this reprint of the text from the Clarendon edition, the editor gives an account of Charlotte Brontë's revisions. In "Note to the Text" in the "Introduction," she gathers important attitudes from critics over the years.

A178   Solomon, Eric. "*Jane Eyre,* Fire and Water." *College English,* 25 (1964), 215-217.

Solomon finds a "hard coherence of thematic and symbolic pattern" in *Jane Eyre:* the five-part division, contrasting characters, and foreshadowing. The main theme — the search for a home — is supported by two pervasive images: fire (of passion) and water (of pure reason), between which "love must find a middle way." In an attempt to show Charlotte Brontë's intensified use of imagery as structure, the critic makes this oversimplification: "Basically, the novel is divided into four acts and a brief conclusion. In each act the same scenes are played out. Jane comes into conflict with authority, defeats it by her inner strength, and departs into exile."

A179   Stedman, Jane W. "Charlotte Brontë and Bewick's 'British Birds.'" *BST,* 15 (1966), 36-40.

Stedman offers an explanation of the influence of Bewick on the three drawings. Not only in the presence of bird images but even in her diction, Charlotte Brontë shows that Bewick's book has become part of the protagonist's mode of expression. The author uses Bewick's technical term "irid" in describing the painting.

A180   Stein, Sondra Gayle. "'Woman and her Master': the Feminine Ideal as Social Myth in the Novels of Charles Dickens, William Thackeray and Charlotte Brontë." Unpublished doctoral dissertation, Washington University, 1976. *DAI,* 37:5149.

Chapter four deals with *Jane Eyre:* "Through a structural analysis of Jane Eyre's relationships with Edward Rochester and St.

John Rivers this chapter explores the way in which Charlotte Brontë, by fusing the identity of woman and worker, responds to the need for radical, social and economic change and, at the same time, rejects the spurious notion of woman's duty which demands that she sacrifice herself to compensate for ruthless self-interest, the ambition for power of her protector, man."

A181   Sue, Eugène. *Kitty Bell: the Orphan.* Ed. Esther Alice Chadwick. London: Sir Issac Pitman, 1914.

Offered by the editors as "possibly an earlier version of Charlotte Brontë's *Jane Eyre*," this story was written about 1844 and published as the work of Eugène Sue. Mrs. Chadwick, an early Brontë authority, sees this as an early story by Charlotte Brontë. This proposal is answered by Sir Tresham Lever in 1969 (A252).

A182   Sullivan, Paula. "Rochester Reconsidered: *Jane Eyre* in the Light of the Samson Story." *BST,* 16 (1973), 192-198.

"*Jane Eyre* is a woman's hostile sexual fantasy about a man," this critic declares. Rochester is patterned on Samson, with the same sin and a similar punishment: his physical weakening, his being blinded, and his being crushed by a building. Jane, as Charlotte Brontë's persona, becomes Rochester's "good angel." The reversal of the male-female role at the end is established as Rochester becomes a figure of "withered vitality." Charlotte Brontë uses the moral framework of reason versus passion to set a "norm of self-government and equality between the sexes."

A183   Swanson, Roger M. "Guilt in Selected Victorian Novels." Unpublished doctoral dissertation, University of Illinois, 1969. *DAI,* 30:342.

"The purpose of this study is to examine the nature of guilt as it is manifested in five novels of the Victorian period of English Literature." Swanson states that in *Jane Eyre,* Charlotte Brontë "establishes the standard of the 'world of spirits' beyond conventional social and religious values as the rule by which human morality is to be judged."

A184   Thorpe, M. "Other Side: *Wide Sargasso Sea* and *Jane Eyre.*" *Ariel,* 8 (July 1977), 99-110.

A comparison of the problem of Rochester's first marriage as seen in the modern novel by Jean Rhys (A162) and in the original story.

A185   Tintner, Adeline R. "Henry James's Use of *Jane Eyre* in *The Turn of the Screw.*" *BST,* 17 (1976), 42-45.

The critic mentions Henry James's attitude toward Charlotte Brontë (see C227 and A159) in discussing James's basis for *The Turn of the Screw* (see also A112). In it he "took possession of the persona of Charlotte Brontë and of certain basic structures in her novel *Jane Eyre.*" The similarities include Charlotte Brontë's age (30), her handwriting, the fact that she was the eldest daughter of a parson and the hints from *Jane Eyre* of the madwoman in the attic and the officiousness of the housekeeper, among other things.

A186   Tompkins, J. M. S. "Jane Eyre's 'Iron Shroud.'" *Modern Language Review,* 22 (1927), 195-197.

The expression is used in Chapter 34: "My iron shroud contracted around me" as Jane feels herself pressed toward marriage with St. John Rivers. The expression is here presented as an allusion to "a story called 'The Iron Shroud' by William Mudford, which appeared in *Blackwood's Magazine* for August 1830."

A187   Vance, N. "Charlotte Brontë's Mr. Brocklehurst." *Notes and Queries,* 24:1 (Jan.-Feb. 1977), 25.

Vance has traced the name Brocklehurst to a story: "An Account of the Conversion and Death of Mr. Edward Brocklehurst" in *Methodist Magazine* which Charlotte Brontë may have seen.

A188   Wagner, Geoffrey. *Five for Freedom: A Study of Feminism in Fiction.* London: George Allen and Unwin, 1972.

The discussion in Chapter Three concerns "*Jane Eyre.* With a Commencement on Catherine Earnshaw: Beyond Biology."

A189   Werkmeister, Lucyle. "The Great Brontë Robbery." *Prairie Schooner,* 31 (1957), 237-246.

Here is a comparison of Martha Finley's *Elsie Dinsmore* and *Elsie's Holiday* with *Jane Eyre*. The critic proves through analysis that the American author "stole ninety percent of the material for the books from *Jane Eyre*, the first American edition of which was hardly two years old at the time" (1868).

A190   West, Katherine. *Chapter of Governesses: A Study of the Governess in English Fiction, 1800-1949.* London: Cohen and West, 1949.

In a survey of the governess in literature, West shows that Jane Eyre suffers many of the trials that beset the typical fictional governess, and yet in many ways she was outside the usual pattern.

A191   Yeazell, Ruth B. "More True than Real: Jane Eyre's Mysterious Summons." *Nineteenth Century Fiction,* 29 (Sept. 1974), 127-143.

The scene in which Jane receives her mysterious summons should not come as a surprise to the reader. Jane has been prepared for such a cry as she has gone through the trials which have made her free to respond. The scene is "the crucial stroke of the novel's psychological design."

A192   Yuen, Maria. "Two Crises of Decision in *Jane Eyre.*" *English Studies,* 47 (June 1976), 215-226.

Twice Jane Eyre asserts her independence and moves forward in establishing her individual identity. The ideals of Charlotte Brontë are reflected in Jane's resolution. In her dramatic departure from Thornfield Hall, Jane is asserting her independent will, vital to her self-respect. This same will is called forth when she refuses the self-annihilating relationship offered by St. John Rivers. The crises are faced with similar resolve.

Criticism of *Shirley*

A193   Ankenbrandt, Katherine Ware. "Charlotte Brontë's *Shirley* and John Leyden's 'The Cout of Keeldar.'" *Victorian Newsletter,* 34 (Fall 1968), 33-34.

The source of Shirley's family name may be an old poem used by Scott in *Minstrelsy of the Scottish Border,* Part III and *The Lady of the Lake.*

A194   Anon. "The Last of the *Shirley* Curates." *BST,* 4 (1914), 82-83.

A report is made on the death of the last of the people thought to have been represented by the curates in *Shirley.* Charlotte Brontë's husband Arthur Bell Nicholls is supposed to have been the model for the curate Macarthey, "decent, decorous, and conscientious."

A195   Bentley, Phyllis. *The English Regional Novel.* London: G. Allen and Unwin, 1941.

Miss Bentley, a fervid Brontë supporter, includes the novels of Charlotte Brontë in her study of the origins and development of the regional novel in England. She finds that *Shirley* is the "first great English regional novel." *Wuthering Heights* cannot be considered a "regional" novel except in setting, as the author's intention is not to depict people and incidents representative of an area.

A196   Briggs, Asa. "Private and Social Themes in *Shirley.*" *BST,* 13 (1958), 203.

This valuable article suggests the three themes in *Shirley* and evaluates the novel as "perhaps the first impressive regional novel in the English language," a statement similar to that made by Miss Bentley in 1941 (see A195). Briggs finds Charlotte Brontë "particularly sensitive to the ambivalent attitudes of the mill owners she was describing." In the novel Charlotte Brontë's statement of the issues was liberal and enlightened, though not her solution. Briggs discusses the historical accuracy of the treatment of the Luddite riots.

A197   Cazamian, Louis. *Le Roman Social en Angleterre, 1830-1850.* Paris: Librairie Georges Bellais, 1903. Reissued in English as *The Social*

Novel in England, 1830-1850. Trans. and Ed. Martin Fido. London: Routledge and Kegan Paul, 1973.

Includes a discussion of *Shirley* as a social study.

A198   Clapham, Barbara. "Charlotte Brontë and Oakwell Hall." *BST,* 17 (1978), 210-213.

A discussion of the home which has been identified as the original of "Fieldhead" in *Shirley.* (See also A213 and A219.)

A199   Copley, J. "The Portrayal of Dialect in *Wuthering Heights* and *Shirley." Transactions of the Yorkshire Dialect Society,* 14 (1976), 7-16.

An authority looks into Charlotte Brontë's handling of dialect, comparing it to the dialect recorded by Emily Brontë in *Wuthering Heights.* Vol. also listed as B113.

A200   Ferrett, Mabel. *Shirley Country: The Brontës in the Spen Valley.* Youlgrave: Hub, 1973.

An environmental study of the countryside in which *Shirley* takes place.

A201   Gary, Franklin. "Charlotte Brontë and George Henry Lewes." *PMLA,* 51 (June 1936), 518-542.

The critic argues that Charlotte Brontë wrote *Shirley* in answer to Lewes' criticism of *Jane Eyre* (see A53).

A202   Girdler, Lew. "Charlotte Brontë's *Shirley* and Scott's *The Black Dwarf." Modern Language Notes,* 71 (March 1956), 187.

Girdler thinks Charlotte Brontë found the name "Keeldar" in Scott's story. He compares *Shirley* with this story and Charlotte Brontë's "The Green Dwarf" with one incident in *Ivanhoe.* (See also Dry's suggestion that *The Black Dwarf* was the chief source of *Wuthering Heights,* B138.)

A203   Grayson, Laura. "*Shirley:* Charlotte Brontë's Own Evidence." *BST,* 14 (1963), 31.

This critic casts doubt on Ivy Holgate's theory (A205) that Francis Butterfield persuaded Charlotte not to use the Chartists and on this advice the author chose the Luddites.

A204   Heaton, H. "The Economic Background of *Shirley.*" *BST,* 8 (1932), 3-19.

In this discussion of labor conditions in West Riding at the time of the action of the novel, the writer emphasizes the shift of cottage industry to factory and mill, the problems of child labor, and the workers' resistance to the coming of the machine. These major problems come clearly to us from the pages of the novel.

A205   Holgate, Ivy. "The Structure of *Shirley.*" *BST,* 14 (1962), 27-35.

Miss Holgate suggests that there was a shift in location and emphasis from the York Chartists problem to the Luddite uprisings in "the Heavy Woollen districts of West Riding" where Charlotte Brontë's friends the Taylors lived. In her article she refers to Emily Brontë as the heroine of the novel. It is thought that Shirley is a depiction of Emily Brontë (as shown through her independence, love of nature, and pantheism) and of Mary Taylor (with her energy, practicality, and feminism). Does this combination of characteristics of two people account for the inconsistency and unbelievability of the protagonist?

A206   Jeffares, A. Norman. "*Shirley* – A Yorkshire Novel." *BST,* (1969), 281-293.

Shirley is considered to be Charlotte Brontë's most feministic novel. She had intended a novel about social conditions; she wrote about what she knew: "the differences between men and women and their relationships." Her major achievement is in creating Shirley, "one of the early spirited heroines of the English novel," and in picturing "the plight of intelligent women in the nineteenth century."

A207   Kneis, Earl Allen. "Art, Death, and the Composition of *Shirley.*" *Victorian Newsletter,* 28 (Fall 1965), 22-24.

Another study of the relationship between the deaths in the Brontë family and the resultant critical supposition that there are biographical echoes in *Shirley* shows, by scholarly investigation, the time lapse between fictional recounting and the events themselves. In spite of critics who base their supposition on Mrs. Gaskell's "facts," Kneis shows that only one volume had been completed before Branwell's death and Louis Moore had already been mentioned. That Charlotte Brontë's "vision was primarily private" has been proved by her composition of *Jane Eyre* and *Villette.*

A208   Korg, Jacob. "The Problem of Unity in *Shirley.*" *Nineteenth Century Fiction,* 12 (Sept. 1957), 125-136.

Unity as seen through patterns of characters, related to the romantic precept of egoism, is here presented with interesting implications. Korg divides the characters into three groups: (1) the Romantics: Shirley, Caroline, the Moore brothers, the Yorke children, (2) the unimaginative Yorkshiremen: Mr. Helston, the elder Yorkes, Joe Scott, and (3) the effete and over-civilized outsiders: the Curates and the Sympsons.

A209   Lane, Margaret. "Introduction" in Charlotte Brontë. *Shirley.* Everyman Edition. London: J. M. Dent and Sons, 1908. Reprinted 1962.

This knowledgeable critic sees Shirley as a pioneer, the "first of that long line of boyish, independent heroines." She finds, however, that *Shirley* is not quite a great novel: "it attempts too much; with two heroes and two heroines, with a historical-industrial theme, and a subsidiary thread of contrasting the futile curates with the Christian practice of the despised old maids in the village."

A210   Passel, Anne W. "The Three Voices in Charlotte Brontë's *Shirley.*" *BST,* 15:4 (1969), 323-326.

In this article the novel is presented as being built around a three-part theme: (1) that man is isolated, (2) that he needs independence and self-respect, and (3) that man seeks his counterpart in woman, and she in him.

A211   Rosengarten, Herbert J. "Charlotte Brontë's *Shirley* and the *Leeds Mercury.*" *Studies in English Literature: 1500-1900,* 16 (Autumn 1976), 591-600.

In assessing the historicity of *Shirley,* the critic suggests that while the facts are accurate (based on Charlotte Brontë's research in the *Leeds Mercury* in the years 1812-1814) the author's own interest and sensitivity have created the novel as a work of literature.

A212   Shapiro, Arnold. "Public Themes and Private Lives: Social Criticism in *Shirley.*" *Papers on Language and Literature,* 4 (1968), 74-84.

Shapiro feels that the "theme of selfishness, the lack of sympathy between people, connects everything − public or private − in the novel."

A213   Sprittles, J. *History and Description of Oakwell Hall and Manor.* Batley, 1963.

More about the original home which appears as "Fieldhead" in *Shirley.* See also Clapham (A198) and Woledge (A219).

A214   Summers, Chris. *Reflections on the Brontës in Spen Valley and District.* Cleckheaton: John H. Hirst, 1973.

Giving a clear picture of the district in which the action of *Shirley* takes place, this brief book adds both historic and geographic background for the events in the novel.

A215   Todd, William B. "An Early State of Charlotte Brontë's *Shirley,* 1849." *Book Collector,* 12 (1963), 355-356.

A textual study of the changing form of the novel.

A216   Tompkins, J. M. S. "Caroline Helstone's Eyes." *BST,* 14 (1961), 18-28.

This article is based on the biographical approach which suggests that the character of Caroline is built on Anne Brontë. This contention is supported by internal evidence from the novel. The main proof is that after the date of Anne's death the author refers to Caroline Helstone's eyes as blue, although they had been brown. There is also the thought that in the original plan Caroline (based on Anne) was to remain single, but Charlotte Brontë gave her a "happier fate" to counteract the tragedy of Anne's death.

A217   Vicinus, Martha, ed. *Suffer and Be Still: Women in the Victorian Age.* Bloomington: Indiana University Press, 1972.

In her introduction on "The Perfect Victorian Lady," the editor cites Shirley Keeldar as an example of the freedom-seeking young woman: "more outspoken . . . longing for a richer life." Vicinus remarks that in her novels Charlotte Brontë dwelt on "unrequited or false love."

A218   Westbrook, James Seymour, Jr. "Sensibility and Society: A Study in Themes," Unpublished doctoral dissertation, Columbia University, 1964.

This dissertation shows how five novelists handle sensibility within a social framework. *Shirley* is used to demonstrate "the difficulties encountered by strongly individual sensibilities as they come face to face with convention."

A219   Woledge, Geoffrey. *Oakwell Hall.* Huddersfield: Kirklees Metropolitan Council Library, 1978.

Details of the home used by Charlotte Brontë as a model for "Fieldhead" in *Shirley.* See also Clapham (A198) and Sprittles (A213).

A220   Arndt, F. C. "*Villette:* Another Turn of the Wheel." Unpublished doctoral dissertation, Duke University, 1973. *DAI*, 34:718.

Arndt argues that all four novels "present life as a moral pilgrimage, often consisting of a series of tests by which an isolated individual proves his, or more often, her integrity and triumphs over the solitude an inimical society forces upon him by finding and winning a correspondingly sensitive and sympathetic love. In *The Professor, Jane Eyre,* and *Shirley* this movement toward union becomes progressively more difficult and culminates in the failure of human love to redeem one from loneliness in *Villette.*"

A221   Bedick, David B. "The Changing Role of Anxiety in the Novel." Unpublished doctoral dissertation, New York University, 1975. *DAI*, 36:3682.

Bedick observes that "anxiety has gained thematic stature within the novel while once it merely enhanced narrative patterns. Aspects of this changing role are developed through an examination of ten novels. . . . In section two, the anxious state of living with deferred hope is studied from the vantage point of Charlotte Brontë's *Villette.*"

A222   Briet, Suzanne. "'Villette,' le Roman de Charlotte Brontë, a-t-il influencé quelques poèmes d'Arthur Rimbaud?" *Revue d'Histoire Littéraire de la France,* 68:834-840.

This French scholar suggests the influence on the imagist poet and parallels Rimbaud's *Scène Parada* with *Villette.*

A223   Burkhart, Charles. "Brontë's *Villette.*" *Explicator,* 21:1 (Sept. 1962), Item 8.

A suggestion that the moon imagery forms the basic symbolism in the novel.

A224   Burkhart, Charles. "George Eliot's Debt to *Villette.*" *Victorian Newsletter,* 52 (Fall 1977), 10-14.

George Eliot wrote in a review in the *Westminster Review,* 1856, about *Villette:* "which we, at least, would rather read for the third time than most new novels for the first." Burkhart points out the use of quotations from *Villette* in *Middlemarch* and the parallel of the characters Lydgate and Bretton.

A225   Burkhart, Charles. "The Nuns of *Villette.*" *Victorian Newsletter,* 44 (Fall 1973), 8-13.

In supporting the idea that "*Villette* concerns life-engagement vs. life-detachment," the critic shows that the role of the nun reinforces the "psychological and philosophical . . . development of its heroine, Lucy Snowe." Burkhart points out the parallel between the five appearances of the nun with the "sexual as well as spiritual" history of the protagonist. The critic concludes that "the nun is the operative device" by which Lucy "attains adulthood and . . . a wise acceptance of those deprivations for which she was, from the beginning, intended."

A226   Charlier, Gustave. "La vie bruxelloise dans *Villette.*" *Passages: essais.* Bruxelles: La Renaissance du Libre, 1947. Reprinted in translation in *BST,* 12 (1955), 386.

Extracts of the essay in Professor Charlier's *Passages* published in Brussels in 1947 have been translated by Dr. Phyllis Bentley. Charlier again attempts to equate the incidents in the story with actual happenings in Brussels, particularly in his description of the Brussels salon of 1842.

A227   Colby, Robert A. *Fiction with a Purpose: Major and Minor Nineteenth Century Novels.* Bloomington: Indiana University Press, 1967.

Chapter VI, about *Villette,* is called "Lucy Snowe and the Good Governess." It is a discussion of the novel, comparing Lucy with other governesses in literature and in life. Colby feels that *Villette* is a "sermon against despair." Lucy "represents, among other things, the conflict between the 'night-side' and the 'day-side' of nature." The critic credits *Villette* with opening up "the subconscious to later novelists." In discussing the total view of Charlotte Brontë as novelist, Colby finds her novels socially relevant. The date of *Jane Eyre* is the same as the founding of the Governesses' Benevolent Institute and of Queens College for Women. Charlotte Brontë writes of the school: "our heroes and heroines really never close the classroom door behind them." Also closely related to its time, *Villette* reflects the anti-Catholic scare of the 1850's.

A228   Colby, Robert A. "*Villette* and the Life of the Mind." *PMLA*, 74 (Sept. 1960), 410-419.

As a literary biography, this study avoids a literal treatment of Charlotte Brontë's personal life, dealing entirely with her creative life. In the study Colby traces Lucy Snowe's emotional development and finds it parallel to Charlotte Brontë's artistic development.

A229   Coursen, Herbert R., Jr. "Storm and Calm in *Villette*." *Discourse*, 5 (Summer 1962), 318-333.

Calm and storm, which play such a large part in the ambiance of all of Charlotte Brontë's novels, are here presented as the thematic opposites which give dimension to *Villette*. The patterning of these extremes marks the maturation of the protagonist.

A230   Dunbar, Georgia S. "Proper Names in *Villette*." *Nineteenth Century Fiction*, 15 (1960), 77-80.

Although on the surface this seems to be a study of the names used in the novel, this article also suggests the basic intent of the novel. The critic seeks to find ironic and symbolic intent in the choice of proper names, particularly through translation from the French.

A231   Goldfarb, Russell. *Sexual Repression and Victorian Literature.* Lewisburg, Pennsylvania: Bucknell University Press, 1970.

Chapter Seven is on *Villette*, giving the author much room for psychological speculation. He contends that "as a psychological study of sexual frigidity, *Villette* is a remarkable book." Lucy needs to repress her emotions but cannot. Finally her "repressed libidinal energies" are discharged by "an imagined sexual experience." Then Lucy is free to accept man.

A232   Hoar, Nancy Cowley. "'And My Ending is Despair': *Villette* — Charlotte Brontë's Valediction." *BST*, 16 (1973), 185-191.

Matthew Arnold had earlier suggested that *Villette* is "disagreeable" because "the author's mind contains nothing but hunger, rebellion and rage." Hoar, quoting Prospero's epilogue, says not "rage" but bitterness. The last word in *Villette* is "Farewell," perhaps indicating the solitude and loneliness of these years. August 1852, while she was working on *Villette*, Charlotte Brontë wrote: "My life is but a pale blank, and often a very weary burden and the future sometimes appals me." By the end of May, ten months later, Charlotte Brontë was caught up emotionally with Mr. Nicholls. He proposed just two weeks after she mailed volume three of *Villette* to the publisher.

A233   Hook, Andrew D. "Charlotte Brontë, the Imagination, and *Villette*" in *The Brontës: A Collection of Critical Essays*. Ed. Ian Gregor. Englewood Cliffs, New Jersey: Prentice-Hall, 1970.

The critic believes that the basic theme of *Villette* is the conflict in "the choice between the ecstasies of imagination and the stern voice of reason." In the novel, romantic excitement is internalized in Lucy. It is a psychological novel in that Lucy as narrator and protagonist is externally passive and internally passionate. The inner conflict is resolved when a balance is achieved between romanticism and reality.

A234   Johnson, D. H. "'Daring the Dread Glance': Charlotte Brontë's Treatment of the Supernatural in *Villette*." *Nineteenth Century Fiction*, 20:4 (March 1966), 325-336.

The thematic function of the subplot of the ghostly nun is analyzed as a device for marking the successive stages by which Lucy Snowe reaches self-realization. The four-part structure of the plot is also presented.

A235   Lederer, Clara. "'Little God-Sister.'" *Trollopian*, 2 (Dec. 1947), 169-175.

The biographical elements in *Villette* are discussed, particularly as they affect the characterization of M. Paul.

A236   Millett, Kate. *Sexual Politics*. New York: Doubleday, 1970.

According to this feminist view, *Villette* is a book "too subversive to be popular." It is a study of the effect which "life in a male-supremacist society has upon the psyche of a woman." We see Lucy as a passive observer, especially of men. Bretton is seen as an egoist and Paul Emanuel as a chauvinist, afraid of competition with women. Lucy puts up with this state and finally wins freedom through education and money. "Escape is all over the book."

A237 Pascal, Roy. "The Autobiographical Novel and Autobiography." *Essays in Criticism,* 9 (1959), 134-150.

The autobiographical novelist seeks "something general, representative, within his own experience, the deeper logic within his character, which life itself may in certain respects distort. . . ." With this definition in mind, the critic concludes that *Villette* transcends autobiography.

A238 Platt, Carolyn V. "How Feminist is *Villette?*" *Women and Literature,* 3 (1975), 16-27.

The author feels that there are certain feminist elements in Lucy Snowe's desires: her independence, experience, growth, and her ambition for "a school of her own." However, she also longs to adore a dominating lover. The novel ends with a cooperative association, but still a dominant-submissive relationship and belief that to be fulfilled woman needs the love of a man. The critic sees Lucy's struggle as the same as that of women today.

A239 Tillotson, Geoffrey. "Introduction," in Charlotte Brontë's *Villette.* Riverside Edition. Boston: Houghton Mifflin, 1971.

A brief introduction to this edition proposes that the novel is a "homely" novel, not a "sensational" one, devoted to the study of the mind of the protagonist, emphasizing her courage. Tillotson points out the poetic quality of the prose and praises the unity in the construction of the novel.

A240   Brammer, Margaret M. "A Critical Study of Charlotte Brontë's *The Professor.*" Unpublished master's thesis, Bedford College, University of London, 1958.

George Sand's *Consuelo* is suggested as the source of this novel. Miss Brammer gives details of the manuscript of *The Professor* and sets up a parallel of the imagery with that in *Villette.*

A241   Brammer, Margaret M. "Manuscript of *The Professor.*" *Review of English Studies,* n.s. 11 (May 1960), 157-170.

Going beyond the ideas presented in her master's thesis (A240) this scholar adds to our understanding of the original story of *The Professor.*

A242   Lane, Margaret. "Introduction" in Charlotte Brontë. *The Professor.* Everyman Edition. London: J. M. Dent and Sons, 1910. Reprinted in 1954.

This short introduction suggests that traditionally the first novel "lies close to the author's own experience." The critic refers to Charlotte Brontë's weakness in the stories of Angria: "Imagination, which was her genius, was also her temptation." She tried to subdue it in *The Professor* with mixed results. The book is pitched in a minor key; "the tone is quiet."

A243   Wheeler, Michael. "Literary and Biblical Allusion in *The Professor.*" *BST,* 17 (1976), 46-57.

Wheeler detects reference to the Bible and to *Pilgrim's Progress* among the allusions in the novel. He is particularly interested in the way in which the allusions are incorporated into the novel. He finds Charlotte Brontë's technique halfway between that used in her juvenilia and that used in *Jane Eyre.* He identifies three kinds of allusions: those set off in quotation marks, those which are unmarked quotations, and those which are references to the original material.

Criticism of Other Writings

A244   Bellour, R. and H. "Le jeu des Jeunes Hommes: Introduction à l'analyse comparée des écrits de jeunesse de Charlotte et Branwell Brontë." *La Revue d'Esthétique,* 22 (1970), 337-362.

The French criticism compares the youthful writing of Charlotte with that of her brother in the juvenilia "The Game of the Young Men."

A245   Blom, M. A. "Apprenticeship in 'The World Below': Charlotte Brontë's Juvenilia." *English Studies in Canada,* 1 (1975), 290-303.

An authority writes on the juvenilia.

A246   Chernaik, Judith. "Unpublished Tale by Charlotte Brontë." *Times Literary Supplement,* 72 (Nov. 23, 1973), 1453-1454.

Following an introduction which gives the history of "An Interesting Passage in the Lives of Some Eminent Men of the Present Time," written in 1830 when Charlotte Brontë was fourteen, this article presents a transcription of the juvenile tale.

A247   Dessner, Lawrence Jay. "Charlotte Brontë's 'Le Nid,' an Unpublished Manuscript." *BST,* 16 (1973), 213-218.

A critical analysis which includes the author's translation from the original French. His comments help us understand the kind of teacher and human being Heger was. Additional parallels are cited of the influence of French authors on Charlotte Brontë's fiction.

A248   Drew, Philip. "Charlotte Brontë as a Critic of *Wuthering Heights.*" *Nineteenth Century Fiction,* 18:4 (March 1964), 365-381.

"She identifies the novel's main source of evil energy and its central metaphor," is Drew's summary of Charlotte Brontë's criticism in the preface to the 1850 edition of her sister's novel. She speaks of the strong language and rusticity, which she apologizes for, and she praises Nelly Dean, a character which tends to irritate modern readers. Her "literally accurate description" of Heathcliff earns great praise from the critic. (See also B49.)

A249   Hannah, Barbara. "The Animus in Charlotte Brontë's 'Strange Events.'" *Harvest* (London: Analytical Psychology Club), 10 (1964), 1-12.

This Jungian critic relates the archetypal animus to the revelation of Charlotte Brontë in this minor work.

A250   Jones, Bernard. "Charlotte Brontë." *Books and Bookmen,* 17 (Nov. 1971), 10-13.

A brief discussion of Charlotte Brontë and a review of her recently published *Five Novelettes.* (See also A40.)

A251   Lane, Margaret. "Charlotte Brontë: Emma, a Fragment" in *Purely for Pleasure.* London: Hamish Hamilton, 1966.

This fragment of a proposed novel, abandoned at the author's death, consists of the first two chapters of a work to have been called "Emma" or "Willie Ellin." It was first published five years later in *Cornhill* (A11).

When Charlotte Brontë read it to Mr. Nicholls he remarked, "The critics will accuse you of repetition." There is no way to know from these chapters who Emma is.

A252   Lever, Sir Tresham. "Charlotte Brontë and Kitty Bell." *Times Literary Supplement,* 68 (March 13, 1969), 267.

This brief study claims that *Kitty Bell, the Orphan* is not an early draft of *Jane Eyre.*

A253   Monahan, Melodie June. "Ashworth: An Unfinished Novel by Charlotte Brontë, Edited with an Introduction." Unpublished doctoral dissertation, University of Rochester, 1976. *DAI,* 37:2899.

"This dissertation is a critical edition of an unfinished novel, here called *Ashworth,* which Charlotte Brontë wrote, probably in December and January, 1839-1840. . . . *Ashworth* is the earliest known manuscript in which Charlotte Brontë adapts Angrian characters and plot lines to an English setting."

A254   Ratchford, Fannie E. "Introduction: The History of Angria" in *Legends of Angria: Compiled from the Early Writings of Charlotte Brontë.* New Haven: Yale University Press, 1933.

In presenting these five tales from the early writings, Miss Ratchford brings the readers the information they need to understand the ambiance which produced the juvenilia. Her understanding of these works causes her to assert that "it is not too much to say that if the novels [of Angria] are read as a series they become the most informing and illuminating of Brontë documents."

A255   Van Doran, Dorothy, ed. *The Lost Art: Letters of Seven Famous Women.* New York: Coward-McCann, 1929.

Charlotte Brontë is here treated as novelist and letter-writer, with discussion of her style and her life story.

A256   Adams, Maurianne. "Family Disintegration and Creative Reintegration: the Case of Charlotte Brontë and *Jane Eyre.*" *The Victorian Family: Stress and Structure.* Ed. Anthony Wohl. London: Croom Helm, 1978.

In discussing the disintegration of the Brontë family, through death and other adversities, the critic presents her belief that it was the determination of the sisters to survive through writing. Through this determination the family unit did survive.

A257   Allott, Miriam, ed. *Charlotte Brontë: Jane Eyre and Villette, a Casebook.* London: Macmillan, 1973.

This material prepared for students is divided into three sections: first the early opinions, then later Victorian assessments, and finally "some twentieth century views."

A258   Andrews, W. Linton. "Charlotte Brontë: the Woman and the Feminist." *BST,* 12 (1955), 351-360.

In considering the novelist and the question of feminism, the critic comes to the conclusion that she was a feminist, but a non-active one.

A259   Arnitt, A. "Charlotte Brontë and Jane Austen," *Modern Review,* 3 (1882), 384-396.

Charlotte Brontë had a confessed lack of sympathy for Jane Austen ("no open country, no fresh air, no blue hill, no bonny beck," only a "carefully-fenced, highly-cultivated garden"). The critic compares their attitudes and accomplishments.

A260   Auerbach, Nina. "Charlotte Brontë: The Two Countries." *University of Toronto Quarterly,* 42 (Summer 1973), 328-342.

The critic identifies the main metaphor of cold and heat, representing thematic conflict in both *Villette* and *Jane Eyre.* She notes the "perpetual war between fire and ice, within the isolated and estranged self."

A261   Beer, Patricia. "Jane Austen and Charlotte Brontë: An Imaginary Conversation." *Listener and BBC Television Review*, 94 (1975), 144-147.

In answer to Charlotte Brontë's entreaty, "Pray let us speak of books," a wholly imaginary Jane Austen and an equally valid but ghostly Charlotte Brontë carry on a delightful conversation about themselves, literature and life (which is called, according to Miss Austen, "the Woman Question").

A262   Beer, Patricia. *Reader, I Married Him: A Study of the Women Characters in Jane Austen, Charlotte Brontë, Elizabeth Gaskell and George Eliot.* London: Macmillan Press, 1974.

This book, which suffers from oversimplification, approaches the problem of the delineation of women characters by the four leading women novelists of the nineteenth century. Beer is best in her analysis of Shirley Keeldar. Lucy Snowe is criticized for her anti-Catholic neuroses, and for being more Protestant than Christian.

A263   Benson, A. C. "The Message of Charlotte Brontë to the Nineteenth Century." *BST*, 5 (1915), 107-115.

An analysis of the contemporary point of view shows Charlotte Brontë's attitude toward such social questions as the place of woman.

A264   Bentley, Phyllis. "The Novels of Charlotte Brontë" in *The Enduring Brontës*. Ed. Linton Andrews. Shipley: Outhwaite Brothers, 1951.

This expert on the Brontës discusses the four novels of Charlotte Brontë.

A265   Bjork, Harriet. *The Language of Truth: Charlotte Brontë, The Woman Question, and the Novel.* Lund: Gleerup, 1974.

"Charlotte Brontë's sensitive response to contemporary currents of thought " is discussed in this book. They include female education and employment, and the relationship between the sexes.

A266   Blom, Margaret A. *Charlotte Brontë.* English Authors Series. New York: Twayne, 1977.

This study of the author shows insights into the psychological and feminist overtones in her writings but doesn't seem to go beyond the restrictions of the format of the series. Blom's approach indicates an understanding of Charlotte Brontë and a sensitivity to the basic content of the novels.

A267   Blom, Margaret A. "Charlotte Brontë, Feminist *Manqué*." *Bucknell Review,* 21 (Spring 1973), 87-102.

Charlotte Brontë writes of woman's agonized search for identity and self-realization in a male-dominated society. The view of women as dolls or angels on the one hand or fiends on the other comes from an innate fear of female sexuality which is supported by Judeo-Christian theology. Charlotte Brontë is both victim and critic, wanting equality but needing to be dominated. This ambivalent attitude is present in all her works.

A268   Bonnell, Henry Hudson. *Charlotte Brontë, George Eliot, Jane Austen: Studies in their Works.* New York: Longmans Green and Company, 1902. Reissued, New York: Folcroft, 1974.

This well-known collector of Brontëana presents a study of three great nineteenth-century women novelists. He declares that Charlotte Brontë is "the greatest writer of pure passion in the English tongue."

A269   Brayfield, Peggy Lee. "A New Feminist Approach to the Novels of Charlotte Brontë." Unpublished doctoral dissertation, Southern Illinois University, 1973. *DAI,* 34:1850.

"There is little in the canons of Brontë criticism to suggest that Charlotte's works actually had any effect on feminist movements. But her novels are based on the sure sense that women exist as beings in and for themselves, and they implicitly insist that the thoughts, feelings and aspirations of woman are a topic worthy of minute fictional study."

A270   Bromley, Laura Ann. "(1) Continuity in Milton's Sonnets. (2) Attitudes Toward Love in'Venus and Adonis.'(3) The Victorian 'Good Woman' and the Fiction of Charlotte Brontë." Unpublished doctoral dissertation, Rutgers University, 1973. *DAI,* 34:3336.

Part three ". . . explores the extent to which the heroines of Charlotte Brontë's novels *Jane Eyre* and *Villette* are conventional Victorian 'good women' of the type made familiar by Dickens."

A271   Burkhart, Charles. *Charlotte Brontë: A Psychosexual Study of Her Novels.* London: Victor Gollancz, 1973.

Burkhart finds Charlotte Brontë a "deeply-human writer" who shares with modern writers "an aesthetic of self." Her work was long considered "coarse" because of the sexuality unconsciously written into the novels. Her eroticism begins with *The Professor* in which the master-pupil relationship demonstrates the "joy of sexual combat." *Shirley* "has the topic of marriage and spinsterhood as its thematic center. It is the one organizing force in a story that otherwise touches too lightly on too much." The novel is against marriage until the double-marriage ending perhaps added to compensate for Anne's death. "The novel abounds in bad marriages and urgings of celibacy." Shirley is the prototype of Sue Bridehead and later liberated women.

A272   Capetanakis, Demetrios. *A Greek Poet in England.* London: John Lehmann, 1947.

In a chapter on Charlotte Brontë, the poet tells about her life and gives his subjective reaction to her writings.

A273   Cecioni, Cesare G. *La narrativa di Charlotte Brontë.* Firenze: Valmartina, 1961.

An Italian work on Charlotte Brontë. Noted but not inspected.

A274   Chesterton, G. K. "Charlotte Brontë as a Romantic" in *Charlotte Brontë, 1816-1916: A Centenary Memorial.* Ed. Butler Wood. Foreword, Mrs. Humphry Ward. London: T. F. Unwin, 1918.

Chesterton's belief that "Romance is a spirit; and as for realism it is a convention" helps him see Charlotte Brontë as adventurous in an intensely individualistic and intensely womanly way.

A275   Chesterton, G. K. "Charlotte Brontë and the Realists." *BST,* 4 (1907), 6-11.

This is merely a paraphrased report of an address given by Chesterton, in which he attacks the advice given to Charlotte Brontë by George Henry Lewes who urged the writer to "be realistic."

A276   Clement, David. "Note the Literary Allusions." *English Journal,* 54 (Jan. 1965), 59-60.

This reference to the allusions in *Jane Eyre* – from Bewick's *History of British Birds* to Gulliver – stresses the importance of noticing what the character reads into the allusion and how it affects the action and theme and dramatizes the psychological state of character.

A277   Cunliffe, J. W. "Charlotte and Emily Brontë." *Leaders of the Victorian Revolution.* New York: Appleton-Century, 1934.

This short chapter hails Charlotte Brontë as a superior novelist. In spite of the title, the chapter hardly mentions Emily's *Wuthering Heights.*

A278   Davis, Joe Lee. "Introduction" in Charlotte Brontë. *Jane Eyre.* New York: Rinehart, 1963.

This preface analyzes Charlotte Brontë's craftsmanship.

A279   Dessner, Lawrence Jay. *The Homely Web of Truth: A Study of Charlotte Brontë's Novels.* The Hague: Mouton, 1975.

This publication of Dessner's doctoral dissertation (New York University, 1969. *DAI,* 31:3500) is an overall study of Charlotte Brontë as a writer. Dessner discusses the juvenilia and the author's reading. He believes her to be influenced by George Sand and Walter Scott, an opinion based on similarities of plot and characters. In discussing the four novels, Dessner has much to say on the narrators in *Jane Eyre* and *Villette.* He is repelled by the "tone of anger" in *Shirley.*

A280   Diskin, Patrick. "Joyce and Charlotte Brontë." *Notes and Queries,* 13 (1966), 94-95.

Diskin feels that Joyce was influenced by the Brontës. *Portrait of the Artist as a Young Man* echoes *Jane Eyre* and "The Dead" echoes *Villette* and has something from Emily Brontë's poem "The Prisoner."

A281   Eagleton, Terry. "Class, Power, and Charlotte Brontë." *Critical Quarterly*, 14 (Autumn 1972), 225-235.

This Marxist critic sees Charlotte Brontë's characters as caught between the urge for emotional fulfillment and the wish to conform to their social restrictions. Emily Brontë's characters are not. Charlotte's characters also demonstrate a need to be dominated. The result is an internal conflict between self-assertion and submission.

A282   Egg, Ines. "Die Bestimmung des Frauenbildes in viktorianischen Roman durch Charlotte Brontë und George Eliot." Unpublished doctoral dissertation, University of Zurich, 1949.

This study is limited to an analysis of the women characters in the Victorian novels of Charlotte Brontë and George Eliot.

A283   Faber, Richard. *Proper Stations: Class in Victorian Fiction.* London: Faber and Faber, 1971.

In Chapter Three the critic discusses Charlotte Brontë's social outlook, along with that of Mrs. Gaskell and George Eliot.

A284   Falconer, J. A. "*The Professor* and *Villette:* A Study of Development." *English Studies,* 9 (April 1927), 33-37.

The critic attempts a comparison by relating both novels to the biographical facts of the author's life. The article suggests that *The Professor* became *Villette* by the addition of "incidents of a purely romantic and rather hackneyed kind."

A285   Fisher, Catherine L. "Charlotte Brontë: Formalist: A Study of the Novels as Thematic Unities." Unpublished doctoral dissertation, State University of New York at Albany, 1975. *DAI,* 36:5314.

The author contends that a "formal, or thematic, approach explains more successfully than do other critical approaches the novels' varying purposes and consequent varying qualities. Each novel takes its shape from a unifying idea, and each develops a pattern of moral growth on the part of two or more central characters."

A286   Fitch, George Hamlin. "Charlotte Brontë and Her Two Great Novels" in *Modern English Books of Power.* San Francisco: Paul Elder, 1912.

This critical article first appeared in the *San Francisco Chronicle* in Fitch's series "Great Books and Their Writers."

A287   Garnett, Richard. "The Place of Charlotte Brontë in Nineteenth Century Fiction" in *Charlotte Brontë, 1816-1916: A Centenary Memorial.* Ed. Butler Wood. London: T. Fisher Unwin, 1918.

The author suggests that Charlotte Brontë's writing is subjective, as it delineates mental states and "only uses incidents as a means of producing those states." He suggests that Charlotte Brontë is distinguished by her subjectivity. In her novels "the predominant character is passion" but "she is deficient in invention and creative imagination."

A288   Gronemeyer, Liesel. "Die Darstellung der Frau in den Romanen der Charlotte Brontë." Unpublished doctoral dissertation, University of Munster, 1948.

Another German study of woman's place as revealed by the characters in Charlotte Brontë's novels.

A289   Hardy, Barbara. *Tellers and Listeners: The Narrative Imagination.* London: Athlone Press, 1975.

In discussing the position of the story teller as closing "the gap between happening and interpretation," Professor Hardy uses examples from Charlotte Brontë's major novels.

A290   Harrison, Frederic. *Studies in Early Victorian Literature.* London and New York: Edward Arnold, 1895.

The chapter "Charlotte Brontë" is a general discussion of the writer and her work, reprinted from *Forum,* 1895.

A291   Heilman, Robert B. "Charlotte Brontë's 'New' Gothic" in *From Jane Austen to Joseph Conrad.* Eds. R. C. Rathburn and Martin Steinmann, Jr. Minneapolis: University of Minnesota Press, 1958.

This is a discussion of the anti-Gothic approach used by Charlotte Brontë in her treatment of symbolic dreams. The critic defines the author's "new" Gothic as "the new sense of the dark side of feeling and personality." Throughout the novels Heilman sees the author behind every first-person narrator.

A292   Heilman, Robert B. "Charlotte Brontë, Reason, and the Moon." *Nineteenth Century Fiction*, 14 (March 1960), 283-302.

Basing his interpretation on the moon symbolism in the novels of Charlotte Brontë, Heilman brings out the ever-present conflict between reason and intuition. The moon "represents another realm than the 'reason' where she at times aspired to dwell."

A293   Heindl, Elisabeth. "Charlotte Brontë und der franzosische Geist." Unpublished doctoral dissertation, University of Vienna, 1944.

This dissertation points out the similarity between the attitudes displayed by Charlotte Brontë in her novels and the feeling being revealed in French writing of the time.

A294   Hoffeld, Laura D. "The Servant Heroine in Eighteenth and Nineteenth Century British Fiction: The Social Reality and Its Image in the Novel." Unpublished doctoral dissertation, New York University, 1975. *DAI*, 36:3730.

Discusses the "nature of the servant heroine in specific works of fiction, and the relationship between social history — the real position of the servant and public awareness of her — and the manner in which the author treats her and her aspirations." Charlotte Brontë's heroines are "women whose virtuous behavior is exemplary. Here women as mother figures, the caretakers of children, replace women as sexual objects."

A295   Howard, Margaret Adelia. "Charlotte Brontë's Novels: An Analysis of Their Thematic and Structural Patterns." Unpublished doctoral dissertation, University of Washington, 1962. *DAI,* 24:728.

Although the title might lead one to suppose that the dissertation would be on the structural patterns of the novels, actually it is a study of the search-for-love theme in the novels and its relation to the author's style.

A296   Jack, Ian. "Physiognomy, Phrenology, and Characterisation in the Novels of Charlotte Brontë." *BST,* 15 (1970), 377-391.

Charlotte Brontë's characters have a "visual dimension," according to Jack. Like the author, the characters study the faces of other characters and reach conclusions about their nature.

A297   Johnson, Reginald Brimley. *The Women Novelists.* London: W. Collins Sons, 1918.

He finds Charlotte Brontë "a lonely soul," middle-class in outlook but with a spirit that was in revolt against the prejudices of the times. He makes much of the anti-feminine criticism she received.

A298   Junge, Hans. "Der Stil in den Romanen Charlotte Brontës." Unpublished doctoral dissertation, University of Halle, 1912.

A dissertation on the style of Charlotte Brontë analyzes the diction and effects created by language.

A299   Katz, J. N. "Rooms of Their Own: Form and Images of Liberation in Five Novels." Unpublished doctoral dissertation, Pennsylvania State University, 1973. *DAI,* 34:1283.

A discussion of symbols of freedom in the novels of Fanny Burney, Jane Austen, Charlotte Brontë, George Eliot, and Virginia Woolf.

A300   Kinkead-Weekes, Mark. "This Old Maid: Jane Austen Replies to Charlotte Brontë and D. H. Lawrence." *Nineteenth Century Fiction,* 30 (Dec. 1975), 399-419.

An imaginary response by Jane Austen to Charlotte Brontë's request that she probe more thoroughly the "hidden and private consciousness of her characters." In this defense Miss Austen claims that she does so increasingly as her style progresses from *Pride and Prejudice* to *Persuasion.*

A301   Knies, Earl A. *The Art of Charlotte Brontë.* Athens, Ohio: Ohio University Press, 1969.

This appeared first as "The Art of Charlotte Brontë: A Study of Point of View in her Fiction." Unpublished doctoral dissertation, University of Illinois, 1964. *DAI,* 25:6596. In a continuing study of narrator and point of view, Dr. Knies examines all of Charlotte Brontë's novels. He feels that *The Professor* does not work because the author fails at a masculine point of view. Knies also treats the various points of view in *Villette,* but he concludes that *Jane Eyre* is the most successful of all. *Shirley* is considered to be weak because of the third-person narration.

A302   Knies, Earl A. "The Artistry of Charlotte Brontë: A Reassessment." *Ohio University Review,* 7 (1966), 21-39.

A303   Kroeber, Karl. *Styles in Fictional Structure: The Art of Jane Austen, Charlotte Brontë and George Eliot.* Princeton: Princeton University Press, 1971.

This collection of computer data includes 80 pages of tables analyzing words, dialogue, sentence structure, time structure, metaphor, etc. Kroeber draws conclusions about the author's interest based on frequency tables. In *Villette,* he reports, "Brontë's expressiveness takes the form of a tension between the narrator and her language."

A304   Lewes, George H. "The Lady Novelists." *Westminster Review,* 58 (Oct. 1852), 70-77.

This reviewer, who had attacked Charlotte Brontë two years earlier for her womanly way of writing (A83), now declares that since novels depend on emotion, women are good novelists as they are more emotional and less intellectual than men.

A305   Linder, C. A. "The Ideal Marriage as Depicted in the Novels of Jane Austen and Charlotte Brontë." *Standpunte*, 96 (1971), 20-30.

In this excellent comparison, Linder identifies certain qualities in the ideal marriage: "Charlotte Brontë recognized the need for a woman's emotional fulfillment through marriage and emphasized its psychological effect." However, in revealing her own concept of the ideal wife, Charlotte Brontë emphasizes "the moral superiority of the female."

A306   Linder, C. A. *Romantic Imagery in the Novels of Charlotte Brontë.* London: Macmillan; New York: Harper and Row, 1978.

This study of all four of the novels discusses structure, imagery, and narration. Through careful analysis of the imagery, the critic shows that, far from being a haphazard collation of personal experiences and anecdotes, these are novels carefully constructed by a talented and imaginative craftsman.

A307   McDaniel, Judith A. "Fettered Wings Half Loose: Female Development in the Victorian Novel." Unpublished doctoral dissertation, Tufts University, 1975. *DAI,* 36:1530.

"This thesis suggests that the three major novels of Charlotte Brontë provide a paradigm for female development within the novel."

A308   Maddox, James Hunt, Jr. "The Survival of Gothic Romance in the Nineteenth Century Novel: A Study of Scott, Charlotte Brontë, and Dickens." Unpublished doctoral dissertation, Yale University, 1970. *DAI,* 32:442.

"This dissertation attempts to define the characteristics of the Gothic romance, largely in terms of plot, and to explore the prevalence of this plot in later, more realistic works." Charlotte Brontë "adapts Gothic material in order to present the imprisoned, claustrophobic minds of her heroines."

A309   Malham-Dembleby, John. *The Confessions of Charlotte Brontë, with the Amazing Revelation that She Herself is "Young Soult," "the rymer and tragedian" and "Northangerland."* Bradford, Yorkshire: published privately by Mrs. Leah Malham-Dembleby, 1954.

This unusual publication "proves" that Charlotte Brontë wrote Emily Brontë's poetry and *Wuthering Heights* — in fact, everything attributed to any of the Brontës.

A310   Martin, Hazel T. *Petticoat Rebels: A Study of the Novels of Social Protest by George Eliot, Elizabeth Gaskell, and Charlotte Brontë.* New York: Helios, 1968.

The critic comes to some conclusions about the Victorian woman based on the characters in these novels. Her considerations are in three categories: the passionate governess, the blessings of marriage, and the educated woman. Of Charlotte Brontë she says, "Her characters cried for the majority of the women of the age." She admires the character of Jane Eyre who "had no fear of anything."

A311   Martin, Robert Bernard. *Accents of Persuasion: Charlotte Brontë's Novels.* London: Faber and Faber, 1966.

This critic treats the complete adult novels of the author, offering some interesting suggestions, but also summarizing plots and entering into the familiar speculation concerning the relationship between "reality and truth." He reacts against twentieth-century psychology being applied to these novels. He sees all four novels as seeking a balance between reason and passion. *Jane Eyre* is "largely a religious novel, concerned with the meaning of religion to man and its relevance to his behavior." It is a version of "the great archetypal pattern of sin, suffering, and redemption."

A312   Martineau, Harriet. "Death of Currer Bell." *Daily News,* April 6, 1855, p. 5. Reprinted in *Biographical Sketches.* London: Macmillan, 1869.

In a summary of the writing career of Charlotte Brontë, Martineau declares, "Her heroines love too readily, too vehemently, and sometimes after a fashion which their female readers may resent; but they do their duty through everything, and are healthy in action, however morbid in passion."

A313   Mason, Leo. "Charlotte Brontë and Charles Dickens." *Dickensian,* 43 (Summer 1947), 118-124.

In a study of Charlotte Brontë and Dickens, the critic makes a comparison of the way the two authors treat schools and young girls and how they make use of the autobiographical form. The suggestion is made that those three elements in *Jane Eyre* influenced Dickens in the writing of *David Copperfield*.

A314 Moers, Ellen. *Literary Women: The Great Writers.* Garden City, New York: Doubleday, 1976; London: W. H. Allen, 1977.

In a rich tapestry presentation of women writers – their lives, work, heroines, metaphors, *etc.* – references to the Brontës are interwoven throughout. Charlotte Brontë, whose canon is carefully considered, is particularly praised for *Shirley.* Vol. also listed as B454.

A315 Moers, Ellen. "Money, the Job, and Little Women." *Commentary,* 55 (1973), 57-65.

The middle third of this article analyzes Charlotte Brontë's attitude toward work and its importance in establishing a woman's self-esteem.

A316 Momberger, Philip. "Self and World in the Works of Charlotte Brontë." *English Literary History,* 32 (Sept. 1965), 349-369.

An evaluation of the introspective quality of Charlotte Brontë's style shows her response to the outer world. The critic suggests that "all of Charlotte Brontë's protagonists might be described as a version of a single type: the outcast." He feels that the Tory journals were right in censoring Jane Eyre's "undue reliance on self." Charlotte Brontë speaks for the "outcast hero," describing his social and love relationship.

A317 Moss, Frederick Keith. "Characterization in Charlotte Brontë's Fiction." Unpublished doctoral dissertation, University of Wisconsin-Madison, 1969. *DAI,* 31:363.

"A comparison of Charlotte Brontë's juvenile stories and her novels shows that she worked with a limited repertoire of characters. . . . Each character searches for a complex combination of independence and dependence in his relationships with other characters. . . . The origin of this persistent theme lies in Charlotte Brontë's juvenilia."

A318   Oliphant, Margaret. "The Old Saloon: The Literature of the Last Fifty Years." *Blackwood's Magazine,* 141 (June 1887), 737-761.

Love is Charlotte Brontë's theme, Mrs. Oliphant declares; the message and writing are inferior to that of George Eliot.

A319   Passel, Anne Wonders. "Charlotte Brontë's Novels: the Artistry of their Construction." Unpublished doctoral dissertation, University of the Pacific, 1967. *DAI,* 28:1444.

A study of the construction of the four novels of Charlotte Brontë with an emphasis on balance and patterning.

A320   Peters, Margot. *Charlotte Brontë, Style in the Novel.* Madison, Wisconsin: Wisconsin University Press, 1972.

In a volume of great interest to linguistic scholars as well as literary ones, Professor Peters analyzes the way in which Charlotte Brontë uses language to achieve her effects. The areas researched are (1) the emphatic adverb, (2) syntactic inversion, (3) antithesis, and (4) courtroom language. Peters concludes that there is a high proportion of inverted sentences, many short clauses strung together, frequent use of intensifying adverbs in positions of stress, many negative statements, and antithesis in vocabulary, theme, and structure. The resulting style is tense and uneven, yet vital.

A321   Peters, Margot McCullough. "Four Essays on the Style of Charlotte Brontë." Unpublished doctoral dissertation, University of Wisconsin-Madison, 1969. *DAI,* 31:379.

Peters asserts that the "author's personal tensions, reflected in the tensions of her style, are largely responsible for the vitality of her novels, which, unlike much Victorian fiction, do not degenerate into a simplified and sentimental mediocrity."

A322   Pollard, Arthur. *Charlotte Brontë* in Profiles in Literature series. London: Routledge and Kegan Paul, 1968.

Pollard explicates characters, plot, setting through an analysis of passages.

A323   Praz, Mario. *The Hero in Eclipse in Victorian Fiction.* Translated by Angus Davison. London: Oxford University Press, 1956.

The critic uses Charlotte Brontë to illustrate various points in discussing other novelists, but merely refers in passing to Emily Brontë's "vehemence" and "truth."

A324   Putzell, Sara Moore. "Victorian Views of Man in the Novels of Charlotte Brontë and George Eliot." Unpublished doctoral dissertation, Emory University, 1977. *DAI,* 38:4851.

Discusses Charlotte Brontë's "latitudinarian view of human nature and George Eliot's Hegelian one. Both novelists portray isolated individuals who suffer as they act to realize their ideas of themselves and to do their duty; these individuals have quite different ideas, however, about who they are, why they suffer, and what they should do with their lives."

A325   Ralli, Augustus. "Charlotte Brontë." *Fortnightly Review*, 100 (Sept. 1913), 524-538.

The critic comments on Charlotte Brontë's use of obvious sexual symbols in *Villette.* An autobiographical reading of Charlotte Brontë's novels reveals the "disharmonies" of her life.

A326   Roscoe, W. C. "Miss Brontë." A review of Mrs. Gaskell's *Life of Charlotte Brontë. National Review,* 54 (July 1857), 127-164.

The critic deals with the problem in separating the author's life from her writing.

A327   Schreiber, Annette. "The Myth in Charlotte Brontë." *Literature and Psychology,* 18 (1968), 48-67.

The Electra myth, in which a girl who hates her mother marries a father surrogate, lies at the base of the novels of Charlotte Brontë, as it also functions in the stories of Jane Austen. But Charlotte Brontë's works are "not only more complex, multifaceted and

ambivalent" but also "more destructive, self-destructive and tragic."
Jane Eyre and *Villette* obviously fit this pattern and so does *Shirley*
when Louis Moore appears. The novels demonstrate a woman
searching for a "ruthlessly masculine" man to dominate her. A hatred
for women pervades *Villette*. The "psychic allegory" in Charlotte
Brontë's novels opens the way for writers like Virginia Woolf and
Dorothy Richardson.

A328   Schwartz, Roberta Christine. "The Search After Happiness: A Study
        of Charlotte Brontë's Fiction." Unpublished doctoral
        dissertation, Wayne State University, 1968. *DAI*, 29:3587.

        Schwartz states that Charlotte Brontë "produced a more
        complex and harmonious world view than critics have recognized thus
        far. Charlotte's fiction suggests not a progressive darkening in her
        outlook but a somber attitude toward existence indicative of her
        increased unwillingness to accept pat solutions to the serious problems
        of life."

A329   Seccombe, Thomas. "Place of the Brontës Among Women Novelists
        of the Last Century." *BST*, 5 (April 1913), 8-12.

        This is primarily a discussion of Charlotte Brontë.

A330   Senseman, Wilfred M. "Charlotte Brontë's Use of Physiognomy and
        Phrenology." *Papers of the Michigan Academy of Science, Art
        and Letters*, 38 (1952), 475-486.

        Background of the pseudo-sciences prepares us for a view into
        Charlotte Brontë's use of physiognomy and phrenology to reveal the
        complexity of her characters and to confirm "her belief that human
        character commonly lacks that monolithic simplicity with which
        novelists have so often endowed it."

A331   Shapiro, Arnold. "A Study in the Development of Art and Ideas in
        Charlotte Brontë's Fiction." Unpublished doctoral dissertation,
        Indiana University, 1965. *DAI*, 26:2730.

        The author attempts to trace the development of Charlotte
        Brontë and to indicate her growth as an artist, pinpointing her
        characteristic themes: the isolated individual in the world, her

criticism of society, and her view of personal relationships and their necessity. He concentrates on Charlotte Brontë's use of the first-person narrator.

A332   Sharma, P. P. "Charlotte Brontë: Champion of Woman's Economic Independence." *BST,* 14 (1965), 38-40.

This critic sees the continuing interest in Charlotte Brontë to be the result of her basic attitude. "All Charlotte Brontë's heroines demand equal rights with men, especially as to economic independence. As a result, her women are relevant today." Charlotte Brontë's heroines are early examples of "modern womanhood striving for economic emancipation."

A333   Showalter, Elaine. "Charlotte Brontë's Use of French." *Research Studies,* 42 (1974), 225-234.

A close examination of French expressions and allusions reveals a remarkable relationship between content, mood, and expression. Charlotte Brontë's use of French increases from novel to novel. In each case the use of foreign words symbolizes passion and immorality, a reflection of Victorian prejudice against French culture. For Charlotte Brontë the language also represented Catholicism. In *Jane Eyre* and *Villette* the author uses French when she wants to express Jane and Lucy's struggle against repressed passion.

A334   Sigel, John E. "Passionate Craftsmanship: The Artistry of Charlotte Brontë's *Jane Eyre* and *Villette.*" Unpublished doctoral dissertation, State University of New York at Binghamton, 1976. *DAI,* 37:1571.

Sigel asserts that the "passion and power of Charlotte Brontë's major fiction are due to her artistry and craftsmanship. More specifically, the novels' imaginative and almost poetic intensity is the result of the careful patterning of motifs and structuring of imagery."

A335   Smith, George Barnett. "The Brontës." *Cornhill Magazine,* 28 (July 1873), 54-71.

The critic finds Charlotte Brontë's writing "masculine in power." Miss Brontë, though more gifted than most novelists, had limited experience, which kept her from being a novelist of the highest rank. This study was reprinted in *Poets and Novelists: A Series of Literary Studies,* London: Smith, Elder, 1875.

A336   Smith, Leroy. "Charlotte Brontë's Flight from Eros." *Women and Literature,* 4 (Spring 1976), 30-44.

Another analysis of Charlotte Brontë's struggle to convey the needs of passion while writing of self-sufficiency.

A337   Snowden, J. K. "The Brontës as Artists and Prophets." *BST,* 4 (1909), 78-92. Reprinted in *Charlotte Brontë, 1816-1916: A Centenary Memorial.* Ed. Butler Wood. London: T. Fisher Unwin, 1918.

The author distinguishes between Charlotte Brontë's romantic "yarns" and her stories "of real life." He finds *Shirley* without plot and without structure. He also gives an overview of criticism of Charlotte and Emily Brontë's novels.

A338   Spens, Janet. "Charlotte Brontë." *Essays and Studies of the English Association,* 12 (1929).

The critic talks about the influence of *Pamela* and other early novels on the writing of Charlotte Brontë. Her conclusion is that *Villette* is Charlotte's finest novel.

A339   Stang, Richard. *The Theory of the Novel in England, 1850-1870.* New York: Columbia University Press, 1959.

The author points out the influence of Thackeray on Charlotte Brontë and briefly discusses her role as an author. The critics' reaction to *Jane Eyre* is also mentioned.

A340   Stebbins, Lucy Poate. *A Victorian Album: Some Lady Novelists of the Period.* New York: Columbia University Press, 1946.

In this sentimental approach to the novels, Stebbins goes over the childhood writings of the Brontës and suggests that an understanding of the Angria stories will help explain Charlotte Brontë's major novels.

A341   Stephen, Sir Leslie. "Charlotte Brontë." *Cornhill*, 36 (Dec. 1877), 723-729. Reprinted in *Hours in a Library*, London: Smith, Elder, 1879.

In this rebuttal to Swinburne (see A344), the critic points out Charlotte Brontë's sense of duty in life. He defends her withdrawal from society. He finds that she did not see life as joyful, but that, to her distorted and morbid view, life was unjust.

A342   Stewart, G. "Teaching Prose Fiction: Some 'Instructive' Styles." *College English*, 27 (Dec. 1975), 383-401.

Using examples from *Jane Eyre*, along with *Pride and Prejudice* and *Great Expectations*, this teacher suggests ways to understand meaning through a study of syntax, diction, imagery, and metaphor. He closely analyzes a passage from *Jane Eyre*, Chapter 12, beginning, "I lingered at the gates . . ." pointing out that the "psychic center" of the passage rests in the word "expanded." He believes in searching in a work for its "poetic patterning," thus gaining an understanding of the work through the mode of expression.

A343   Sullivan, Paula. "Studies in Charlotte Brontë." Unpublished doctoral dissertation. Harvard University, 1974.

Of particular interest is one chapter entitled "The Pictorial Mode of Vision in the Novels."

A344   Swinburne, Algernon Charles. *A Note on Charlotte Brontë*. London: Chatto and Windus, 1977. Reprinted in *Complete Prose Works*. Vol. IV. Bonchurch Edition. Ed. Sir Edmund Gosse and T. J. Wise. London: William Heinemann, Ltd., 1926.

Swinburne sees the everlasting quality of Charlotte Brontë's work and expresses his flowery opinion that the novels are evidence of a "noble fruitful genius which found in the frail temple of her mortal life a minister so high and pure of spirit, so faithful and heroic of heart." In praising her moral elevation he continues: "I cannot think of any great good quality most proper to the most noble among women which was not eminent in the genius as in the nature of Charlotte Brontë."

A345   Toth, Emily. "The Independent Woman and 'Free' Love." *Massachusetts Review*, 16 (Autumn 1975), 647-664.

This feminist declares that "Charlotte Brontë, too, focuses on the incompatibility between love and freedom for women." One solution she tried was the use of asexuality (maimed men). Jane Eyre accepts a compromise while Shirley Keeldar discovers that men do not take her seriously. When Charlotte Brontë's friend, Mary Taylor, read the ending of *Shirley* she wrote its author: "You are a coward and a traitor."

A346   Unger, William E. "Implied Authors and Created Readers in Thackeray, Trollope, Charlotte Brontë, and George Eliot." Unpublished doctoral dissertation, Ohio State University, 1974. *DAI*, 35:2956.

"This study is a comparison of the techniques employed by the four major Victorian novelists indicated in the title as they attempted to create readers who would fully share the values advocated by the novels themselves."

A347   Utter, Robert P. and Gwendolyn B. Needham. *Pamela's Daughters*. New York: Macmillan, 1937.

The authors show the heroine in her relationship to the basic prototype presented in *Pamela*. Lucy Snowe is suggested as fitting the pattern, as does Jane Eyre. The fact that the heroines are governesses is considered to be important.

A348   Ward, Barbara. "Charlotte Brontë and the World of 1846." *BST*, 11 (1946), 3-13.

Charlotte Brontë's work has a strongly subjective quality as she was aloof from the events of her day and influenced very little by the outside world. It is the experiential nature of novels which keeps them from being a conventional reflection of the times.

A349   Ward, Mrs. Humphry. "Introduction" in Charlotte Brontë. *Jane Eyre, Shirley, Villette, The Professor* and *Poems* and Mrs. Gaskell's *Life of Charlotte Brontë*. London: Haworth Edition, 1899-1900.

This great Brontë authority of her time gives an overall view of Charlotte Brontë, pointing out the Celtic element in her style and contrasting Emily and Charlotte, as personalities and writers. Charlotte Brontë liked French Romantic literature, Mrs. Ward declares, and did not hesitate to use autobiographical elements in her novels.

A350   Ward, Mrs. Humphry. "Some Thoughts on Charlotte Brontë" in *Charlotte Brontë, 1816-1916: A Centenary Memorial.* Ed. Butler Wood. London: T. Fisher Unwin, 1918.

Among her praises of Charlotte Brontë, Mrs. Ward points out the weaknesses in the novels, especially the function of the curates in *Shirley.*

A351   West, Rebecca. "Charlotte Brontë" in *The Great Victorians.* Ed. Harold Massingham. London: I. Nicholson and Watson, 1932.

In balancing an evaluation of Charlotte Brontë, Rebecca West finds that her most serious defect is a sentimentality perhaps caused by emotionalism. The merits are her truth and candor, and, at special moments, the poetry in her novels.

A352   Widmer, Eleanor J. "Love and Duty: The Heroines in Jane Austen and Charlotte Brontë." Unpublished doctoral dissertation, University of Washington, 1958. *DAI,* 19:3297.

"The purpose of this study is to examine the significance of the heroine in the works of Jane Austen, Charlotte Brontë and more briefly in related novelists, where the heroine is the focus of the novels' coherent values. On the hypothesis that the English novel of the nineteenth century has a distinctively limited moral and domestic view, our problem is to reveal how the heroines of Jane Austen and Charlotte Brontë become major exemplifications of the domestic-moral affirmation."

A353   Wills, Jack Charles. "Charlotte Brontë's Literary Theories." Unpublished doctoral dissertation, University of Delaware, 1966. *DAI,* 28:1413.

The author states that while Charlotte "occasionally employs the methods of such disparate literary types as the Gothic romance and European Realism, her art is solidly built on a philosophic substructure which is virtually identical to that of the English Romantic poets."

A354　Wills, Jack C. "The Shrine of Truth: An Approach to the Works of Charlotte Brontë." *BST,* 15 (1970), 392-399.

Here is a comment on Charlotte Brontë's "determination to be truthful." Such reverence for truth is bound to Arnold's "high seriousness." Charlotte Brontë was basically an intense Romantic, believing that "true artistic creation . . . resulted from divine inspiration."

A355　Woolf, Virginia. *A Room of One's Own.* London: Hogarth Press, 1929.

Among her comments about women writers and their plight, Virginia Woolf suggests that Charlotte Brontë's weaknesses – her anger, her ignorance – were caused by her response to her sequestered life. "She will write in a rage where she should write calmly," Virginia Woolf declared. "She is at war with her lot."

A356　Youngren, Virginia Rotan. "Moral Life in Solitude: A Study of Selected Novels of Jane Austen, Charlotte Brontë, Elizabeth Gaskell and George Eliot." Unpublished doctoral dissertation, Rutgers University, 1977. *DAI,* 38:814.

Youngren asserts that Austen, Charlotte Brontë, Gaskell, Eliot "moved out of the home and into what Mrs. Humphry Ward referred to as the characteristically masculine subjects of 'manners, politics, and adventure.' But they maintained a point of view as novelists which was consistent with feminine and domestic preoccupations. This point of view emphasizes the value of introspection and a private moral perspective and is articulated by an essentially private writing voice."

A357　Zagarell, Sandra Abelson. "Charlotte Brontë from Fantasy to Social and Psychological Reality." Unpublished doctoral dissertation, Columbia University, 1976. *DAI,* 37:6521.

Zagarell contends that although Charlotte Brontë "has traditionally been seen as an idiosyncratic romantic writer . . . her works show a development from an early and private world to an increasingly mature vision, both psychological and social."

A358   Allott, Miriam Farris. *Elizabeth Gaskell.* Writers and Their Works Series, British Council and National Book League. London: Longmans, Green, 1960.

In discussing the works of Mrs. Gaskell, the critic includes much of the life of Charlotte Brontë as it pertains to the biography.

A359   Aoyama, S. "Charlotte Brontë and Currer Bell: Biographical Study of Charlotte Brontë's Works." *Collected Essays by the Members of the Faculty.* No. 11. Kyoritsu, Japan: Kyoritsu Women's Junior College, 1968.

Noted but not inspected.

A360   Bache, Kentish. "Notes on the Reverend A. B. Nicholls." *BST,* 4 (1912), 236.

An early study of the curate Charlotte Brontë married sheds some light on the last months of the author's life.

A361   Ball, Margaret. "Introduction" in Charlotte Brontë. *Jane Eyre.* Modern Readers' Series. New York: The Macmillan Company, 1931.

This is a clear presentation of the biographical background of the novelist used to support the critic's analysis of the novel. She points out Charlotte Brontë's conscious presentation of "the modern characteristics of her heroines."

A362   Bellour, R. *Charlotte Brontë: Patrick Branwell Brontë.* Mayenne, 1972.

A French critic discusses the relationship between the novelist and her brother.

A363   Benson, Arthur C. "Charlotte Brontë: A Personal Sketch." *Charlotte Brontë: A Centenary Memorial.* London: T. Fisher Unwin, 1917.

Benson gives a clear view of the private person who was Charlotte Brontë.

A364   Benson, E. F. *Charlotte Brontë.* London: Longmans, Green, 1932.

Admired by some (Burkhart, A271, calls this "one of the most judicious and sophisticated of modern studies"), it is nonetheless written by one of Charlotte Brontë's bitterest condemners. One of the negative aspects covered is the relationship of both Emily and Charlotte with their brother. Benson compares the treatment of Lockwood in the first two chapters of *Wuthering Heights* with the same character at the end of the novel and concludes that the beginning must have been written by Branwell. The critic also questions Charlotte's attitude toward Branwell's affair and compares that situation to the Charlotte Brontë-Heger relationship. The book of criticism offers interpretations not put forth elsewhere.

A365   Birrell, Augustine. *Life of Charlotte Brontë.* London, 1887. Reissued, Ann Arbor, Michigan: Finch Press, 1972.

This excellent early biography includes one of the best early bibliographies, compiled by John Parker Anderson.

A366   Bostridge, Mark. "Charlotte Brontë and George Richmond: Idealisation in the Sitter." *BST,* 17 (1976), 58-60.

Charlotte Brontë was thirty-four and at the peak of her career when she sat for the famous portrait now at the National Portrait Gallery in London. George Richmond, we are reminded by this critic, was famous for idealizing the subjects of his portraits. We should not be surprised then that the handsome sitter shows so little resemblance to the person of Charlotte Brontë as she describes herself. Of the portrait, the forthright Mary Taylor said, "I had rather the mouth and eyes had been nearer together and shown the veritable square face and large disproportionate nose."

A367   Bradby, Godfrey Fox. "Charlotte Brontë and Mr. Nicholls" in *The Brontës and Other Essays.* London: Oxford University Press, 1932.

This biographer tries to give a true-to-life representation of Charlotte Brontë and her husband.

A368   Brash, W. Bardsley. "The Brontës of Haworth – Through Trials to Triumph." *London Quarterly and Holborn Review*, 167 (Jan. 1942), 57-66.

Here is another emotional retelling of the Brontë story, one which centers on Charlotte Brontë as the main character. He finds that the understanding which binds the sisters is "a triple cord which cannot be broken."

A369   Brendon, John Adam. *Twelve Great Passions*. London: Hutchinson, 1912.

Among others presented, the relationship between Charlotte Brontë and Mr. Nicholls is covered in the chapter "The Husband of Charlotte Brontë."

A370   Byron, May. *A Day with Charlotte Brontë*. London: Hodder and Stoughton, 1912. Reissued, New York: R. West, 1974.

Writing under the pseudonym of Maurice Clare, this biographer prepared a study of Charlotte Brontë for A Day with Great Writers Series, for which she regularly wrote. Her understanding of the series was greater than her understanding of Charlotte Brontë.

A371   Carus-Wilson, William. *A Refutation of the Statements in "The Life of Charlotte Brontë" Regarding the Casterton Clergy Daughters' School, When at Cowan Bridge*. Weston-Super-Mare: J. Whereat, (n.d., c. 1857 following the publication of Mrs. Gaskell's *Life of Charlotte Brontë*).

A hard-to-find item of extreme interest: the head of the school attacks Mrs. Gaskell's statements about it in the biography.

A372   Chadwick, Esther Alice. "Charlotte Brontë and Thackeray." *BST*, 4 (1911), 167-188.

Mrs. Chadwick, who frequently writes about the Brontës, offers this biographic study to clarify our understanding of the interrelationship of these two great contemporaries.

A373   Childe, Wilfred R. "The Literary Background of the Brontës." *BST*, 10 (1944), 204-208.

Speculating in an area of great interest to many Brontë scholars, Childe offers an interesting supposition as to what the family members read. He is able to be most factual about Charlotte Brontë's literary background.

A374 Crompton, Margaret. *Passionate Search: A Life of Charlotte Brontë.* London: Cassel, 1955.

The biographer comes to her own personal conclusions about Charlotte Brontë's relationship with a series of people: her father, Ellen Nussey, her suitors, M. Heger, Branwell, her sisters, her friends, and Arthur Bell Nicholls. Crompton believes: "It was the tragedy of Charlotte's life that few of the people she loved were capable or desirous of the intensity of affection which she herself was anxious to bestow."

A375 Curtis, Myra. "Charlotte Brontë in her Letters." *BST,* 13 (1960), 411-424.

Here is an interesting view of Charlotte Brontë's letters, not as biographical source material, but "as one of her achievements in authorship." The critic discerns an intensity and fervor in the letters and notes a certain stiffness of style. Of course, these observations naturally lead the reader to some biographical conclusions.

A376 Curtis, Myra. "Cowan Bridge School: an Old Prospectus Re-examined." *BST,* 12 (1953), 187-192.

Here Dame Myra pens an answer to Mrs. Weir's *BST* article of 1946 (A437), suggesting a reconsideration of the "old documents" about the school. Both the Prospectus and the song, she assures us, are lampoons: the facts of the Prospectus are preposterous and are meant to be funny. She recommends a closer examination of the genuine records from the school archives.

A377 de Knevett, Edgar. "Charlotte Brontë's School in Brussels." *BST,* 6 (1923), 129-134.

This is a discussion of the photo of the school which had just been discovered. The visualization of the building gives a certain veracity to Charlotte Brontë's experience and her novels *The Professor* and *Villette.*

A378   Dooley, Lucille. "Psycho-Analysis of Charlotte Brontë as a Type of the Woman of Genius." *American Journal of Psychology,* 31 (July 1920), 221-272. Originally a doctoral dissertation, Clark University, 1916. *DAI,* 50 (1920), 32.

This Freudian approach suggests that Charlotte Brontë's love for her father is transferred into fantasy within the novels.

A379   Dunlop, Agnes Mary Robertson. *Girl with a Pen: Charlotte Brontë.* New York: Holt, Rinehart and Winston, 1965.

First published under the pseudonym Elizabeth Kyle, this is juvenile biographical fiction.

A380   Duthie, Enid L. "Charlotte Brontë and Constantin Heger." *Contemporary Review,* 187 (March 1955), 169-173.

This biographical analysis of M. Heger is one of the most vivid and seems likely to be true to his character. He is shown to be a man of integrity and fast faith. The writer confirms his reputation as an excellent teacher.

A381   Duthie, Enid L. *The Foreign Vision of Charlotte Brontë.* London: Macmillan, 1975.

An expert on this period of Charlotte Brontë's life, Dr. Duthie believes that the trip to Belgium resulted in "the broadening of a receptive mind." She reviews the influence of this experience on *The Professor* and *Villette.* In a sensible suggestion Dr. Duthie asks scholars and students to put less emphasis on the emotionalism of the Heger experience and more on the Brussels experience as enlightening and cultural.

A382   Easson, A. "Substantive Misprints and a Deletion in Mrs. Gaskell's *Life of Charlotte Brontë." Notes and Queries,* 23 (Feb. 1976), 61-62.

The alert critic notes eight misprints uncorrected in the third edition of the biography.

A383   Eliot, George. *Letters.* Vol. II. Ed. Gordon Haight. New Haven: Yale University Press, 1954-1955.

At the time when she was first reading Charlotte Brontë's novels, George Eliot gives this second-hand report of Charlotte's looks, in a letter to Charles and Cara Bray: "Lewes was describing Currer Bell to me yesterday as a little, plain, provincial, sickly-looking old maid. Yet what passion, what fire in her! " Vol. also listed as A61.

A384   Gaskell, Elizabeth Cleghorn. *The Letters of Mrs. Gaskell.* Eds. J. A. Chapple and Arthur Pollard. Manchester: Manchester University Press, 1966.

Charlotte Brontë's famous biographer was first a friend and confidante of Charlotte's, and they had the same publisher, Smith, Elder. Many of Mrs. Gaskell's letters tell about their association, report on the response of literary England to Charlotte, and are gossipy and informative.

A385   Gaskell, Mrs. Elizabeth. *Letters on Charlotte Brontë by Mrs. Gaskell.* Ed. Thomas J. Wise. Privately printed, 1914.

One of Wise's suspect publishing ventures resulted in this non-commercial book.

A386   Gaskell, Mrs. Elizabeth. *The Life of Charlotte Brontë: Author of Jane Eyre, Shirley, Villette, etc.* 2 vols. London: Smith, Elder, 1857. Reprinted many times.

Commissioned by the Reverend Brontë shortly after Charlotte Brontë's death, this classic among biographies is partisan and enthusiastic. Forthright in the first edition, Mrs. Gaskell was threatened with law suits and made two revised editions within the first year. The suppressed passages were reprinted in *BST* in 1921 (see A387). Accurate after her fashion, Mrs. Gaskell had met many of those she wrote about, having known Charlotte and her family personally. Her lack of perspective is apparent. Her inaccuracies, resulting from her persuadability, centered around Branwell, Heger, the Cowan Bridge School, and the Robinson family. She had the Angrian material available, but did not connect it with Charlotte's published writing. Dr. Donald Hopewell, former president of Brontë Society, once said of her: "Mrs. Gaskell was the first and greatest of Brontë legend-mongers."

A387   Gaskell, Mrs. Elizabeth. "Suppressed Passages: A Collation of the Earlier and Later Editions of Mrs. Gaskell's *Life of Charlotte Brontë*." *BST*, 6 (1921), 50.

Of interest to Brontë and Gaskell scholars, this article shows the dangers and trials of biography.

A388   Gérin, Winifred. *Charlotte Brontë: The Evolution of Genius.* London: Oxford University Press, 1967.

Long years of research and ten years of writing produced the second memorable biography of Charlotte Brontë. This celebrated Brontë historian has been painstaking in her homework and sensitive in her perception. Her conclusion: the Brontës cannot be separated from their environment. The weaknesses of the biography are twofold: she has not been able to make Arthur Bell Nicholls seem to be a real human being, and her tone – kept in moderate control through most of the book – becomes emotionally fraught at the end.

A389   Goldring, Maude. *Charlotte Brontë: The Woman.* London: Elkin Mathews, 1915. Reissued, New York: R. West, 1974.

One of the old biographies gives us the opportunity to see how Charlotte Brontë was "appreciated."

A390   Gosse, Edmund. "The Challenge of the Brontës." *BST*, 2 (1904), 195-202. Reprinted in *Some Diversions of a Man of Letters.* London: Heinemann, 1919.

This literary gentleman in a patronizing tone tells about his estimation of Charlotte Brontë. He reveals her "defiance, rebellion, narrowness, pride, and indignation." He finds that all the sisters have "pride and stubbornness," and "imperviousness to public opinion."

A391   Harland, Marion. *Charlotte Brontë at Home.* New York: G. P. Putnam's Sons, 1899. Reprinted, New York: Richard West, 1974.

Another early personal account of what Charlotte Brontë must have been.

A392   Harrison, Brett. "The Real Miss Temple." *BST,* 16 (1975), 361-364.

Here is another attempt to locate the identity of the person on whom Charlotte Brontë's fictional character was modeled. Harrison is in disagreement with Pollin whose article in *BST,* 16 (1973), had proposed a candidate. As examples of scholarly sleuthing, both of these articles are interesting. (See also A415.)

A393   Hastings, Selina. "Supplanting Mr. Rochester." *Daily Telegraph Magazine,* Dec. 7, 1973, pp. 15-16, 18.

This is a reappraisal of Arthur Bell Nicholls, partially based on interviews with people who knew him, in an attempt to understand what kind of man Charlotte Brontë married.

A394   Holloway, Laura C. *An Hour with Charlotte Brontë or Flowers from a Yorkshire Moor.* Philadelphia: J. W. Bradley, 1882. Reissued, New York: Richard West, 1974.

Another early biography of Charlotte Brontë now available.

A395   Howells, William Dean. *The Life of Charlotte Brontë: the Famous Authoress of "Jane Eyre."* London: Ward, Lock, 1882.

Part of the series "Ward and Lock's Penny Books for the People," this biography tells Charlotte Brontë's story on a popular level.

A396   Huxley, Leonard. *The House of Smith Elder.* London: privately printed, 1923.

Under the heading "Four Friends," the author describes Charlotte Brontë's life story, including her place in the history of her publisher.

A397   Isenberg, David R. "Charlotte Brontë and the Theatre." *BST,* 15 (1968), 237-241.

Isenberg points out that Charlotte Brontë had a lack of sympathy for the theatre, but was fascinated by the actress Rachel whose performance she saw in London in 1851. Isenberg suggests that Charlotte Brontë fears that a "free portrayal of what she considered evil might be immoral."

A398   Lane, Margaret. *The Brontë Story: a Reconsideration of Mrs. Gaskell's Life of Charlotte Brontë*. London: Heinemann, 1953.

Though sympathetic with Mrs. Gaskell's problems, this critic sets straight some of the earlier biographer's inaccuracies. The updating is based on the current understanding of the juvenilia which was unavailable to Mrs. Gaskell.

A399   Lane, Margaret. "The Hazards of Biography: Mrs. Gaskell and Charlotte Brontë." *Cornhill Magazine*, 993 (Autumn 1952), 154-179.

The story of the creation of the work which was "to display to the world a hidden life," as she composed "the portrait of a woman of genius." Of particular interest are the details concerning Reverend Brontë's reaction to the biography, the comparison of the Clergy Daughters' School with Lowood, and some further discussion of the validity of Mrs. Gaskell's report of the Branwell-Mrs. Robinson affair.

A400   Lane, Margaret. "Mr. Nicholls." *Cornhill Magazine*, 983 (Summer 1950), 351-375.

This factual, sympathetic biography is based on the facts supplied by Mrs. Gaskell.

A401   Langbridge, Rosamond. *Charlotte Brontë: a Psychological Study*. Garden City, New York: Doubleday, Doran, 1929.

This early psychological study, though angry and inaccurate, was very influential at the time of publication. Many of the so-called "facts" which caused such a stir were disproved in subsequent publications.

A402   Larken, Geoffrey. "Charlotte Brontë and Catherine Crowe." *BST*, 17 (1978), 205-209.

The critic speculates on the possible results of a furthering of the acquaintance of these two ladies who met on June 12, 1850, at a "hen-party" given by Thackeray at No. 13, Young Street.

A403   Lee, P. F. "Charlotte Brontë and the East Riding." *BST*, 1 (1896), 20-25.

One of the very first articles published by the Brontë Society.

A404   Lee, Sir Sidney. "Charlotte Brontë in London" in *Charlotte Brontë, 1916-1916: A Centenary Memorial*. Ed. Butler Wood. London: T. Fisher Unwin, 1918. Originally published in *BST*, 4 (1909), 95-120.

Fifty-four years after Charlotte Brontë's death, Sir Sidney Lee talked with those who had known her, including George Smith and Thackeray's daughter. Mr. Smith was thought to be the model for Dr. John Bretton.

A405   Lerner, Lawrence. "The Tremulous Homely-faced Creature: Charlotte Brontë and Her Critics." *Encounter*, 45 (July 1975), 60-66.

Here the critic reviews three recent publications on Charlotte Brontë. After discussing the difference between Charlotte's personal approach to the position of women and Harriet Martineau's more feminist approach, the reviewer explains the weaknesses of Millett (A236), Patricia Beer (A262), and Terry Eagleton (C76).

A406   Lever, Tresham. "Charlotte Brontë and George Smith." *BST*, 17 (1977), 106.

This article by the late president of the Brontë Society was to be chapter seven of an unfinished book, *The Life of George Smith*. In it, Sir Tresham discusses the professional and romantic relationship between Charlotte Brontë and her publisher. The biographer tells of a recently discovered letter from Charlotte Brontë to George Smith implying that in September, 1851, he was on the point of proposing.

A407   Macdonald, Frederica. *The Secret of Charlotte Brontë: Followed by Some Reminiscences of the Real Monsieur and Madame Heger.* London and Edinburgh: T. C. and E. C. Jack, 1914.

This author had been a pupil at Heger Pensionnat in the 1860's. She disagrees completely with Charlotte Brontë's depiction of the Hegers in her novels. This gossipy revelation discusses Charlotte Brontë's "honorable" love for the Belgian teacher. The book is an enlargement of "The Brontës at Brussels," an article in *Woman at Home* in 1894.

A408   Moglen, Helene. *Charlotte Brontë: The Self Conceived.* New York: Norton, 1976.

This modern biography, which avoids both sentimentality and clinical psychology, makes Charlotte Brontë's concerns and creativity understandable. The two areas of her life which remain clouded — the Brussels experience and Charlotte's relationship with Branwell — are carefully explored. The combined critical-biographical study fuses the writer with her work.

A409   Nussey, Ellen. "Miss Nussey's 'Reminiscences.'" *Scribner's Monthly,* 2 (May 1871), 18-31. Reprinted as "Reminiscences of Charlotte Brontë" (A410).

Charlotte's close friend Ellen Nussey tells intimate details about her association with the novelist. Her innate gentility caused her to censor names, dates, and identifiable details. (See also A410 and A420.)

A410   Nussey, Ellen. "Reminiscences of Charlotte Brontë." *BST,* 2 (1899), 58-83. Reprint of A409.

A first-hand account of the understanding Ellen Nussey had of the personality of Charlotte Brontë, with all references to people and incidents removed to avoid offending anyone. (See also A420.)

A411   Offor, Richard. "The Brontës — Their Relation to the History and Politics of Their Time." *BST,* 10 (1943), 150-160.

The critic-historian writes primarily about Charlotte Brontë as there is little information about her sisters in relation to the history and politics of the time.

A412   Pearson, Frederick Richard. *Charlotte Brontë on the East Yorkshire Coast.* No. 7 of the East Yorkshire Local History Series. Micklegate: East Yorkshire Local History Society, 1957.

Biographical background is offered to clarify the literary material of the Brontës.

A413   Peters, Margot. *Unquiet Soul: A Biography of Charlotte Brontë.* New York: Doubleday, 1975.

A book designed for those who know only a little about the author, this biography is direct, clear, and believable. After a thorough investigation and a clear visualization, Dr. Peters brings to the reader a real person: Charlotte. The clouded areas of her life require speculation and Dr. Peters must do her share, but her view of Branwell begins to make his motivations and reactions a little clearer. With restrained feminism, the writer shows Charlotte's feelings as a plain but vigorously independent woman struggling against male dominance.

A414   Pollard, Arthur. "Admiration and Exasperation: Charlotte Brontë's Relationship to William Makepeace Thackeray." *BST,* 17 (1978), 171-181.

Originally given as an address to the Brontë Society, June 3, 1978, this scholarly work covers the history of the association between these two great authors, quoting from their own words on the subject as well as the letters and memoirs of those who knew them. Professor Pollard quotes from the Shakespeare Head editors, "It cannot be said that Charlotte Brontë and Thackeray gained by personal contact," and reminds us of her disappointment in the man whose work she so admired. Pollard concludes: "When admiration bowed out, exasperation flew in."

A415   Pollin, Burton R. "Two Letters Concerning Charlotte Brontë in Contemporary American Journals." *BST,* 16 (1973), 205-212.

The first is a letter of 1850 discussing "The Author of *Jane Eyre.*" The second is the full text of a letter from Ann Evans reported to be "Maria Temple" in *Jane Eyre.* In the letter she "discreetly denies her role in the novel," as reported by Pollin.

A416   Preston, Benjamin. "On the Death of Charlotte Brontë" in *A Garland of Poetry; by Yorkshire Authors, or Relating to Yorkshire.* Ed. Abraham Holroyd. Saltaire: Abraham Holroyd, 1873.

This biographical description accompanies other editorial comments about the Brontë poetry.

A417   Ratchford, Fannie E. "Some New Notes on the Brontë-Heger Letters." *Bookman* (London), 85 (1933), 180-182.

Miss Ratchford discusses the tone of the letters and the question of M. Heger's connection with the fictional Paul Emanuel.

A418   Reid, T. Wemyss. *Charlotte Brontë: a Monograph.* London: Macmillan, 1876.

Expanded from his articles in *Macmillan's Magazine*, 34 (Sept. 1876), 385-401; 34 (Oct. 1876), 481-499; and 35 (Nov. 1876), 1-18, about Charlotte Brontë and Heger, this early revelation was based on 100 letters from Charlotte Brontë to Ellen Nussey which were not included in Mrs. Gaskell's book.

A419   Robinson, Dennis. "Elizabeth Gaskell and a Few Words about *Jane Eyre.*" *Notes and Queries,* 23 (Summer 1976), 396-398.

Suggests that "Few Words" was not written by Mrs. Gaskell (as has been suggested) but by Catherine Winkworth, copying parts of a letter from Mrs. Gaskell (A73). Vol. also listed as A165.

A420   Scruton, W. "Reminiscences of the Late Miss Ellen Nussey." *BST,* 1 (1898), 23-42.

Following the appearance of these "Reminiscences" in *Scribner's Monthly* in May 1871 (A409), Scruton brings the facts to *Transaction* readers. (See also A410.)

A421   Shelston, Alan. "A Letter from Charlotte Brontë." *Times Literary Supplement,* March 25, 1977, p. 344.

This letter, dated May 28, 1853, is from Charlotte Brontë to a Mrs. Holland. In it the author defines her understanding of the novelist's role. The critic suggests that this letter may have been written to Miss Lucy Holland, Mrs. Gaskell's cousin, who is thought by some to be portrayed as Miss Matty in *Cranford.*

A422   Shepheard, Henry. *A Vindication of the Clergy Daughters' School, and of the Reverend W. Carus Wilson, from Remarks in "The Life of Charlotte Brontë."* London: Kirkby, Lonsdale, 1857.

The Chaplain and honorary secretary of the school discusses Charlotte Brontë's life there and defends the school from the attack on it in Mrs. Gaskell's biography of Charlotte Brontë.

A423   Sinclair, May. "Introduction," in Elizabeth Gaskell. *Life of Charlotte Brontë.* London: J. M. Dent and Sons, 1908.

The editor discusses Mrs. Gaskell's problem: the influence which the personality of Branwell had on the biographer's understanding of events. Branwell's behavior was to blame for an evil atmosphere in the parsonage. But for Mrs. Gaskell, "the more she exposed Branwell the more she defended Charlotte." The editor blames her for her "lack of a judicial attitude."

A424   Smith, George Murray. "Charlotte Brontë." *Cornhill Magazine,* 82, n.s. 9 (July-Dec. 1900), 778-795.

An account by Charlotte Brontë's publisher of his association with her, including such personal reminiscences as their visit to the phrenologist Dr. T. P. Browne and including the doctor's "Phrenological Estimate of a Certain Mr. and Miss Fraser" (the publisher Smith and Charlotte Brontë).

A425   Spielmann, M. H. "Charlotte Brontë in Brussels" in *Charlotte Brontë, 1816-1916: A Centenary Memorial.* Ed. Butler Wood. London: T. Fisher Unwin, 1918. Originally published in the *Times Literary Supplement* for April 13, 1916.

A geographical-biographic supposition which was later refuted by Clement Shorter in the *Sphere.*

A426   Spielmann, M. H. *The Inner History of the Brontë-Heger Letters.* London: Chapman and Hall, 1919.

A clarification of the problem which continues to attract scholars. The critic tells how he got the letters. Reprinted from the *Fortnightly Review,* April, 1919. These are further explicated in Spielmann's introduction to these letters when they are reproduced in *BST,* 5 (1914), 49.

A427   Stead, J. J. "Hathersage and *Jane Eyre.*" *BST,* 1 (1898), 26-28.

Was Hathersage the original Thornfield Hall?

A428   Stead, J. J. "The *Shirley* Country." *BST,* 1 (1897), 3-16. Reprinted in 4 (1907), 26-40.

Identifying the actual ambiance of the fictional setting.

A429   Stevens, J. "A Brontë Letter Misdated." *Notes and Queries,* 19 (1972), 254.

On a letter to Mary Taylor, Charlotte Brontë wrote "March 4, 1852." Stevens has estimated that there was not time enough for a ship to get to England with the news after Ellen Taylor's death. Stevens thinks that Charlotte Brontë may have meant *May* 4, 1852.

A430   Stevens, J. "Charlotte Brontë's Mistake." *Notes and Queries,* 17 (Jan. 1970), 19.

In a letter to Miss Wooler, Charlotte Brontë commented on the forthcoming marriage of Waring Taylor to Mary Knox. Charlotte Brontë erroneously suggests that Miss Knox is the daughter of Dr. Knox. She was in fact his niece.

A431   Stevens, J., ed. *Mary Taylor, Friend of Charlotte Brontë: Letters from New Zealand and Elsewhere.* New York: Oxford University Press, 1972.

This book of letters from Charlotte Brontë's good friend includes 33 letters from 1841-1863. They show strength of character and clear thinking. Mary indicates that she realizes that the Brontës were "outsiders" living in racial and intellectual isolation.

A432   Thackeray, William Makepeace. "The Last Sketch." *BST,* 2 (1899), 84-87. Reprinted from *Cornhill Magazine,* 1 (1860), 485-498.

Remembering the vitality of Charlotte Brontë, Thackeray admits, "I fancied an austere little Joan of Arc marching upon us, and rebuking our easy lives, our easy morals." This *Cornhill* editor pays tribute to Charlotte Brontë in his introduction to the first printing of the posthumous fragment of a novel called "Emma." Vol. also listed as A11.

A433   Tillotson, Geoffrey and Kathleen. *Mid-Victorian Studies.* London: University of London Press, 1965.

A general view of literary life in the mid-nineteenth century gives substance to the atmosphere for writers and readers of the time. Very little is included on Charlotte Brontë specifically.

A434   Tillotson, Kathleen. "A Day with Charlotte Brontë in 1850." *BST*, 16 (1971), 22-30.

This eminent Victorian expert recounts an incident from 1850, described in a two-part article published anonymously in *Free Lance* and written by a 22-year-old John Stores Smith, known as "Little Smith." The two installments appeared on March 7 and 14, 1868, as "Charlotte Brontë" and "A Day with Charlotte Brontë." He was ´a member of a coterie of Currer Bell admirers in Halifax (Yorks.). He dined with Charlotte and the Reverend Brontë, talked with her all afternoon, and left at five. She warned him not to seek a London literary life. "I felt that I had met a Cassandra," he reported.

A435   Tillotson, Kathleen. "'Haworth Churchyard': The Making of Arnold's Elegy." *BST*, 15 (1967), 105-122.

The critic-scholar envisions for us the encounter between Charlotte Brontë and Arnold referred to in the poem and then his later visit to Haworth. (See C232.)

A436   Todd, John and Kenneth Dewhurst. "The Periodic Depressions of Charlotte Brontë." *Perspectives in Biology and Medicine.* Chicago: University of Chicago, 1968.

Two medical practitioners speculate on the past.

A437   Weir, Edith M. "Cowan Bridge: New Light from Old Documents."
        BST, 11 (1946), 16-28.

        The article describes a recently-discovered prospectus and a song,
        both about Cowan Bridge School. The critic restates the facts known
        about the Brontë children at the school. She gives the added
        information that by the end of the year in which the Brontë sisters
        were there, 28 of the 77 pupils "left," either dying or returning home.
        (For an interesting rejoinder, see A376.)

A438   Winnifrith, Tom J. "Charlotte Brontë and Calvinism." *Notes and
        Queries*, 17 (Jan. 1970), 17-18.

        A note on Winifred Gerin's interpretation of the letter which
        Charlotte Brontë wrote to Ellen Nussey, as it is presented in Gerin's
        Charlotte Brontë: The Evolution of Genius (A388).

A439   Winnifrith, Tom J. "Charlotte Brontë's Letters to Ellen Nussey."
        Durham University Journal, n.s. 32:1 (Dec. 1970), 16-18.

        The critic writes about the unpublished letters in Ellen Nussey's
        handwriting, copies of those written by Charlotte Brontë. These had
        been bought by Mrs. Needham in 1898. There seem to be scribal
        inaccuracies, but they also show Miss Nussey as censor. Mostly they
        show the fallability of the *Shakespeare Head Brontë* and Thomas J.
        Wise as "a man who, by splitting up the manuscripts of the letters,
        made any edition of them extremely difficult."

A440   Wood, Butler. "The Brontë Itinerary" in *Charlotte Brontë,
        1816-1916: A Centenary Memorial*. Ed. Butler Wood. London:
        T. Fisher Unwin, 1918.

        An article of interest to those who want to visit the places found
        in the Brontë novels and letters. The volume contains twelve other
        articles, reprints of items found in this listing.

A441   Wroot, Herbert E. "The Persons and Places of the Brontë Novels."
        BST, 3 (1906), 5-237.

Presented in three supplementary parts, this old-fashioned scholarship gives the writer's guess about the factual basis for the fictional representations in all four of Charlotte Brontë's novels: Part (1) *Jane Eyre,* (2) *Shirley,* and (3) *Villette* and *The Professor.*

A442   Wroot, Herbert E. "Persons and Places: Sources of Charlotte Brontë's Novels." *BST,* supplement to 8 (1935), 5-214.

A continuation of the investigations presented in A441.

B. EMILY BRONTË

PRIMARY MATERIAL

Wuthering Heights: Major Editions
Listed in Chronological Order of First Publication

B1   *Wuthering Heights.* Vols. I and II of 3 vols. London: Thomas C. Newby, 1847.

B2   [with Anne Brontë]. *Wuthering Heights, Agnes Grey, together with a selection of Poems by Ellis and Acton Bell. Prefixed with a Biographical Memoir of the authors by Currer Bell.* London: Smith, Elder, 1850.

B3   *Wuthering Heights* in *Wuthering Heights by Emily Brontë (Ellis Bell) and Agnes Grey by Anne Brontë (Acton Bell).* Vol. IV of 7 vols. *The Life and Works of the Brontë Sisters.* Introduction, Mrs. Humphry Ward. New York: Harper Brothers, 1903; reprinted New York: AMS Press, 1973.

      Until the publication of the Clarendon Edition in 1976, this was the most reliable text available.

B4   *Wuthering Heights.* Vol. II of *Complete Works of Emily Brontë.* Ed. Clement Shorter. London: Hodder and Stoughton, 1911.

B5   *Wuthering Heights.* Vol. III of *Shakespeare Head Brontë.* Eds. T. J. Wise and J. A. Symington. Oxford: Shakespeare Head Press, 1931.

B6   *Wuthering Heights.* Ed. Hilda Marsden and Ian Jack, Clarendon Edition. Oxford: Clarendon Press, 1976.

      This has been a difficult novel to re-edit and reprint as the manuscript is missing, and Newby's first edition did not include the author's corrections. In the Smith, Elder 1850 edition Charlotte Brontë made many editorial changes. In this new edition the editors have worked with what material is available, adding seven appendices and using footnotes to explain the variants.

In addition to the six basic editions of *Wuthering Heights* listed here, there has been an ever increasing number of editions each year. Some of these are scholarly, some are from the popular presses, and some — in each category — are edited by Brontë scholars and include valuable comments, criticisms, and analyses. In this bibliography the editions with the most valuable introductions have been included and will be found under the name of the editor preparing the critical material. See also works under Brontë Family.

Poetry: Major Editions
Listed in Chronological Order

B7   [with Charlotte and Anne Brontë]. *Poems by Currer, Ellis, and Acton Bell.* London: Aylott and Jones, 1846.

B8   [with Charlotte and Anne Brontë]. *Poems by Currer, Ellis, and Acton Bell.* London: Aylott and Jones, 1848.

B9   *Poems* in *Wuthering Heights* and *Agnes Grey*. London: Smith, Elder, 1850.

B10   *Poems*. Ed. Arthur Symons. London: Heinemann, 1906.

B11   *Poetry*. Vol. I of *Complete Works of Emily Jane Brontë*. Ed. Clement Shorter. London: Hodder and Stoughton, 1910.

           This volume contains 139 new poems not published earlier as well as 39 from *Poems by Currer, Ellis, and Acton Bell* (B7) and 17 from Emily Brontë's *Poems* edited by Charlotte Brontë in 1850 (B9).

B12   *Complete Poems*. Ed. Clement Shorter. Arranged and collected with Bibliography and Notes by C. W. Hatfield. London: Hodder and Stoughton, 1923.

B13   *Complete Poems*. Vol. I, *Shakespeare Head Brontë*. Eds. T. J. Wise and J. A. Symington. Oxford: Shakespeare Head Press, 1934.

B14   *Gondal Poems: Now First Published from the MS. in the British Museum*. Eds. Helen Brown and Joan Mott. Oxford: Shakespeare Head Press, 1938.

B15   *The Complete Poems of Emily Jane Brontë.* Ed. C. W. Hatfield. London: Oxford Press and New York: Columbia University Press, 1941.

Still the most reliable edition of her collected poetry, these poems are transcribed from the manuscript and carefully documented.

B16   *Poems in The Brontës.* Heather Edition. Ed. Phyllis Bentley. London: A. Wingate, 1949.

B17   *Selected Poems.* Ed. Philip Henderson. London: Lawson and Dunn, 1947.

B18   *Complete Poems.* Ed. Philip Henderson. London: The Folio Society, 1952.

Based on a re-examination of the Brontë manuscript, the editor presents the poems in chronological order, mixing Gondal poems with non-Gondal.

B19   *A Selection of Poems.* Ed. Muriel Spark. London: Grey Walls Press, 1952.

B20   *Poems.* Ed. Rosemary Harthill. London: Tom Stacey, 1973.

B21   *Five Late Romantic Poets: George Darley, Hartley Coleridge, Thomas Hood, Thomas Lovell Beddoes, Emily Brontë.* Ed. J. Reeves. London: Heinemann, 1974.

Other Writings
Listed in Chronological Order

B22   "A Diary Paper." *BST,* 12 (1951), 15.

One dated June 26, 1837, is deciphered. The article by Fannie Ratchford includes a facsimile of the original.

B23   *Five Essays Written in French.* Translated Lorine W. Nagel. Austin: University of Texas Press, 1948.

These include "The Cat," "Portrait: King Harold," "Filial Love," "A Letter from One Brother to Another," and "The Butterfly."

103

B24   "Three Essays." *BST,* 11 (1950), 337-341.

These are "The Cat," "A Letter from One Brother to Another," and "The Butterfly."

SECONDARY MATERIAL

Poetry: Nineteenth-Century Reviews
Listed in Chronological Order

B25   [Dobell, Sydney]. "Poetry of the Million," *Athenaeum,* 975 (July 4, 1846), 682.

One of the first three published reviews which the Brontës read. The critic calls theirs "a family in whom appears to run the instinct of song. It is, however, by the three brothers — as we suppose them to be — in very unequal portion . . . rising" in the case of Ellis, "into an inspiration, which may yet find an audience in the outer world." He speaks of the "fine, quaint spirit" of Ellis Bell and of the "impression of originality" which he conveys.

B26   Butler, William Archer. "Evenings with Our Younger Poets." A review of *Poems by Currer, Ellis, and Acton Bell. Dublin University Magazine,* 28 (Oct. 1846).

One of the three published reviews (of the poems) reported to have been read by the Brontës. The reviewer, as Charlotte Brontë says in a letter (see Gaskell A386), "conjectured that the *soi-disant* three personages were in reality but one."

B27   Anon. A review of *Poems by Currer, Ellis, and Acton Bell. Spectator,* Nov. 11, 1846, pp. 1094-1095.

Noted but not read. Listed in Parkison, D17.

B28   Anon. A review of *Poems by Currer, Ellis, and Acton Bell. Critic,* 1846.

One of the three published reviews of the poems which the Brontës read, according to T. J. Wise and J. A. Symington. *The Brontës: Their Lives, Friendships and Correspondence,* vol. 2, p. 102. Oxford: The Shakespeare Head Press, 1932 (C7).

The reviewer comments that "in these compositions" the alert reader will recognize "more genius than it was supposed this utilitarian age had devoted to the loftier exercise of the intellect. . . ."

B29   Anon. A review of *Poems by Acton, Currer, and Ellis Bell. Spectator,*
        Nov. 18, 1848, pp. 1094-1095.

        As Charlotte Brontë reports in a letter to Mr. Williams of Smith,
        Elder (the publisher of the second edition of the poems) in Oct.
        1848 (C2): "The *Spectator* consistently maintains the tone it first assumed
        regarding the Bells."

Wuthering Heights: Nineteenth-Century Reviews Listed in Chronological Order

B30   Anon. "Our Library Table." A review of *Wuthering Heights* (and
        Agnes Grey). *Athenaeum,* Dec. 25, 1847, pp. 1324-1325.

        The critic suggests that all Brontë novels are written by the same
        hand. He comments on the vulgarity and bad taste of all Brontë
        novels. He finds *Wuthering Heights* "disagreeable . . . eccentric" and
        "unpleasant."

B31   Anon. A review of *Wuthering Heights. Spectator,* 20 (Dec. 1847),
        1217.

        The review states that "The success is not equal to the abilities
        of the writer . . . the incidents and persons are too coarse and
        disagreeable to be attractive." He concludes, though: "The execution,
        however, is good: grant the writer all that is requisite as regards
        matter, and the delineation is forceful and truthful."

B32   Anon. A review of *Wuthering Heights. Examiner,* Jan. 8, 1848, pp.
        21-22.

        One of the five reviews which Emily Brontë read and kept, now
        found in the Brontë Parsonage Museum. The *Examiner*'s reviewer
        finds that although "the book has the merit . . . of avoiding the
        commonplace and affectation" and "is not without evidence of
        considerable power," it is "a strange book" with elements "coarse
        and loathsome."

B33   Anon. A review of *Wuthering Heights. Britannia,* Jan. 15, 1848, pp.
        42-43.

One of the five reviews Emily Brontë kept, also found now in the Brontë Parsonage Museum. Granting that the author "displays considerable power in his creations" which are "strangely original," the critic nonetheless finds the novel full of "evil impulses" which are "the natural offspring of the unregulated heart."

B34   Anon. A review of *Wuthering Heights. Douglas Jerrold's Weekly Newspaper,* Jan. 15, 1848, p. 77.

One of the five reviews which Emily Brontë kept, now to be found in the Brontë Parsonage Museum. The reviewer claims that he was "shocked, disgusted, almost sickened."

B35   Anon. A review of *Wuthering Heights. Atlas,* Jan. 22, 1848, p. 59.

One of the five reviews which Emily Brontë read, and kept, now in the Bonnell Collection in the Brontë Parsonage Museum. Although the critic speaks of the "rugged power" and "unconscious strength," he claims that "*Wuthering Heights* casts a gloom over the mind" and "sadly wants relief."

B36   Anon. A review of *Wuthering Heights. Economist,* 6 (Jan. 29, 1848), 126.

The reviewer finds the characters strong but the theme and plot unpleasant.

B37   Anon. A review of *Wuthering Heights. New Monthly Magazine and Humorist,* 82 (Jan. 1848), 140.

The reviewer finds that in reading *Wuthering Heights* the "mind shrinks from mansion and tenant."

B38   Anon. A review of *Wuthering Heights. Tait's Edinburgh Magazine,* 15 (Feb. 1848), 138-140.

According to this review, the novel proves that Satan is master of the law of entail.

B39   **Anon. A review of** *Wuthering Heights. Peterson's Magazine* (Philadelphia), 13 (March 1848), 229.

The critic finds the work "coarse" and the villain "base."

B40   Anon. A review of *Wuthering Heights*. *Literary World* (New York), 2 (April 29, 1848), 243.

After quoting from the novel, the critic condemns it for its coarse dialogue and improbable plot.

B41   [Briggs, Charles F.]. "Review of *Wuthering Heights*." *Holden's Dollar Magazine* (New York), 1 (June 1848), 370-372.

The reviewer mistakenly claims the same author wrote *Jane Eyre* and *Wuthering Heights*. He admires *Wuthering Heights* for its directness, crediting the author with being "honest in his purpose and sincere in his manner of dealing with you."

B42   Von Frank, Albert J. "An American Defense of *Wuthering Heights* – 1848." *BST*, 16 (1974), 277-283.

B43   Peck, W. G. A review of *Wuthering Heights*. *American Review* (New York), 7 (June 1848), 572-585.

After praising the immense power of the book, Peck comments on the coarseness of language and manners and the untruthfulness of the passions.

B44   Anon. "Review of New Books." A review of *Wuthering Heights*. *Graham's Gentlemen's Magazine* (Philadelphia), 33 (July 1848), 60.

An unsympathetic review suggesting that all Brontë novels are by the same writer.

B45   Whipple, E. P. A review of *Wuthering Heights*. *North American Review*, 67 (Oct. 1848), 354-360.

The reviewer denounces the brutality and spiritual wickedness of Heathcliff while admitting that the author is "a man of uncommon talents." He continues, "The truth is, that the whole firm of Bell & Company seem to have a sense of the depravity of human nature peculiarly their own. It is the yahoo, not the demon, that they select for representation; their Pandemonium is of mud rather than fire."

B46   Rigby, Elizabeth (later Lady Eastlake). A review of *Jane Eyre*, with comments on *Wuthering Heights*. *Quarterly Review*, 84 (1848), 153-185.

She finds Catherine and "Heathfield" [sic] "too odiously and abominably pagan to be palatable" and accuses the author of adapting "all the unscrupulousness of the French school of novels." The reviews comments on the book's "repulsive vulgarity in the choice of its vice."

B47   Anon. A review of *Wuthering Heights* (source unknown, c. 1848) cited in Charles Simpson. *Emily Brontë.* London: Country Life, 1829.

The fifth review which Emily Brontë kept and which is now in the Brontë Parsonage Museum in Haworth. This unidentified review is reprinted in Charles Simpson's *Emily Brontë* (B507).

B48   Dobell, Sydney. A review of work by Currer Bell, including *Wuthering Heights. Palladium,* Sept. 1850, pp. 161-175. Reprinted as "Sydney Dobell's Article on Currer Bell, contributed to the *Palladium* in 1850," *BST,* 5 (1918), 210-136.

Lyric praise for *Wuthering Heights* carries over into a criticism of all the Brontë novels. Dobell believes that the others are "rough and earlier statues from the hand which later shaped *Jane Eyre* and *Shirley*" while *Wuthering Heights* is "the masterpiece of a poet rather than the hybrid creation of a novelist."

B49   Brontë, Charlotte. "Editor's Preface to the New Edition of *Wuthering Heights.*" *Wuthering Heights* (second edition). London: Smith, Elder, 1850.

Charlotte Brontë's naive assumption that Emily Brontë was unaware of what she was doing when she wrote *Wuthering Heights* has set the tone for much subsequent negative criticism. (See also B2.)

B50   Anon. A review of *Wuthering Heights* (and *Agnes Grey*). *Examiner,* Dec. 21, 1850, p. 815.

An argument concerning the critics' attitude toward the Brontës.

B51   Lewes, G. H. A review of *Wuthering Heights* (and *Agnes Grey*). *The Leader,* Dec. 28, 1850, p. 953.

In this early review praising the novel, Lewes says, "We cannot deny its truth: sombre, rude, brutal, yet true." He declares that "the power, indeed, is wonderful" and concludes that "in the treatment of this subject . . . Ellis Bell shows real mastery, and it shows more genius . . . than you will find in a thousand novels. . . ."

B52   Anon. A review of *Wuthering Heights* (and *Agnes Grey*). *Athenaeum,* Dec. 28, 1850, pp. 1368-1369.

A discussion of whether or not the author is a woman.

B53   Anon. A review of *Wuthering Heights* (and *Agnes Grey*). *Economist,* Jan. 4, 1851, p. 15.

Emphasis on Yorkshire quality of the novels.

B54   Anon. A review of *Wuthering Heights. Eclectic Review,* n.s. 1 (Feb. 1851), 222-227.

The reviewer finds *Wuthering Heights* to be a "repellent book." The author's powers are "not only premature but misdirected." According to him, the characters "are devoid of truthfulness, are not in harmony with the actual world, and have, therefore, but little power to move our sympathies. . . ."

B55   Dallas, Eneas Sweetland. A review of *Jane Eyre* with comments on *Wuthering Heights. Blackwood's Magazine,* 82 (July 1857), 77-94.

He speaks of the writing of these novels as an outlet for the intellectual energy of the Brontës.

B56   Montégut, Emile. Comments on *Wuthering Heights* in a review of Mrs. Gaskell's *Life of Charlotte Brontë. La Revue des Deux Mondes,* July 1857. Reprinted in *Ecrivains Modernes d'Angleterre,* 1st ser. Paris: Hachette, 1885.

The French critic finds Emily Brontë's work "the most remarkable" of all the sisters' novels. "Emily had the gift that the

English define as 'genius.'" He calls her "la petite soeur d'Hoffmann."

B57   Dearden, William. "Who Wrote *Wuthering Heights?*" [letter]. *Halifax Guardian,* June 15, 1867. Reprinted in *BST.* (See also B74.)

This letter is strong in its support of Branwell Brontë's authorship of *Wuthering Heights.*

B58   Stephen, Leslie. "Charlotte Brontë." *Cornhill,* 36 (Dec. 1877), 723-739. Reprinted in *Hours in a Library.* London: Smith, Elder, 1879.

While discussing Charlotte Brontë, the reviewer adds that "Emily Brontë's feeble grasp of eternal facts makes her book a kind of baseless nightmare."

B59   Williams, Alexander Malcolm. "Emily Brontë." *Temple Bar Magazine,* 98 (July, 1893), 431.

In a general study of women writers, the critic discusses the style and content of *Wuthering Heights.* The article was later reprinted in *Our Early Female Novelists and Other Essays,* Glasgow: James Maclehose, 1904.

B60   Mackay, Angus Mason. *The Brontës, Fact and Fiction.* London: Service and Paton, 1897.

An attempt to differentiate between history and supposition.

B61   Swinburne, Algernon Charles. "Emily Brontë." *Miscellanies.* London: Chatto and Windus, 1886.

This literary essay deals with the works of Emily Brontë in a wholly ornate style, with more concern for Swinburne's language than for content. He calls *Wuthering Heights* "a poem in the fullest and most positive sense of the term." First published in the *Athenaeum,* June 16, 1883, pp. 762-763.

B62   Pollin, Burton. "Brontës in the American Periodicals Press of Their Day." *BST,* 16 (1975), 383-399.

A thoroughly researched listing of critical reviews in 19th-century American press, with brief annotations.

111

B63   Adams, Ruth M. *"Wuthering Heights*: The Land East of Eden."
       Nineteenth Century Fiction, 13 (June 1958), 52-62.

       Here the critic assigns Genesis 4:24 as the text for Rev.
       Branderham's sermon (see Shannon, B297, for another opinion). The
       critic feels that this novel is devoid of conventional morality as
       Catherine and Heathcliff themselves illustrate the "perverse values that
       prevail in *Wuthering Heights.*"

B64   Allott, Kenneth, ed. "Introduction." *Victorian Prose: 1830-1880.* Ed.
       Kenneth and Miriam Allott. Harmondsworth, Middlesex:
       Penguin, 1956.

       The editor speaks of "the modification of style by emotion"
       in the last sentence of *Wuthering Heights* as "an imaginative effect
       seemingly beyond the powers of any English novelist of the eighteenth
       century."

B65   Allott, Miriam. *Emily Brontë: Wuthering Heights: A Casebook.*
       London: Macmillan, 1970.

       Some fifty critical approaches to *Wuthering Heights* are included
       in this helpful book for students of the novel.

B66   Allott, Miriam. "Mrs. Gaskell's 'The Old Nurse's Story': a Link
       between *Wuthering Heights* and *The Turn of the Screw." Notes
       and Queries,* 18 (March 1961), 101-102.

       Two years after she read *Wuthering Heights,* Mrs. Gaskell
       published this story in the 1852 Christmas Number of Dickens'
       Household Words. Her story, in turn, is thought to have inspired
       Henry James' *Turn of the Screw.*

B67   Allott, Miriam. *"Wuthering Heights*: the Rejection of Heathcliff?"
       Essays in Criticism, 8 (1958), 27-47.

       Dr. Allott approaches the problem of Heathcliff's rejection and
       suggests that by the end of the novel "the tones are those of someone
       aware that the claims of the head and heart remain unreconciled."

B68   Anderson, Quentin. "Introduction" in Emily Brontë. *Wuthering Heights.* New York: Collier Books, 1962.

The editor states that Emily Brontë succeeded in revealing the realities of life far more clearly than in "any other novel of the century."

B69   Anderson, W. E. "Lyrical Form in *Wuthering Heights.*" *University of Toronto Quarterly,* 47 (Winter 1977-1978), 112-134.

The critic suggests that *Wuthering Heights* is written in "a radically new form." Emily Brontë, he feels, "shifts the planes of reality to such a degree that ordinary life gradually comes to seem less vital than death." Through this shift, she creates a novel in which "we have, in place of logical structure and a realistic plot, a symbolic action progressing towards 'lyric' revelation," as opposed to those logically progressive plots of Fielding or Austen.

B70   Ankenbrandt, Katherine Ware. "Songs in *Wuthering Heights.*" *Southern Folklore Quarterly,* 33 (June 1969), 92-115.

Wuthering Heights includes three folksongs which echo relationships in the novels. They reinforce three major themes in the novel: cruelty to motherless children, lack of harmony between Cathy and Hareton, and the resolution in their predicted marriage.

B71   Anon. "Brontë Discoveries." *Bookman* (New York), 33 (May 1911), 228.

Here is the news in 1911 that J. Malham-Dembleby has found correlations between "Charlotte Brontë's *Wuthering Heights*" and *Jane Eyre.* This article ends with a tourist guide to Brontë country.

B72   Anon. "The Genius of the Moors." *Academy and Literature,* 65 (Oct. 3, 1903), 333-334.

This early article insists that Branwell did not write *Wuthering Heights.* It was written by a woman as proved by the fact that Lockwood's point of view is never male. Further, the article states that Emily Brontë's poetry shows such a strong relationship to the novel that only Emily Brontë could have written *Wuthering Heights.*

113

B73   Anon. "Landscape in the Brontë Novels." *The Academy*, 71 (Sept. 8, 1906), 226-228.

The author points out that the description of landscape in *Wuthering Heights* is brief but effective and essential to the plot.

B74   Anon. "Patrick Branwell Brontë and *Wuthering Heights.*" *BST*, 7 (1927), 97-102.

This is a reprint of the article from *Halifax Guardian*, June 15, 1867 (B57), ascribing *Wuthering Heights*' authorship to Branwell Brontë.

B75   Apter, T. E. "Romanticism and Romantic Love in *Wuthering Heights.*" *The Art of Emily Brontë*. Ed. Anne Smith. London: Vision Press, 1976.

Wuthering Heights expresses romantic imagination while also criticizing the destructive and self-destructive elements of romanticism.

B76   Arnold, Josephine. "Georges Sand's *Mauprat* and Emily Brontë's *Wuthering Heights.*" *Revue de Littérature Comparée*, April-June 1972, pp. 210-218.

This article shows a parallel between the works, *Mauprat* showing the positive side and *Wuthering Heights* the negative side of a "unique and deathless love."

B77   Bataille, Georges. *La Littérature et le Mal.* Paris, 1957. Translated as *Literature and Evil.* London: Calder and Boyars, 1973. Reprinted in *Critique*, 13 (Feb. 1957), 99-112.

This French critic defines the eroticism of Catherine and Heathcliff as "an approbation of life to the point of death."

B78   Bell, Vereen M. "*Wuthering Heights* and the Unforgivable Sin." *Nineteenth Century Fiction*, 17 (Sept. 1962), 188-191.

According to Bell, the unforgivable sin is not — as Shannon suggests — that Catherine marries Edgar Linton. Instead, the theme

114

of the novel is the absence of forgiveness, as demonstrated in Lockwood's first dream.

B79   Bell, Vereen M. *"Wuthering Heights* as *Epos." College English,* 25 (Dec. 1963), 199-208.

This article emphasizes the excellence of the double narrative. Bell suggests that Emily Brontë was influenced by the oral tradition which she had learned through the Celtic tales told by her father and Aunt Branwell. Emily Brontë uses Nelly for her point of view and to present an oral narrative to "give full expression to her limited creative gift."

B80   Benson, E. F. "The Brontës." *The Spectator,* 146 (Feb. 7, 1931), 178-179.

Benson points out that *Wuthering Heights* was misunderstood by readers and critics, especially by Charlotte Brontë.

B81   Bentley, Phyllis. "Introduction" in Emily Brontë. *Wuthering Heights.* London: A. Wingate, 1949.

This reliable Brontë authority suggests the psychological complexities of the novel.

B82   Beversluis, John. "Love and Self-Knowledge: A Study of *Wuthering Heights." English,* 24 (Autumn 1975), 77-82.

Catherine's declaration: "I am Heathcliff," expresses a romantic self-centering, idealized, but not possible to achieve within society. Catherine cannot cast off society while Heathcliff is outside of society.

B83   Black, Michael. *The Literature of Fidelity.* London: Chatto and Windus, 1975.

In a chapter, *"Wuthering Heights:* Romantic Self-commitment," the critic gives an analysis of the force behind the actions within the novel, relating it to the romantic genre of which it is a part.

B84   Blayac, A. on Emily Brontë's *Wuthering Heights* in *Cahiers d'Etudes et de Recherches Victoriennes et Édouardiennes,* No. 3. Montpellier, France: Université Paul Valéry, 1976.

B85   Bleikasten, André. "La Passion dans *Les Haut de Hurlevent.*" *Bulletin de la Faculté des Lettres de Strasbourg,* 36 çpre 1958, 357-364.

B86   Blondel, Jacques. *Emily Brontë: Wuthering Heights: the Main Episode.* Paris: Didier, 1951.

        This critical study is meant for student use with the text of *Wuthering Heights.* The introduction, notes, and exercises are in English.

B87   Blondel, Jacques. "Imagery in *Wuthering Heights.*" *Durham University Journal,* n.s. 37 (Dec. 1975), 1-7.

        Professor Blondel sees a "rapprochement between setting and character" and speaks of "elemental imagery" and the use of "the contraries of frost and fire, storm and sunshine, the wild and the tame, the rocks and the loose earth."

B88   Blondel, Jacques. "Nouveaux regards sur Emily Brontë et *Wuthering Heights.*" *Annales de la Faculté des Lettres et Sciences Humaines d'Aix,* 1961.

B89   Bloomfield, Paul. "To Breathe Lightning." *Time and Tide,* 29 (March 20, 1948), 304.

        This book review of *Wuthering Heights* sees the major tension in Heathcliff's "personal struggle against possession by self-will."

B90   Bluestone, George. *Novels into Film.* Baltimore: The Johns Hopkins Press, 1957.

        This book attempts in part that difficult task of explaining what happened to *Wuthering Heights* when it was transposed from print to film.

B91   Booth, Wayne C. *The Rhetoric of Fiction.* Chicago: University of Chicago Press, 1961.

Booth refers briefly to Emily Brontë as an author who concealed her "commentary by dramatizing it as scenery" in "the natural setting."

B92   Bosco, Ronald. "Heathcliff: Societal Victim or Demon." *Gypsy Scholar*, 2 (Fall 1974), 21-39.

Answering Van Ghent's essay (B326), which suggests that Heathcliff is a combination of classical daemon and evil demon, Bosco proposes another definition: that Heathcliff is, in fact, a societal victim. "Although Heathcliff is shaped initially by the oppression, hunger, dirt, and agony of the city, it is the experience of hate and servitude that he is forced to endure at the hands of Hindley and the others at the Heights that shaped his ultimate course." He adds, "Revenge is Heathcliff's dominant motive for action," but it is his "excessive energy" in carrying out this revenge that makes him appear as "the daemon-demon figure."

B93   Bowlin, Karla J. "The Brother and Sister Theme in Post-Romantic Fiction." Unpublished doctoral dissertation. Auburn University, 1973. *DAI*, 34:1232.

The purpose of this study is "to show that sorrow for the loss of childhood and the subsequent loss of brother or sister emerged as a theme in fiction after the Romantic Movement." Among the novels the author discusses are Emily Brontë's *Wuthering Heights,* George Eliot's *Mill on the Floss,* William Faulkner's *The Sound and the Fury.*

B94   Bradner, Leicester. "The Growth of *Wuthering Heights.*" *PMLA,* 48 (1933), 129-146.

This article shows the relation of Emily Brontë's earlier poetry to the vision of *Wuthering Heights.* One of the best and most comprehensive studies, it covers the suggestion made by earlier critics that the poems in their development reflect the development of *Wuthering Heights.* He also sees the influence of Hoffmann's *Das Majorat* and the Irish tale "The Bridegroom of Barma."

B95   Brick, Allan R. "Lewes's Review of *Wuthering Heights.*" *Nineteenth Century Fiction,* 14 (1960), 355-359.

117

Here is a serious analysis of the early criticism by Lewes which praised many elements in *Wuthering Heights.* Lewes gave "the strange novel, which revolted so many, its due regard."

B96   Brick, Allan R. *"Wuthering Heights*: Narrators, Audience, and Message." *College English,* 21 (Nov. 1959), 80-86.

This approach reveals some of the complexity of the frame-story structure. Brick feels that the narrative form interferes with "essential message." He looks on Lockwood as "personified audience."

B97   Brown, E. K. *Rhythm in the Novel.* Toronto: University of Toronto Press, 1950.

Tribute is paid to Emily Brontë by Brown when he admits that ". . . every time *Wuthering Heights* is reread it releases a little more of its mysterious meaning."

B98   Buchen, Irving H. "Metaphysical and Social Evolution in *Wuthering Heights." Victorian Newsletter,* 31 (Spring 1967), 15-20.

The critic senses the gap between the poetry and fiction of *Wuthering Heights,* seeing both metaphysics and sociology. Emily Brontë integrates these with two love stories.

B99   Buckler, William E. "Chapter VII of *Wuthering Heights*: A Key to Interpretation." *Nineteenth Century Fiction,* 7 (1952), 51-55.

Here it is proposed that the theme is set in Chapter VII when Catherine returns from Thrushcross Grange. Heathcliff's isolation becomes complete, Catherine sets her course, and Nelly is established as the trustworthy narrator.

B100   Buckley, Vincent. "Passion and Control in *Wuthering Heights." Southern Review: An Australian Journal of Literary Studies,* 1 (1964), 5-23.

The critic first studies the prose of *Wuthering Heights* where controlled effects are said to result from "commonsense realism." Then he discusses the nature of the relationship between Catherine and Heathcliff, one which he sees as both sexual and spiritual.

B101   Burkhart, R. E. "The Structure of *Wuthering Heights*," *PMLA* 87 (Jan. 1972), 104-105.

   Burkhart objects to Van Ghent's division of *Wuthering Heights* into two parts, the Catherine-Heathcliff relationship and the "small romances" of Cathy-Linton and Cathy-Hareton. He says that the Catherine-Edgar pairing balances the structure with two pairings in each generation. See also Sonstroem, *PMLA*, 87 (March 1972), 314, who points out other pairings. (See also B326.)

B102   Burns, Wayne. "In Death They Were Not Divided: The Moral Magnificence of Unmoral Passion in *Wuthering Heights*" in *Metapsychological Literary Criticism – Theory and Practice: Essays in Honor of Leonard Folk Manheim.* Ed. M. Goldstein. Hartford, Connecticut: University of Hartford, 1973.

   According to this essay, *Wuthering Heights* expresses what Mark Schorer said no novel can possess: "the moral magnificence of unmoral passion." Whatever Catherine and Heathcliff do, "their love is of such an immaculate nature" that it can only be realized through death.

A103   Burns, Wayne. "On *Wuthering Heights*." *Recovering Literature,* 1 (1972), 5-25.

   This is not a novel about the love of men and women, but about Catherine's immaculate love for Heathcliff. Catherine wants both Heathcliff and Edgar and will not choose between them. But such a love "cannot be achieved by these people at this time." Readers find a rapport with this knowledge because we too "hate our bodies and cherish our souls."

B104   Butterfield, Mary A. *Pondon Hall.* Stanbury, West Yorkshire: Roderick and Brend Taylor, 1976.

   This book describing the locale of the Brontë novels discusses the lives and writings of the Brontës, particularly the possibility that Pondon Hall becomes Wuthering Heights.

B105   Caine, Jeffrey. *Heathcliff.* New York: Knopf, 1977.

   In a fictional off-shoot of *Wuthering Heights,* the author tries to imagine where Heathcliff went on the hegira and what adventures befell him.   119

B106   Carrère, Felix. *"Les Hauts de Hurlevent* d'Emily Brontë, histoire
        d'amour.'' *Annales de la Faculté des Lettres d'Aix,* 32 (1958),
        75-89.

B107   Carson, Joan. "Visionary Experience in *Wuthering Heights.*" *The
        Psychoanalytic Review,* 62 (1975), 131-151.

        "The novel's obscurities and its emotional resonance have
        suggested to me that the reading of this work in the light of some
        of the concepts of Jungian psychology might serve to clarify its
        apparent anomalies" in the belief that "anything that sheds light on
        a literary text is properly part of the act of criticism." This Jungian
        critic studies the novel on three levels: (1) the surface reading, (2)
        a psychological reading (seeing Catherine and Heathcliff regressing
        into childhood), and (3) as an archetypal experience of the night
        sea journey.

B108   Champion, Larry S. "Heathcliff: A Study in Authorial Technique."
        Ball State University Forum, 9 (1968), 19-25.

        The critic sees the author's need to create a world in which
        "Heathcliff's actions can be not merely tolerated but literally
        condoned." To do this, she must first depict Heathcliff "in a world
        in which Christianity is both hypocritical and inept." She then
        concentrates on Heathcliff's struggle for survival, allowing him to
        emerge "as a mortal, fallible man, twisted and tortured by the evil
        which pervades his environment."

B109   Clay, Charles Travis. "Notes on the Chronology of *Wuthering
        Heights.*" *BST,* 12 (1952), 100-105.

        Here is a fully-documented analysis of the chronology in
        Wuthering Heights, with a genealogical table of the Earnshaws and
        the Lintons. Clay's chronology differs slightly from Sanger's. (B290.)

B110   Collard, Millicent. *Wuthering Heights – The Revelation: A Psychical
        Study of Emily Brontë.* London: Regency Press, 1960.

        The revelation is that *Wuthering Heights* is symbolic on all levels;
        the incidents reflect those in the Bible and the characters are in fact
        members of the Brontë family.

B111   Collins, Clifford. "Theme and Conventions in *Wuthering Heights*." *The Critic*, 1 (Autumn 1947), 43-50.

Catherine and Heathcliff are seen as representing life force, ideal in nature. The critic compares *Wuthering Heights* to the works of D. H. Lawrence. The novel is not melodrama "because of its controlled moral intention."

B112   Cooper, Dorothy J. "A French Thesis on Emily Brontë." *BST*, 12 (1954), 268-272.

A review of Jacques Blondel's "Emily Brontë" dissertation at the Sorbonne in 1954. See Blondel, *Emily Brontë: experience spirituelle et création poetic*, Paris, 1955 (B352).

B113   Copley, J. "The Portrayal of Dialect in *Wuthering Heights* and *Shirley*." *Transactions of the Yorkshire Dialect Society*, 14 (1976), 7-16.

A further examination of local dialect used in the novels and an evaluation of the authors' skill in presenting valid dialect.   Vol. also listed as A199.

B114   Corr, Patricia. *Emily Brontë: Wuthering Heights*. Harrap's Study Guide series. London: Gill and Macmillan, 1972.

Material for the student first approaching the novel.

B115   Cott, Jeremy. "Structures of Sound: The Last Sentence of *Wuthering Heights*." *Texas Studies in Literature and Language*, 6 (Summer 1964), 280-289.

This excellent linguistic analysis of the single sentence begins with structural grammar and concludes by relating language to poetic sensibility.

B116   Cowhig, Ruth M. "*Wuthering Heights* — An Amoral Book?" *Use of English*, 17 (Winter 1965), 123-126.

In answering this question, Professor Cowhig reminds us that Emily Brontë, according to Charlotte, combined "deep compassion

121

with stern severity." Her characters reflect this attitude. Although *Wuthering Heights* seems "closely related to the world of Greek tragedy . . . this novel does not end in tragedy" but in "reconciliation and forgiveness, essentially within the Christian tradition." In fact "the scenes of violence, injustice, oppression and hatred are always seen against an implied background of humane standards." Professor Cowhig points out that "Emily Brontë does not judge her characters . . . she does not need to. They are inexorably and relentlessly judged by life itself."

B117   Crehan, T., ed. *Wuthering Heights: With a Critical Commentary.* London: University of London Press, 1962.

Emily Brontë succeeds in establishing both the misanthropy of Heathcliff and the strange love of Catherine and Heathcliff. She also handles excellently the factual elements of the law and time relationships. Much of what is found in *Wuthering Heights* is anticipated in her poetry.

B118   Crothers, George Dunlap, ed. *Invitation to Learning: English and American Novels.* New York and London: Basic Books, 1966.

One of two roundtable discussions of the Brontë novels: originally presented on CBS. *Wuthering Heights* is the subject discussed by Harriet van Horn, Walter Allen, and George D. Crothers. Vol. also listed as A106.

B119   Dahm, Hildegard. "Die Technik der Charakterdarstellung und das Künstlerische Gesamtbild der Charaktere im Roman *Wuthering Heights* von Emily Brontë." Unpublished doctoral dissertation, University of Innsbruck, 1955.

A120   Daiches, David. "Introduction" in Emily Brontë. *Wuthering Heights.* Harmondsworth, Middlesex: Penguin, 1965.

This respected critic brings the new reader of *Wuthering Heights* an awareness of the modern approaches to the novel.

B121   Daley, A. Stuart. "The Date of Heathcliff's Death: April, 1802." *BST,* 17 (1976), 15-19.

Daley suggests the importance of knowing the date to gain a proper feeling toward the final scenes – was the dying long or short? C. P. Sanger and S. A. Powers say May 1802, based on Nelly's report on Sept. 16, 1802, that it was "three months since."

B122   Daley, A. Stuart. "The Moons and Almanacs of *Wuthering Heights.*" *Huntington Library Quarterly*, 37 (1974), 337-353.

Emily Brontë based a fictive 1802 on the actual 1837 according to Daley's study. Throughout the novel the chronology is carefully controlled, relying on three harvest moons. The action fits the almanacs of 1836-1837, thus relating *Wuthering Heights* to the earlier Gondal writings.

B123   Davenport, Basil. "Emily Brontë" in Emily Brontë. *Wuthering Heights.* New York: Dodd, Mead, 1942.

This biographical approach raises the question: is Heathcliff based on M. Heger? As Emily Brontë nursed Charlotte when they returned from Brussels, the critic proposes a biographical source for the narrating nurse.

B124   Davies, Cecil W. "A Reading of *Wuthering Heights.*" *Essays in Criticism*, 19 (July 1969), 254-272.

Catherine and Heathcliff's relationship is at the heart of the novel's construction; it does not have a dualistic construction (see Cecil, C58). Through identification with each other, Catherine and Heathcliff demonstrate the force of love.

B125   Davies, Cecil. "Art within a Tradition: *Wuthering Heights* and the German 'Novelle.'" *BST*, 17 (1978), 197-204.

Here *Wuthering Heights* is presented as being "within a firm literary tradition," a tale in the manner of the German *Novelle*: with a limitation of material, a relationship with reality, a careful construction, a basis in an "extraordinary event," and a steady "climactic build." By analyzing character, setting, symbolism, and form, Davies concludes that *Wuthering Heights* is indeed a part of a great tradition.

B126   Davis, R. G. "The Sense of the Real in English Fiction." *Comparative Literature,* 3 (1951), 200-217.

B127   Dean, Christopher. "Joseph's Speech in *Wuthering Heights.*" *Notes and Queries,* 7 (Feb. 1960), 73-76.

This discussion stresses the accuracy and consistency of West Riding dialect in Joseph's speech. Although the dialect is not pure, it gives a valid atmosphere to the novel.

B128   De Villiers, J. *"Wuthering Heights."* Standpunte, 11 (1956-1957), 15-25.

In response to Stanford's "uncritically conventional" judgments, de Villiers offers what were, at the date of publication, new interpretations of the characters of *Wuthering Heights.* He sees Lockwood as "the perpetual bachelor, the perennial adolescent," a "very limited human being." Joseph is "obsessed with sin," the "complete immoral egocentric," while Nelly is recognized as one who is "re-interpreting the past in the light of the present."

B129   Devlin, James E. "*Wuthering Heights*: The Dominant Image." *Discourse: A Review of the Liberal Arts,* 5 (Summer 1962), 337-346.

There is a "thick web of imagery of restraint" in *Wuthering Heights.* The novel concerns the frustration of psychic forces which are revealed through complex and skillful imagery.

B130   Dingle, Herbert. "The Origin of Heathcliff." *BST,* 16 (1972), 131-138.

Dingle favors the interpretation that Heathcliff is Mr. Earnshaw's illegitimate son. He bases his assumption on the lack of sexual desire in the relationship of Catherine and Heathcliff. In discussing the improbability of Emily Brontë's story, Dingle suggests that details are supplied to warn us of the improbability of the tale.

B131   Diskin, Patrick. "Some Sources of *Wuthering Heights.*" *Notes and Queries,* July-Aug. 1977, pp. 354-361.

Here Diskin suggests that Emily Brontë may have been influenced by stories she read in the *Dublin University Magazine* between 1835 and 1840.

B132   Dobrée, Bonamy. "Introduction" in Emily Brontë. *Wuthering Heights.* London: Collins, 1952.

Among other aspects of the novel, Dobrée discusses the role of the narrator. He finds that Nelly Dean contributes emotionally within the plot as well as being a literary device. He points out the "metaphysical" considerations along with the modern symbolism.

B133   Dobrée, Valentine. "Introduction" in Emily Brontë. *Wuthering Heights.* New York and London: Knopf, 1927.

Wuthering Heights is related to poetry because of its "preoccupation with metaphysical problems."

B134   Dodds, Madeleine Hope. "Heathcliff's Country." *Modern Language Review,* 39 (April 1944), 116-129.

Heathcliff's mysterious home (which he came from and returned to during his absence) is derived from Gondal. The critic disagrees with Ratchford about Gondal, finding no dominating single character in the poems.

B135   Drew, Arnold P. "Emily Brontë and *Hamlet.*" *Notes and Queries,* 1 (1954), 81-82.

In Catherine's mad scene, the speech she makes while pulling feathers from the pillow is modeled on Ophelia's flower speech.

B136   Drew, Elizabeth. "Emily Brontë: *Wuthering Heights*" in *The Novel: A Modern Guide to Fifteen English Masterpieces.* New York: Norton, 1964.

Here is a brief review of modern criticism which concludes that Emily Brontë is appreciated more than Charlotte Brontë. *Wuthering Heights* is still mysterious today, though Heathcliff loses sympathy through his cruelty. The critic defends Charlotte Brontë's editing of the novel.

B137   Drew, Philip. "Charlotte Brontë as a Critic of *Wuthering Heights.*"
        Nineteenth Century Fiction, 18:4 (March 1964), 365-381.

        The critic finds that Charlotte Brontë's remarks were valid and
        perceptive. "She identifies the novel's main source of evil energy and
        its central metaphor." (See also B49.)

B138   Dry, Florence Swinton. *The Sources of Wuthering Heights.*
        Cambridge, England: W. Heffer and Sons, 1937.

        In an attempt to identify the literary sources, the critic discusses
        Scott's *Black Dwarf,* the names of the characters and the revenge
        plot and theme. She also suggests Tennyson's "Locksley Hall."

B139   du Maurier, Daphne. "Introduction" in Emily Brontë. *Wuthering
        Heights.* London: Macdonald, 1955.

        While making some sage statements about the novel, du Maurier
        primarily discusses the date of composition of the novel, proposing
        1841.

B140   Dunn, Richard J. "The Feeling of *Wuthering Heights.*" *Research
        Studies,* 45 (1977), 160-167.

        A discussion of the emotional content of the novel.

B141   Edgar, Pelham. "Judgments on Appeal: II. The Brontës." *Queen's
        Quarterly,* 39 (Aug. 1932), 414-422. Reprinted in *The Art of
        the Novel,* New York: Macmillan, 1933.

        Edgar sees a need for detachment between the work and Emily
        Brontë's biography. He feels that in *Wuthering Heights* Nelly Dean's
        narrative is a formal flaw, but the book survives anyway. Nelly's role
        is unbelievable. The reader loses interest in the story when Catherine
        dies.

B142   Edgerley, C. Mabel. "Ponden Hall and the Heatons." *BST,* 10 (1945),
        265-268.

        Here a local home is identified as Wuthering Heights from a
        description of its exterior. The writer gives a history of the estate.

B143 Efron, Arthur. "'Paunch,' *Wuthering Heights* and the Body." *Paunch,* 40-41 (1975), 166-171.

Part of an unresolved debate on *Wuthering Heights* going on in this journal since 1964. The contention is about "the necessary but hidden critical assumption . . . that characters in fiction must be understood as having human bodies."

B144 Empson, William. *Some Versions of Pastoral.* London: Chatto and Windus, 1950 (second edition).

Empson points out that "*Wuthering Heights* is a good case of double plot in the novel . . . telling the same story twice with the two possible endings."

B145 Everitt, Alistair G. "Preface" to *Wuthering Heights: An Anthology of Criticism.* New York: Barnes and Noble, 1967.

Everitt suggests that the criticism of *Wuthering Heights* is marked by dissent over the meaning of the novel. He suggests that an overview of the critical essays will reflect the complexity.

B146 Fadiman, Clifton. "Afterword" in Emily Brontë. *Wuthering Heights.* New York: Macmillan, 1963.

This brief essay in a popular style calls *Wuthering Heights* "a nightmare that makes perfect sense."

B147 Fenton, Edith Maud. "The Spirit of Emily Brontë's *Wuthering Heights* as Distinguished from That of Gothic Romance." *Washington University Studies*, Humanities Series, 8 (1920), 103-122.

This forward-looking study gives a Freudian interpretation of the dreams in *Wuthering Heights.* Fenton points out the similarities between this novel and the Gothic Romance.

B148 Fenton, Edith Maud. "The Tempestuous Novel." Unpublished Master's thesis, University of California, 1919.

What must have been preparatory work for B147.

B149   Fike, F. "Bitter Herbs and Wholesome Medicines: Love as Theological Affirmation in *Wuthering Heights.*" *Nineteenth Century Fiction,* 23 (Sept. 1968), 127-149.

"Theological affirmation" in love is portrayed in *Wuthering Heights.* The writer sees "Christian reality" in Catherine and Heathcliff, and in Cathy and Hareton.

B150   Fine, R. E. "Lockwood's Dreams and the Key to *Wuthering Heights.*" *Nineteenth Century Fiction,* 24 (June 1969), 16-30.

A Freudian analysis of the dreams presents the theme of two lovers in an endless search for one another.

B151   Flahiff, F. R., ed. "Introduction" in Emily Brontë. *Wuthering Heights.* Toronto: Macmillan, 1968.

Flahiff discusses Heathcliff's actions as they relate to the themes of the novel. He suggests that although Catherine has been aware of the "substantial identification" between herself and Heathcliff since their childhood, Heathcliff only becomes aware of this unity at the end of the novel.

B152   Ford, Boris. "An Analysis of *Wuthering Heights.*" *Scrutiny,* 7 (March 1939), 375-389.

This respected scholar sees the novel as based on a relationship between Catherine and Heathcliff which is sexless and rather inhuman. In attempting to find the "something wrong" with *Wuthering Heights,* Ford acknowledges the "rigid control" and the "clarity of execution" that are "truly remarkable." He compares the Catherine-Heathcliff relationship with that of Cathy-Hareton.

B153   Fotheringham, James. "The Work of Emily Brontë and the Brontë Problem." *BST,* 2 (1901), 116.

The "problem" is finding the source of *Wuthering Heights*: this article proposes (1) the Yorkshire ambiance, (2) Emily Brontë's imagination, and (3) the deterioration of Branwell. Emily Brontë's character is seen as being bound in with the novel. But Fotheringham finds the theme harsh along with "faults of style and defects of construction."

B154   Franke, Wolfgang. "'Halbert and Hob': Browning at *Wuthering Heights.*" *Browning Society Notes* (London), 5:3 (Dec. 1975), 3-8.

The Browning dramatic idyl about evolution is set in the north of England, which causes the critic to comment on "the extraordinary doings at Wuthering Heights." He suggests that "the Victorian imagination contrived to transform even the industrial north into a kind of residual saga-world of heathen amorality."

B155   Fraser, J. "The Name of Action: Nelly Dean and *Wuthering Heights.*" *Nineteenth Century Fiction,* 20 (Dec. 1965), 223-226.

Here is praise in defense of Nelly Dean's conduct. Fraser finds the critical attacks on this character symptomatic of the "too-common sentimentality about wickedness."

B156   Froese, Fritz. "Untersuchungen zu Emily Brontës Roman *Wuthering Heights.*" Unpublished doctoral dissertation, University of Königsberg, 1920.

B157   Fulcher, Paul M. "Introduction" in Emily Brontë. *Wuthering Heights.* Modern Readers' Series. New York: Macmillan, 1929.

The edition finds the "faults of craftsmanship" as obvious as the "merits" of the novel: Nelly is too literary, the narrative method too complex. However, among the merits he admires the way the characters are mirrored in one another. On second reading he finds *Wuthering Heights'* "full power."

B158   Garrett, P. K. "Double Plots and Dialogical Form in Victorian Fiction." *Nineteenth Century Fiction,* 32 (June 1977), 1-17.

The form of a novel is "shaped by the tensions between structural principles," and *Wuthering Heights* plays "double- against single-focus narrative." The disruption of the Healthcliff story forms a non-chronological narrative, allowing two plots to unfold concurrently in "dramatic confrontations."

B159   Garrod, H. W. "Editor's Introduction" in Emily Brontë. *Wuthering Heights.* London: Humphrey Milford, 1930.

This is a "novel of edification" for Lockwood, who serves as an instrument for the moral of its story. Through him Emily Brontë is able to teach the reader what love is. However, the editor advises that the novel is "ill-constructed, and in its detail often complicated and obscure."

B160   Gates, Barbara. "Suicide and *Wuthering Heights.*" *Victorian Newsletter,* 50 (Fall 1976), 15-19.

Ms. Gates discusses the two possible suicides in *Wuthering Heights* — the death of Hindley and that of Catherine — to show the relationship of the act to the plot. For reasons of inheritance Hindley's death must be established as natural. Catherine's concern just before her death is that, having taken her own life, she will be forced to return as a ghost.

B161   Gettmann, Royal A. "Introduction" in Emily Brontë. *Wuthering Heights.* New York: Modern Library, 1950.

In discussing the position of *Wuthering Heights* as a Victorian novel, the editor mentions that nature is not described but "felt on every page." He notes minor errors but says the theme is in Heathcliff; Nelly functions to "control passions, bring out their meanings, and make them beautiful" and Hareton is there "to effect harmony."

B162   Gilbert, B. and P. C. Cross. "Farewell to Hoffmann." *BST*, 15 (1970), 412-416.

In examining the suggestions which have been made over the years as to what works influenced Emily Brontë in the composition of *Wuthering Heights,* the authors list: (1) May Sinclair: the Gondal poems, (2) William Wright: the Irish background, (3) Charles Simpson: a story heard at Law Hill, (4) Mrs. Ward and Romer Wilson: the German romanticism of Hoffmann, (5) Leicester Bradner: a story in *Blackwood's,* and (6) John Hewish: Hoffmann's "The Devil's Elixir." Their conclusion is that Hoffmann may have influenced Emily Brontë, but there is no evidence that she read him.

B163   Gillie, Christopher. "The Heroine Victim." *Character in English Literature.* London: Chatto and Windus; New York: Barnes and Noble, 1965.

Catherine Earnshaw is compared with Emma Woodhouse as a central character.

B164   Gillie, Christopher. "Satan Against Society." *Character in English Literature*. London: Chatto and Windus; New York: Barnes and Noble, 1965.

The critic estimates Heathcliff's credibility and discusses the five styles of "sexual emotion" in *Wuthering Heights*.

B165   Girdler, Lew. "*Wuthering Heights* and Shakespeare." *Huntington Library Quarterly*, 19 (Aug. 1956), 385-392.

This critic suggests that the plays of Shakespeare naturally sprang to Emily Brontë's mind and colored her writing. He notes the allusions, verbal echoes, and "general resemblance in characters, plot, structure, and theme." He finds allusions to *Twelfth Night, King Lear, The Taming of the Shrew,* and *Hamlet*. Charlotte Brontë too, in a letter to Ellen Nussey, compared *Wuthering Heights* to a Shakespearean work.

B166   Gleckner, Robert F. "Time in *Wuthering Heights.*" *Criticism*, 1 (Fall 1959), 328-338.

This Blake scholar analyzes the novel, suggesting that the time theme accounts for the character of Heathcliff, as the past presses on present both in the narrative and in Heathcliff's mind. Gleckner says that the window and the mirror are the key temporal images.

B167   Goldstone, Herbert. "*Wuthering Heights* Revisited." *English Journal*, 48 (April 1959), 175-185.

This practical approach urges high school teachers to avoid complex interpretations (such as those of Cecil and Van Ghent) and teach the book simply, as "the view of life in the book is direct, simple, very comprehensive, and clearly presented."

B168   Goodridge, Jonathan Francis. *Emily Brontë: Wuthering Heights.* London: Edward Arnold, 1964.

Here is a chapter-by-chapter analysis of *Wuthering Heights* as fiction, showing that Nelly "brings us very close to the action and is, in one way, deeply engaged in it." Her air of "righteous superiority towards Catherine and Heathcliff" is supported by her "commonsense point of view." The critic feels that Emily Brontë controls her readers' response by making us feel "more perceptive and imaginative than her narrators."

B169   Goodridge, Jonathan Francis. "A New Heaven and a New Earth." *The Art of Emily Brontë*. Ed. Anne Smith. London: Vision Press, 1976.

Here Goodridge defines the subject matter of romantic novels and concludes that *Wuthering Heights* is not a romantic novel.

B170   Gose, Elliott B., Jr. *Imagination Indulged: The Irrational in the Nineteenth-Century Novel*. Montreal: McGill-Queen's University Press, 1972.

In discussing this theme in literature, the critic includes a study of irrationality in *Wuthering Heights*.

B171   Gose, Elliott B., Jr. "*Wuthering Heights*: The Heath and the Hearth." *Nineteenth Century Fiction*, 21 (June 1966), 1-19.

This is a discussion of *Wuthering Heights* on four levels: (1) as a fairy tale, (2) in relation to religion and the Bible, (3) concerning the traditional elements of nature, and (4) as an example of the process of initiation. He sees the hearth related to the weak characters like the Lintons and the heath as "strong" like Heathcliff. He compares the patterning of the Catherine-Heathcliff story with that of Cathy-Hareton. He finds the climax of this tension in the scene in which Cathy uproots Joseph's mulberry bushes: " . . . someone has finally resisted tyranny, and Heathcliff, seeing the pattern of his youth repeated, gives up."

B172   Gould, Gerald Lynn. "Emily Brontë's Relation to Gondal as Subject of *Wuthering Heights*." Unpublished doctoral dissertation, City University of New York, 1974. *DAI*, 35:1655.

Gould discusses *Wuthering Heights* as "an attempt to resolve the conflict between the death-and-child-oriented, solipsistic religion of Gondal and the world of ordinary consciousness and adulthood."

B173   Grabo, Carl H. "Technical Characteristics of *Wuthering Heights.*" *The Technique of the Novel.* New York: Gordian Press, 1928.

Worst among technical devices are the narrators: Nelly is not very effective, while Lockwood gets in the way and "is of no value whatsoever." However, the critic concludes that "the structural inadequacies" of the novel are "insignificant when weighed with its great merits."

B174   Grazhdanskaya, S. "Emily Brontë and her Novel *Wuthering Heights.*" Translated from the Russian by Ethel Bronstein. *BST*, 17 (1976), 21-29.

The theme of the novel is the moral downfall of man. Heathcliff is seen as the avenger who would destroy those who destroyed him. The critic comments on the "workers and peasants" in this novel of social consciousness. He finds, though, that Emily Brontë's faith in mankind is revealed as the errors of Catherine are redeemed by her daughter.

B175   Gregor, Ian. "Introduction" in *The Brontës: A Collection of Critical Essays.* Englewood Cliffs, New Jersey: Prentice-Hall, 1970.

The editor's primary interest is in the various interpretations of *Wuthering Heights,* in the "extreme diversity of view."

B176   Grove, Robin. "*Wuthering Heights.*" *Critical Review,* 8 (1965), 71-87.

This article investigates the bond and relationship between Catherine and Heathcliff, which is the "great fact and focus" of *Wuthering Heights.* Emily Brontë is concerned with the unnaturalness of their love. The Cathy-Hareton love becomes an anti-masque or counterfeit of the central relationship of Catherine and Heathcliff.

B177   Grudin, Peter D. "*Wuthering Heights*: The Question of Unquiet Slumbers." *Studies in the Novel,* 6 (Winter 1974), 389-407.

Is this novel pagan or Christian? The critic points out the folkloric basis of the after-death walks of the lovers on the moor. Lockwood, in contrast, notes that they are sleeping quietly in their graves. But he is wrong to assume that there is no ghostly afterlife in the novel. Emily Brontë has given us cause and effect, prophecy and fulfillment. It is Heathcliff's final experience which gives the novel integrity.

B178   Guérard, Albert J. "Preface" in Emily Brontë. *Wuthering Heights.* New York: Washington Square Press, 1960.

Perhaps the insufficiencies in Emily Brontë's life are compensated for in *Wuthering Heights,* that "dark, splendid, imperfect novel." Its imperfection is shown in the creation of Heathcliff whose delineation is "erratic and uncertain."

B179   Hafley, James. "The Villain in *Wuthering Heights.*" *Nineteenth Century Fiction,* 13 (Dec. 1958), 199-215.

In this article which has caused controversy over the years, Hafley suggests that Nelly Dean is the true villain. He argues that she is in a position to interfere with the actions of the characters. She shows herself to be resentful and ambitious because of her position in the family. She manipulates people so that finally, after Catherine's death, she becomes mistress of the Grange.

B180   Hagan, John. "Control of Sympathy in *Wuthering Heights.*" *Nineteenth Century Fiction,* 21 (March 1967), 305-323.

Hagan shows how Emily Brontë controls the readers' double vision as they disapprove of Catherine and Heathcliff's actions but never lose sympathy for the characters. There is a "blend of moral disapproval and compassion" as the readers see that the cruelty is the consequence of extreme suffering.

B181   Hanson, T. W. "The Local Colour of *Wuthering Heights.*" *BST,* 6 (1924), 201-219.

Hanson relates *Wuthering Heights* and some of Emily Brontë's poetry to the landscape and climate of Yorkshire.

B182   Hardy, Barbara. *Wuthering Heights.* Notes on English Literature series. London: Blackwell, 1963.

Designed to be used as a teaching aid, this book points out the importance of Chapter XVIII as a transitional chapter in the structure of the novel. Professor Hardy believes that *Wuthering Heights* gives the reader an "inner adventure" as he sifts the evidence and makes judgments.

B183   Harvey, W. J. *Character and the Novel.* Ithaca, New York: Cornell University Press, 1965.

Wuthering Heights is used as an illustration of the important issues which are to be faced in considering the novel in terms of characters, reality, time, identity, freedom, essence, and existence.

B184   Hatch, Ronald B. "Heathcliff's 'Queer End' and Schopenhauer's Denial of the Will." *Canadian Review of Comparative Literature,* 1 (1974), 49-64.

A close reading of Heathcliff's actions, especially those near the end of the novel, suggests that Emily Brontë "deliberately eschews all overt explanation of Heathcliff's behavior, leaving it open to the reader's interpretation." Hatch's explanation is that Heathcliff changes as he begins "to perceive that *all* individuals are mere objectifications of the single world force." Heathcliff's "new knowledge of the nature of the world" quiets his "will," in a manner explained by Schopenhauer in his major work *Die Welt als Wille und Vorstellung (The World as Will and Idea).*

B185   Hoffmann, L. N. "A Delicate Balance: The Resolutions to Conflict of Women in the Fiction of Four Women Writers of the Victorian Period." Unpublished doctoral dissertation, University of Indiana, 1975. *DAI,* 35:4432.

Emily Brontë's work is considered along with that of George Egerton (Mary Dunne Bright), George Eliot, and Olive Schreiner.

B186   Holderness, Graham. *A Study Guide to Wuthering Heights.* Bletchley: Open University Press, 1973.

A helpful approach to *Wuthering Heights* is presented for the student first studying the novel.

135

B187   Holloway, Owen E. "*Wuthering Heights*: A Matter of Method."
        Northern Miscellany of Literary Criticism, 1 (Autumn 1953),
        65-74.

        The critic discusses the position of *Wuthering Heights* in literary
        history. He indicates some of the strengths in the method of
        narration: (1) the protagonist is hardly present at all, and (2) the
        order is not chronological: it needs reader participation. The present
        represents "appearance," a narrated past is "reality," and then Emily
        Brontë shifts to the reality of the future.

B188   Homans, Margaret. "Repression and Sublimation of Nature in
        Wuthering Heights." *PMLA*, 93 (Jan. 1978), 9-19.

        In what has been called "an audacious and marvelously
        interesting essay" – a Freudian and structuralistic approach to the
        novel – Homans points out the "avoidance of direct presentation"
        of nature. Emily Brontë "does not consider language to be adequate
        to the task of representing nature," but uses instead "constructive
        figurative language," in what Freud would consider "successful
        repression."

B189   Howells, William Dean. "Heroines of Nineteenth Century Fiction.
        XIX: The Two Catherines of Emily Brontë." *Harper's Bazaar*,
        33 (Dec. 29, 1900), 2224-2230.

        Wuthering Heights is here compared with *Jane Eyre*. Howells
        condemns the double narrative: "Seldom has a great romance been
        worse contrived." His praise of Emily Brontë comments favorably
        on the non-intrusive authorship and the "unfaltering truth of her
        scenes." Reprinted in *Heroines of Fiction.* New York and London:
        Harper and Brothers, 1901.

B190   Insh, G. P. "Haworth Pilgrimage." *BST*, 10 (1944), 209-213.

        Insh identifies borrowings from Shakespeare in Chapter II of
        Wuthering Heights on the theme of ingratitude: (1) when Lockwood
        is attacked by the dogs (from *Lear*), and (2) when he meets the
        cat "Grimalkin" (from *Macbeth*).

B191   Johnson, James William. "Nightmare and Reality in *Wuthering Heights*" in Emily Brontë. *Wuthering Heights.* Boston: Houghton Mifflin, 1965.

Emily Brontë uses irrational emotions which are shown through dreams and ghosts. While the characters form the central nucleus, continuity is established through weather, landscape, family lines, and reports of events.

B192   Jordan, J. E. "Ironic Vision of Emily Brontë." *Nineteenth Century Fiction,* 20 (June 1965), 1-18.

In contrast with Cecil's attitude, Jordan finds *Wuthering Heights* "a fabric of ironies" with "more than meets the eye." He sees Lockwood as a "city slicker in the haunted house," and credits Emily Brontë with irony in her delineation of Cathy, Nelly Dean, and Lockwood, as well as in their comments and narration.

B193   Junkin-Hill, M. "Myths and Fallacies in *Wuthering Heights.*" *Louisiana University Review,* 3 (1970), 46-55.

B194   Justus, James. "Beyond Gothicism: *Wuthering Heights* and an American Tradition." *Tennessee University Studies in Literature,* 5 (1960), 25-33.

There are elements in *Wuthering Heights* which "make it vital in man's experience," according to this author. He sees these same basic elements in the development of the American writing of Hawthorne, Melville, Dreiser, and Faulkner.

B195   Kavanagh, Colman. *The Symbolism of Wuthering Heights.* London: John Long, 1920.

Emily Brontë is referred to as a "Celtic genius" in this work of fifty-some years ago which offers a beginning for what has developed into a popular area of investigation. Earnshaw, the father of Heathcliff, is seen to leave a "legacy of woe." Hindley symbolizes the "sin of despair," Catherine the "sin of pride," while Edgar Linton is seen as a "good angel" for Catherine and Heathcliff.

B196   Keppler, Carl Francis. *The Literature of the Second Self.* Tucson: University of Arizona Press, 1972.

In this exploratory inquiry into the "second self" in literature, Keppler speaks of many forms of second self, among them the basic concept of the self divided in two, constantly seeking to be rejoined — "the search for the Beloved." Heathcliff serves to illustrate this concept, as one "who from the first breeds bad feeling in the house" is "the invader from the dark who has brought with him, for the people who have taken him in, the darkness of their doom."

B197   Kermode, Frank. "A Modern Way with the Classic." *New Literary History,* 5 (Spring 1974), 415-434.

In discussing *Wuthering Heights* as a "classic," the critic is particularly interested in Q. D. Leavis' "Fresh Approach to *Wuthering Heights*" (B215). The divergent interpretations by critics over the years form part of this presentation which was originally given as the last of the T. S. Eliot Memorial Lectures of 1973.

B198   Kettle, Arnold. "Emily Brontë: *Wuthering Heights* (1847)." *An Introduction to the English Novel.* Vol. I, Part III. London: Hutchinson House, 1951.

In his Marxist approach to the novel, Kettle comments on the "rebellion of the spirit" in it. He proposes that Emily Brontë works in symbols, not ideas. He sees a similarity to *Oliver Twist* in that "*Wuthering Heights* is about England in 1847." Catherine and Heathcliff are bound by a feeling of "an expression of the necessity of man . . . to revolt against all that would destroy his inmost needs and aspirations . . . to become . . . more fully human." Kettle feels that Heathcliff uses "against his enemies with complete ruthlessness their own weapons . . . of money and arranged marriages."

B199   Kiely, Robert. *The Romantic Novel in England.* Cambridge, Mass.: Harvard University Press, 1972.

In his last chapter the critic discusses *Wuthering Heights,* calling it "one of the few perfect novels in nineteenth-century English." He discusses memories, dreams, imagery and moral significance. He speaks clearly about the tone of the novel when he says that it is "filled with transformations, the fusion of opposites or the interchange of aspects, until there are fewer and fewer clear distinctions."

B200   Klingopulos, D. G. "*Wuthering Heights*: The Novel as Dramatic Poem, II." *Scrutiny*, 14 (Sept. 1947), 269-286.

Readers may dislike *Wuthering Heights* because it is not a moral tale and some passages are too "insistent and deliberate," according to this article, but that is the novel's poetic nature. Amid the tensions and conflicts many statements are like those made "in the finest English dramatic poetry." *Wuthering Heights* is similar to *Macbeth*, though less coherent. The end of the novel is ambiguous.

B201   Knight, Grant C. *Superlatives.* New York: Alfred A. Knopf, 1925.

A discussion of the language used in describing Heathcliff comes under the head of "The Most Terrible."

B202   Knoepflmacher, U. C. *Laughter and Despair: Readings in Ten Novels of the Victorian Era.* Berkeley, California: University of California Press, 1971.

This study of the extremes of emotion in the Victorian novel places *Wuthering Heights* as a "Tragicomic Romance." Comic aspects of the novel are used to disguise thinly the anarchy and decay which Emily Brontë is describing for her readers.

B203   Kolb, Edward. "An Exercise in Dialect Detection." *Transactions of the Yorkshire Dialect Society,* 11 (1955), 11-17.

Joseph's dialect is used as an example of the way dialect can reveal the geographical origin of a person.

B204   Krier, W. J. "A Pattern of Limitations: The Heroine's Novel of the Mind." Unpublished doctoral dissertation, Indiana University, 1973. *DAI,* 34:227.

B205   Krupat, Arnold. "The Strangeness of *Wuthering Heights.*" *Nineteenth Century Fiction,* 25 (Dec. 1970), 269-270.

Wuthering Heights is strange because it is "different from other books" and different from the reader's own life. The author is completely absent and the narrators, though different, share a "single bland speech." Tension is created through "the persistent split between the materials of the book and the style in which they are presented."

139

B206   Kuhlmann, Rudolf. *Der Natur-Paganismus in der Weltarshauung von Emily Brontë.* Bonn: Schloppe, 1926.

Emily Brontë's mysticism is shown to be derived from current German philosophy. This presentation is part of a movement to show that Emily Brontë sought a solution outside the Church of England.

B207   Lane, Margaret. "Emily Brontë in a Cold Climate." *BST,* 15 (1968), 187-200.

According to this authority on the Brontës, *Wuthering Heights* does not take place in a humanized natural world, but amidst nature alien to man. Discussing Gondal sources, characters, and setting, the critic also touches on such details as the books in *Wuthering Heights* and the number of deaths. She comments on its poetic prose and on the criticism the book has aroused.

B208   Lane, Margaret. "Introduction" in Emily Brontë. *Wuthering Heights and Selected Poems.* London: Dent, 1957.

Wuthering Heights is a "completely amoral book, quite free from justification or apology," which seems to account for its popularity today. Vol. also listed as B449.

B209   Langham, F. H. "Thoughts on *Wuthering Heights.*" *Essays in Criticism,* 15 (July 1965), 294-312.

Critics have underestimated the "significance of prose style and narrative method of *Wuthering Heights*" because of the pervasive presence of violence and cruelty. The novel arouses our sympathy for Heathcliff because of Hindley's earlier "brutality, tyranny, and murderous violence" which "far outdo anything" Heathcliff does. The critic concludes by admitting that Heathcliff reveals "an excess from which moral sympathy does turn away."

B210   Lavers, Norman. "The Action of *Wuthering Heights.*" *South Atlantic Quarterly,* 72 (Winter 1973), 43-52.

Heathcliff is shown to be the ruthless but constructive hero in the novel. All action relates to the single aim: "to restore to power the Earnshaw family." Each character does his part in the action, then dies. Heathcliff brings about the restoration of the Earnshaws and, therefore, is the true hero.

140

B211   Law, Alice. "Branwell Brontë's Novel." *The Bookman* (London), 68 (April 1925), 4-6.

A restatement of Alice Law's belief that Branwell wrote *Wuthering Heights*. (See also B212 and B213.)

B212   Law, Alice. *Emily Jane Brontë and the Authorship of Wuthering Heights*. Altham, Accrington: Old Parsonage Press, 1925.

According to this British pamphlet, the idea that Emily Brontë – isolated, undereducated, retiring – wrote *Wuthering Heights* "savours of nothing less than a miracle." The challenge to Emily Brontë's authorship is based on "a careful study of her character" from what must surely be considered scant evidence. The critic sees clearly that Branwell must be the author as it reflects "his own unhappy passion for another man's wife."

B213   Law, Alice. *Patrick Branwell Brontë*. London: A. M. Philpot, 1923. Reissued, New York: Richard West, 1974.

In discussing Branwell's life, the critic argues that he wrote *Wuthering Heights*: first on the evidence that Emily Brontë didn't, second on the evidence that Branwell Brontë did. General reaction to this presentation caused the critic to reinforce it with *Emily Jane Brontë and the Authorship of Wuthering Heights* in 1925 (B212). Vol. also listed as C214.

B214   Leavis, F. R. "The Brontës" in *The Great Tradition*. New York: G. W. Stewart, 1950.

A respected critic presents his evaluation of Emily Brontë, stating that "out of her a minor tradition comes." He coined the statement, so often quoted, that *Wuthering Heights* is "a kind of sport."

B215   Leavis, Q. D. "A Fresh Approach to *Wuthering Heights*" in F. R. and Q. D. Leavis. *Lectures in America*. London: Chatto and Windus, 1969.

New in many ways, this lecture emphasizes the "human centrality" of the novel and proposes among other things that in its original version it was intended to be the story of the position of Heathcliff in the home of his natural father, Mr. Earnshaw.

B216   Lecarme, N. "Le sacré et le profane dans *Wuthering Heights.*" *Etudes Brontëennes.* Eds. Jacques Blondel and Jean-Pierre Petit. Paris: Edition Ophrys, 1970.

B217   Lehman, B. H. "Of Material, Subject, and Form: *Wuthering Heights*" in *Image of the Work: Essays in Criticism.* Berkeley: University of California Press, 1955.

Here the critic attempts to see the work from the author's point of view, emphasizing the function of the narrators. The critic believes that *Wuthering Heights* is not Gothic as it is too universal. Its material is nature and life; its subject matter is that of life renewing itself; its form centers on Nelly Dean as character and as narrator. "Certain universal modes of being pervade" *Wuthering Heights*: the march of generations, the sequence of birth and death.

B218   Lemon, Charles. "Sickness and Health in *Wuthering Heights.*" *BST,* 14 (1963), 23-25.

The state of health of all in *Wuthering Heights* reflects Emily Brontë's familiarity with death through her experiences within the Brontë family.

B219   Lemon, Lee T. "The Hostile Universe: A Developing Pattern in Nineteenth-Century Fiction" in *The English Novel in the Nineteenth Century: Essays on the Literary Mediation of Human Values.* Ed. George V. Goodin. Urbana: University of Illinois Press, 1972.

The theme of hostility and man's reaction to it is discussed in relation to *Wuthering Heights* among other novels.

B220   L'Estrange, Anna (Rosemary Ellerbeck). *Return to Wuthering Heights.* New York: Pinnacle Books, 1977.

Popular fiction of our time explores the question: what happens after the last chapter of *Wuthering Heights*?

B221   Lettis, Richard and William E. Morris. "Introduction" to *A Wuthering Heights Handbook.* New York: Odyssey Press, 1961.

The introduction to the collection suggests that there are many possible approaches to *Wuthering Heights,* through the characters, action, point of view, style, symbolism, and imagery.

B222   Livermore, Ann Lapraik. "Byron and Emily Brontë." *Quarterly Review,* 300 (July 1962), 337-344.

Noting Byron's influence on Emily Brontë's poetry, the critic suggests that Byron also influenced *Wuthering Heights.* "It becomes possible to perceive that probably *Wuthering Heights* was planned as an intertwining of *The Dream* [Byron] with the facts as then known of Byron's ambiguous love for his half-sister, his marriage to Anne Isabella, and her flight from him."

B223   Loe, Thomas B. "The Gothic Strain in the Victorian Novel: Four Studies." Unpublished doctoral dissertation, University of Iowa, 1974. *DAI,* 35:2231-A.

"The first four chapters attempt to isolate the formal narrative patterns that recur in the eighteenth and early nineteenth century Gothic Novel. The rest of this study then deals with individual Victorian novels that appear to contain the recurring Gothic ideological and structural forms. It examines *Wuthering Heights, Great Expectations, Heart of Darkness,* and *Tess of the D'Urbervilles.*"

B224   Longbottom, John. "*Wuthering Heights* and Patrick Branwell Brontë." *Yorkshire Notes and Queries,* 1 (Feb. 1905), 342-346.

Longbottom is so sure that Branwell wrote *Wuthering Heights* that he quotes from the novel as "Biographical Notes."

B225   Loxterman, Alan S. "The Giant's Foot: A Reading of *Wuthering Heights.*" Unpublished doctoral dissertation, Ohio State University, 1972. *DAI,* 32:4007.

The purpose of this dissertation is to "provide a comprehensive reading of *Wuthering Heights* as an ambiguous novel with two

143

different plots which are complementary in structure yet
contradictory in their philosophical implications."

B226   Lucas, Peter D. *An Introduction to the Psychology of Wuthering
        Heights.* London: Guild of Pastoral Psychology, 1943.

        This psychological study suggests that all the characters are, in
        fact, a part of one central figure, that of Catherine.

B227   Macaulay, Rose. "Introduction" in Emily Brontë. *Wuthering Heights.*
        New York: Modern Library, 1926.

        Stating that Emily Brontë is best at creating atmosphere, the
        editor criticizes the characters: Nelly is often too literary, Joseph
        is ill-conceived, and Catherine and Heathcliff represent "false men
        and women." She feels that *Wuthering Heights* developed out of
        Emily Brontë's inherited Celtic mysticism and imagination.

B228   McCaughey, G. S. "An Approach to *Wuthering Heights.*" *Humanities
        Association Bulletin,* 15 (Aug. 1964), 28-34.

        This approach centers on one point: the trials of the Earnshaw
        family, including Hindley's alcoholism and the fact that Catherine
        is drawn to the Linton family. In the end an Earnshaw is again the
        master of Wuthering Heights, ending the series of calamities.

B229   McCullough, Bruce. "The Dramatic Novel" in *Representative English
        Novelists: Defoe to Conrad.* New York: Harper and Brothers,
        1946.

        In showing that *Wuthering Heights* is not like the novels of its
        time, the critic discusses the major techniques used by Emily Brontë
        and the major themes of the novel.

B230   McIlwraith, Jean N. "Introduction" in Emily Brontë. *Wuthering
        Heights.* New York: Doubleday, Page, 1907.

        There is an impersonality that makes *Wuthering Heights* like
        Shakespeare's plays. Emily Brontë uses limited locale and seems to
        demonstrate a "taste for horrors" like that of Holmann.

144

B231   MacKay, Ruth M. "Irish Heaths and German Cliffs: A Study of the Foreign Sources of *Wuthering Heights*." *Brigham Young University Studies*, 7 (Autumn 1965), 28-39.

MacKay proposes that there are two principal sources for *Wuthering Heights*: the German story *Das Majorat* and the anonymous Irish tale "The Bridegroom of Barma," which appeared in *Blackwood's Magazine*. She also suggests that the Catherine-Heathcliff relationship reflects Emily's feelings for her brother Branwell.

B232   MacKereth, James A. "The Greatness of Emily Brontë." *BST*, 7 (1929), 175-200.

In this excellent treatment of the novel, MacKereth voices an objection to biographical and psychological criticism. He feels that Emily Brontë's novel shows that "Man is vaster than any temporal aspects or consciousness of himself."

B233   McKibben, Robert C. "The Image of the Book in *Wuthering Heights*." *Nineteenth Century Fiction*, 15 (Sept. 1960), 159-169.

The critic limits his investigation to one symbol and thoroughly investigates its use in the novel. Its climax is in the later part where the book comes to represent the stabilizing love of Cathy for Hareton.

B234   Madden, David. "Chapter Seventeen of *Wuthering Heights*." *English Record,* 17 (Feb. 1967), 2-8.

The critic feels that this chapter serves as a transition from the first part of the novel to the second. There is more violence in this transition and the symbols are especially powerful.

B235   Madden, William. "The Search for Forgiveness in Some Nineteenth Century English Novels." *Comparative Literature Studies,* 3 (1966), 139-153.

In *Wuthering Heights* forgiveness is the central theme. An early example is found in Jabes Branderham's sermon. The only unforgivable sin, we learn from *Wuthering Heights,* is the refusal to forgive.

B236   Madden, William. "*Wuthering Heights*: The Binding of Passion."
        Nineteenth Century Fiction, 272 (Sept. 1972), 127-154.

        Human action must be directed by a "healthy binding of that
        energy which will lead to constructive action," according to this
        article. Those who refuse to forgive must pay the price of suffering
        and loneliness.

B237   Mais, S. P. B. *Why Should We Read.* London: Richards, 1921.

        In explaining *Wuthering Heights,* this critic asserts that Catherine
        married Edgar in an "attempt to sunder the body from the soul."
        Edgar and Isabelle are used in the novel to set up a contrast with
        the daily life at Wuthering Heights.

B238   Malham-Dembleby, John. *The Key to the Brontë Works.* London:
        Walter Scott, 1911.

        This gentleman "proves" that Charlotte Brontë wrote *Wuthering
        Heights* and she is Catherine to M. Heger's Heathcliff. The critic treats
        the novel as though it were a diary of Charlotte Brontë's love life.
        He refers to "Charlotte Brontë's *Wuthering Heights, Jane Eyre,* and
        her other works" as though there can be no doubt.

B239   Malham-Dembleby, John. "The Lifting of the Brontë Veil."
        Fortnightly Review, 81 (March 1907), 489-505.

        Here Malham-Dembleby makes his declaration that Charlotte
        Brontë wrote *Wuthering Heights.*

B240   Manley, S. M. "'Pale T-Guilp Off.'" *Transactions of the Yorkshire
        Dialect Society,* 13 (1971), 25-28.

        A technical discussion of dialect in *Wuthering Heights.*

B241   Marsden, Hilda. "The Scenic Background of *Wuthering Heights.*" *BST,*
        13 (1957), 111-130.

        The district of Gimmerton in the novel is presented with "precise
        topographical detail," including a map. High Sunderland Hall, which

was demolished in 1950, is suggested as the original Wuthering Heights, and Shibden Hall as the Grange. The theory is substantiated by descriptions from *Wuthering Heights.*

B242   Marshall, William H. "Hareton Earnshaw: Natural Theology on the Moors." *Victorian Newsletter,* 21 (Spring 1962), 14-15.

The critic feels that Hareton sees Heathcliff as a deity and yet retains his native intelligence to "effect his own regeneration." He can be compared to Shakespeare's Caliban but is implicitly like Browning's version.

B243   Mathison, John K. "Nelly Dean and the Power of *Wuthering Heights.*" *Nineteenth Century Fiction,* 11 (1956), 102-129.

That Nelly is an admirable woman is a point of view which the reader must reject on his own analysis. The reader senses the inadequacy of Nelly's wholesome viewpoint and thus becomes the interpreter and judge. The reader remains sympathetic to passions even though he finds them destructive and violent. The structure of the novel maintains the reader's sympathy until the end of the book.

B244   Maugham, W. Somerset. *Great Novelists and Their Novels: Essays on the Ten Greatest Novels in the World and the Men and Women Who Wrote Them.* Philadelphia: John C. Winston, 1948.

Emily Brontë is included in this select group. The chapter "Emily Brontë and *Wuthering Heights*" includes highly individualized criticism and some biography of the Brontë family.

B245   Maugham, W. Somerset. "The Ten Best Novels: *Wuthering Heights.*" *Atlantic Monthly,* 181 (Feb. 1948), 89-94.

This accomplished author gives serious consideration to the various critical areas of *Wuthering Heights* and ends by suggesting one or two conclusions: that the dual narration is in fact a "double mask" because Emily Brontë was both Catherine Earnshaw and Heathcliff. The further conclusion based on this supposition is that Emily and Anne had a lesbian attachment.

B246   Maxwell, J. C. "A Shakespearean Comma in *Wuthering Heights.*" *The Trollopian,* 3 (March 1949), 315.

This is a textual note on the comma used to indicate emphasis in the nineteenth century, similar to Elizabethan use. "Are you, Linton" means "Are *you* Linton?"

B247   Mayne, Isobel. "Emily Brontë's Mr. Lockwood." *BST,* 15 (1968), 207-213.

The article discusses the use of this character as a device to communicate with the reader. It is judged to be a "skillful and realistic technical device."

B248   Meier, T. K. "*Wuthering Heights* and Violation of Class." *BST,* 15 (1968), 233-236.

Heathcliff, Nelly, and Joseph are accused of violation of class, an act which causes moral decline. Linton Heathcliff is seen as central to the major aspects of decay in the novel.

B249   Mendilow, Adam Abraham. *Time and the Novel.* New York: Humanities Press, 1952.

The critic speaks of the complexity of the point of view in *Wuthering Heights,* pointing out the difference between observer-within-the-novel and novelist-outside-the-novel.

B250   Messiaen, P. "Les Hauts-de-Hurle-Vent." *Revue des Cours et Conférences,* 40 (1938), 189-192.

B251   Miller, J. Hillis. "Emily Brontë" in *The Disappearance of God: Five Nineteenth-Century Writers.* Cambridge, Massachusetts: Harvard University Press, 1963.

Miller senses a duality of feeling in Emily Brontë's novel, that of wanting to be controlled by God yet wanting control. He sees her as influenced by her religious education and her Romantic reading. She creates an interest in Heathcliff as a hero with a "permanent and unceasing attitude of aggression," but with the assurance that the suffering which "sin brings will be sufficient expiation for that sin." Thus the sinner will "escape to heaven." Miller proposes that *Wuthering Heights* "is a work with which no reader has felt altogether at ease."

B252 Mitchell, G. "Incest, Demonology and Death in *Wuthering Heights.*" *Literature and Psychology,* 23 (1973), 27-36.

Believing that both Catherine and Heathcliff are aware of their brother-sister relationship, this critic finds the characters ruled by incestuous desire and guilt.

B253 Moers, Ellen. "Female Gothic: Monsters, Goblins, Freaks." *New York Review of Books,* April 4, 1974, pp. 35-39.

In presenting her subject, the critic writes much about Christina Rossetti's "Goblin Market," but refers to *Wuthering Heights* to substantiate her general thesis.

B254 Moglen, Helene. "The Double Vision of *Wuthering Heights*: Clarifying View of Female Development." *Centennial Review,* 15 (Fall 1971), 391-405.

Here the critic finds the movement of *Wuthering Heights* "cohesive and linear, not cyclical." She believes that the theme is the development of the female personality from childhood to maturity.

B255 Moody, Philippa. "The Challenge to Maturity in *Wuthering Heights.*" *Melbourne Critical Review,* 5 (1962), 27-39.

This critic sees that the Catherine-Heathcliff relationship is "extreme, intense" but very like many typical adolescent relationships. Not outside normal experience, it can be sexless and yet credible. It is the central experience in *Wuthering Heights* and demonstrates the value of intense emotion.

B256 Moore, Geoffrey. "Foreword" in Emily Brontë. *Wuthering Heights.* New York: New American Library, 1959.

The editor points to Emily Brontë's romantic imagination and yet her grasp of human realities.

B257   Moser, Thomas. "Introduction" in Emily Brontë. *Wuthering Heights: Text, Sources, Criticism.* New York: Harcourt Brace, 1962.

Moser declares *Wuthering Heights* to be modern because of the intricate techniques used in its construction. He says that the subject matter which is of interest to the twentieth-century reader includes (1) the problem of evil and (2) the power of the unconscious.

B258   Moser, Thomas. "What is the Matter with Emily Jane? Conflicting Impulses in *Wuthering Heights.*" *Nineteenth Century Fiction,* 17 (June 1962), 1-19.

This Freudian psychological reading of *Wuthering Heights* finds that "sex is a central subject." Moser concludes that it is a powerful and imperfect novel.

B259   Muir, Edwin. "Time and Space" in *The Structure of the Novel.* London: Hogarth Press, 1928.

Discussing *Wuthering Heights,* the critic states that it is a dramatic novel and not a novel of character. He deals with those two very modern concerns of Time and Space.

B260   Nelson, Lowry, Jr. "Night Thoughts on the Gothic Novel." *Yale Review,* 52 (Dec. 1962), 236-257.

Heathcliff is presented here as heir to the Gothic hero. *Wuthering Heights* is compared with *Moby Dick* and *Frankenstein,* all "without either God or devil."

B261   Neufeldt, Victor A. "The Shared Vision of Anne and Emily Brontë: The Context for *Wuthering Heights.*" Unpublished doctoral dissertation, University of Illinois, 1970. *DAI,* 31:764.

"It is the contention of this study that a close analysis of all of Anne's and Emily's writings, and of the beliefs and attitudes they shared can shed considerable light on the purpose and meaning of *Wuthering Heights.*"

B262   Nicholson, Norman. "Introduction" in Emily Brontë. *Wuthering Heights.* London: Paul Elek (Camden Classics), 1948.

150

B263   Nicolai, Ralf. "*Wuthering Heights*: Emily Brontë's Kleistian Novel." *South Atlantic Review*, 28 (May 1973), 23-32.

Wuthering Heights is discussed as similar to Heinrich von Kleist's *Der Findling.*

B264   Nixon, Ingeborg. "A Note on the Pattern of *Wuthering Heights*" in *English Studies, Presented to R. W. Zandvoort.* A supplement to *English Studies,* 45 (Supplement, 1964), 235-242.

This study of the structure of *Wuthering Heights* shows that the actions are grouped around "certain lyrical and dramatic passages."

B265   Odumu, O. "Women Talk About Women: The Image of Women in the Novels of Jane Austen and Emily Brontë." *Horizon* (Ibadan), 9 (1973), 47-54.

Noted but not inspected.

B266   Patterson, Charles, Jr. "Empathy and Daemonic in *Wuthering Heights.*" *The English Novel in the Nineteenth Century: Essays on the Literary Mediation of Human Values.* Ed. George V. Goodin. Illinois Studies in Language and Literature No. 63. Urbana, Illinois: University of Illinois Press, 1972.

Characters, action, tone, and atmosphere of *Wuthering Heights* are shaped by "the relentless Romantic drive for experience more richly fulfilling than ordinary life affords." This drive is manifest in two modes: "the daemonic urge to pierce beyond all human limitations in the search for the heart's desire" and the "capacity for empathy" which allows one human being to merge himself with the person he loves, "the transcendental union of the self with the 'other.'"

B267   Pearsall, Robert Brainard. "The Presiding Tropes of Emily Brontë." *College English,* 27 (Jan. 1966), 267-273.

The poetic language in *Wuthering Heights* is analyzed carefully. Characters are seen to speak in "bold metaphors." The critic feels

151

that Emily Brontë "lusted" to reveal her suffering and yet was determined to hide it.

B268   Petit, Jean-Pierre. "La mort dans *Wuthering Heights.*" *Etudes Brontëennes.* Eds. Jacques Blondel and Jean-Pierre Petit. Paris: Edition Ophrys, 1970.

The eminent French scholar discusses the various forms of death in *Wuthering Heights* and the significance of them.

B269   Petit, Jean-Pierre. *L'Oeuvre d'Emily Brontë: La Vision et les Thèmes.* Lyons: Editions L'Hermès, 1977.

One of the major French scholars of Emily Brontë has written a thoroughly researched, carefully substantiated analysis and explication of *Wuthering Heights* and the poems. His own evaluation of Emily Brontë's mysticism and counterbalancing awareness of reality points the way for further exploration into this pervasive duality.

B270   Petyt, K. Malcolm. "The Dialect Speech in *Wuthering Heights*" from *Emily Brontë and the Haworth Dialect* in Emily Brontë. *Wuthering Heights.* Eds. Hilda Marsden and Ian Jack. Oxford: Clarendon Press, 1976.

A careful analysis of Yorkshire "pronunciation . . . morphology . . . semantics . . . vocabulary" selected from the longer study (B271). The conclusion is that Emily Brontë's "observation of dialect seems so keen. . . . She must have listened often to 'the peasantry amongst whom she lived,'" despite Charlotte Brontë's insistence that Emily had no contact with them. The dialect of the second edition is less valid as Charlotte Brontë modified it in editing the book.

B271   Petyt, K. Malcolm. *Emily Brontë and the Haworth Dialect: A Study of the Dialect Speech in Wuthering Heights.* Keighly, York: Yorkshire Dialect Society, 1970.

An expert in the area writes about Emily Brontë's handling of local Yorkshire dialect in the novel. Part reprinted in B270.

B272   Petyt, K. Malcolm. "'Thou' and 'You' in *Wuthering Heights.*" *BST*, 16 (1974), 291-293.

In the nineteenth-century Yorkshire dialect 'Thou' and 'You' were used to indicate social position, servant-master and child-adult relationships. 'Thou' is used about twelve times in the novel, each time correctly: in addressing Joseph or Nelly, when Joseph speaks to a child, and once by Hareton to an adult in anger and scorn. This usage shows Emily Brontë's understanding of dialect.

B273   Phelps, William Lyon. "The Mid-Victorians" in *The Bookman* [pre-1916]. Reprinted in *The Advance of the English Novel.* New York: Dodd, Mead, 1916.

This educator finds *Wuthering Heights* "more hysterical than historical" in revealing human nature. He finds that the novel "has the strength of delirium" and believes the tone of passion is caused by Emily Brontë's personal repression.

B274   Pittock, Malcolm. "*Wuthering Heights* and Its Critics." *Critical Survey*, 5 (Summer 1971), 146-154.

Over the years critics have found various explanations for *Wuthering Heights.* Emily Brontë does not tell us which of three possible interpretations we should believe: (1) that it is a psychological novel, (2) that it is based on traditional religion with moral concepts of right and wrong, or (3) that salvation through faith (antinomianism) is the basic tenet.

B275   Plath, Sylvia. "*Wuthering Heights*" from *Crossing the Water.* London: Faber and Faber, 1971.

Here is a poem ending, "how, in valleys narrow / and black as purses, the house lights / gleam like small change." The whole poem recreates the mood of the novel.

B276   Power, S. A. "The Chronology of *Wuthering Heights.*" *BST*, 16 (1973), 139-143.

A presentation of the discrepancies in ages and dates in *Wuthering Heights.*

B277   Pritchett, V. S. (Victor Sawdon). "Implacable, Belligerent People of Emily Brontë's Novel, *Wuthering Heights*" in "Books in General." *New Statesman and Nation,* 31 (June 22, 1946), 453.

A review of the "zest" of hatred in the novel. Heathcliff's literary ancestor is Lovelace, but Emily Brontë's character is not so admirable as Lovelace. They both possess a maleness "with power of conspiracy and seduction." This article suggests that the imbalance of the first and second part of *Wuthering Heights* results from the uneven feeling toward the ending.

B278   Pritchett, V. S. "Introduction" in Emily Brontë. *Wuthering Heights.* Boston: Houghton Mifflin, 1956.

The subject of *Wuthering Heights* is the self alone, or the soul. The novel is Elizabethan in intensity in presenting the Yorkshire people: taciturn, self-reliant and innately good. Their emotion, once aroused, lasts for a lifetime. Emily Brontë is not afraid to depict cruelty as the elements of cruelty exist in the human soul. The love in *Wuthering Heights* has the "innocent ferocity of childhood." Catherine and Heathcliff "attempt to get back to their childhood and its sexless companionship."

B279   Quennell, Peter. "Foreword" in *Novels by the Brontë Sisters.* London: Pilot Press, 1947.

Did Branwell Brontë write *Wuthering Heights*? If not, this critic assumes that he influenced it. Quennell cites Branwell and Emily's habit of collaboration from childhood. In any case, *Wuthering Heights* merges the human and superhuman, and its setting and lighting are appropriate and unlabored.

B280   Rancy, J. "Gothic et Surnaturel dans *Wuthering Heights.*" *Etudes Brontëennes.* Eds. Jacques Blondel and Jean-Pierre Petit. Paris: Ophrys, 1970.

B281   Rawlings, Carl D. "Prophecy in the Novel." Unpublished doctoral dissertation, University of Washington, 1973. *DAI,* 34:2575.

Attempts to "develop a concept of prophetic fiction." He draws illustrations from E. M. Forster, F. Dostoevsky, D. H. Lawrence, Emily Brontë, and Herman Melville.

B282   Reed, Walter. "Brontë and Lermontov: the Hero In and Out of Time." *Meditations on the Hero: A Study of the Romantic Hero in Nineteenth Century Fiction.* New Haven: Yale University Press, 1974.

Heathcliff fulfills part of the criteria for a hero as a figure of strength and stature. The novel has for its sources works by Shakespeare, Byron, Scott; *Paradise Lost* and "The Bridegroom of Barma." He feels that *Wuthering Heights* "cannot be seen ultimately as a novel of psychological or family conflict. . . . In its structure it belongs to the genre of the meditation on the hero."

B283   Reynolds, Thomas. "Division and Unity in *Wuthering Heights.*" *University Review* (Kansas City, Missouri), 32 (Autumn 1965), 31-37.

Here is a study of the analogies, balances, and counterpoints of *Wuthering Heights* as Emily Brontë works out the love-hate and hate-love relationships.

B284   Rhys, Ernest. "The Haworth Tradition." *BST,* 6 (1922), 88-96. Reprinted in *The Brontës: Then and Now.* Shipley: Outhwaite Brothers, 1947.

The "power of the place" in *Wuthering Heights.* There is a universality felt in the novel due to the language which makes it real.

B285   Roberts, Mark. *The Tradition of Romantic Morality.* London: Macmillan; New York: Harper and Row, 1973.

The critic deals with "The Dilemma of Emily Brontë," suggesting that the "motive power" of *Wuthering Heights* is in the "tension between two opposing conceptions of moral behavior." The "dilemma" of Emily Brontë is based on the difference between traditional values and the values of Romanticism. "It is because she refuses to suggest that there is an easy solution, and because she presents the strengths and weaknesses of the two opposing views with such imaginative power" that there is a "*Wuthering Heights* problem."

B286   Romberg, Bertil. "Studies in the Narrative Technique of the First-Person Novel" in *Emily Brontë: A Critical Anthology*. Ed. Jean-Pierre Petit. Harmondsworth, Middlesex: Penguin, 1973.

A pertinent selection on narration as it applies to *Wuthering Heights*.

B287   Rosenfield, Claire. "The Shadow Within: The Conscious and Unconscious Use of the Double." *Daedalus*, 92 (Spring 1963), 326-344.

In writing *Wuthering Heights*, Emily Brontë has made use of the double personality. Catherine and Heathcliff are doubles, only their sex is different. They can exist as one only in childhood and in death, and this complexity causes the tension in the novel.

B288   Rossetti, Dante Gabriel. *Letters*. Eds. Oswalk Doughty and John Robert Wahl. Volume I. London: Oxford University Press, 1965.

Wuthering Heights is "laid in hell, – only it seems places and people have English names there."

B289   Sager, Keith. "The Originality of *Wuthering Heights*" in *The Art of Emily Brontë*. Ed. Anne Smith. London: Vision Press, 1976.

The critic compares this novel with other Victorian novels and concludes that *Wuthering Heights* is original.

B290   Sanger, Charles Percy [C.P.S.]. *The Structure of Wuthering Heights*. London: Hogarth Press, 1926. Reprinted, Folcroft, Pennsylvania: Folcroft, 1976.

Originally read before the Heretics at Cambridge, this truly great study substantiates the validity of Emily Brontë's understanding of legal background as well as her remarkable control of time. The work includes a family tree of the Earnshaws and Lintons as well as a chronology of the novel showing events from the earliest mentioned (Hindley Earnshaw's birth in 1757) to the last (the anticipated marriage of Cathy and Hareton on January 1, 1803). Sanger indicates in which chapter each event is mentioned.

B291   Scheuerle, William H. "Emily Brontë's *Wuthering Heights.*" *Explicator*, 33:9 (May 1975), item 69.

This note refers to a Yorkshire superstition that pigeon feathers in the pillow delay or prevent death. It explains why Catherine wishes to throw the pillow to the floor saying, "They put pigeon feathers in the pillow – no wonder I couldn't die !"

B292   Schorer, Mark. "Fiction and the 'Analogical Matrix.'" *Kenyon Review*, 11 (Autumn 1949), 539-560.

Schorer identifies the "analogical matrix" as the "whole habit of value association." He analyzes *Wuthering Heights* (along with *Persuasion* and *Middlemarch*) as to animal imagery, discussing the structural functions of verbs, metaphors, and epithets.

B293   Schorer, Mark. "Introduction" in Emily Brontë. *Wuthering Heights.* New York: Rinehart, 1950.

In *Wuthering Heights* we see Emily Brontë emerging from the world of "unmoral passion" (Gondal) into the real world, the moral world. Schorer finds that the power of *Wuthering Heights* lies in its conclusion that "the triumph" of cloddish characters "is not all on the side of convention." He includes a discussion of the structure of the novel and Emily Brontë's use of metaphor.

B294   Schorer, Mark. "Technique as Discovery." *Hudson Review*, 1 (Spring 1948), 67-87.

In *Wuthering Heights,* Emily Brontë attempts to show the "moral magnificence of unmoral passion" in a "world of ideal value." The two elements of narrative perspective, (1) Lockwood's conventional emotions and (2) Nelly's conventional morality, extend over a long period of time. Throughout there is a "tone of somnambulistic excess."

B295   Scrivner, Buford, Jr. "The Ethos of *Wuthering Heights.*" *Dalhousie Review*, 54 (Autumn 1974), 451-462.

The novel demonstrates that we each live in an unchanging world within ourselves, trying to bridge the gap between Being and

Becoming. *Wuthering Heights* is based structurally on dualism, one force countering another, the inner constancy of each character contrasted with his need to exist in the world of social convention. The central ethical failure within the plot is Catherine's decision to marry Edgar, making the unity between Catherine and Heathcliff impossible.

B296   Serlen, Ellen. "The Rage of Caliban: Realism and Romance in the Nineteenth Century Novel." Unpublished doctoral dissertation, SUNY at Stony Brook, 1975. *DAI*, 36:911-A.

Serlen discusses the desire of novelists "to give their public the escape they wanted" and suggests that their desire to "fulfill their function as purveyors of reality created in the novelists a conflict which was transferred to their books." *Wuthering Heights* is one of the novels discussed.

B297   Shannon, Edgar F., Jr. "Lockwood's Dreams and the Exegesis of *Wuthering Heights.*" *Nineteenth Century Fiction,* 14 (Sept. 1959).

In refuting Adams (B63), who says that the sermon text is Genesis 4:24, this critic finds relevance in the dream sermon and suggests that its source is Matthew 18:21-22. Shannon also disagrees with Van Ghent as to the dream interpretation. The thematic problem in *Wuthering Heights* concerns the nature of Catherine's offense. For Heathcliff, hate is the corollary of love as "evil derives solely from separation — from the denial of sympathy and love." The novel "results in a paradigm of love." Emily Brontë shows that Heathcliff "is not innately demonic and that hate is subservient to love."

B298   Shapiro, Arnold. "*Wuthering Heights* as a Victorian Novel." *Studies in the Novel,* 1 (Fall 1969), 284-296.

Because of its ethical and moral concerns, Shapiro finds *Wuthering Heights* to be Victorian in flavor. It attacks society for selfishness and hypocrisy, finding that the master-slave relationship of Heathcliff with others is wrong, and the teacher-pupil relationship of Cathy and Hareton is right.

158

B299   Shorter, Clement. "Introduction" in *The Complete Works of Emily Brontë*, Vol. II, prose. London: Hodder and Stoughton, 1911.

In this edition of *Wuthering Heights* the editors have followed the first edition; Joseph's dialect is amended by Charlotte Brontë in footnotes. Shorter suggests that Reverend Brontë's experiences in Ireland have influenced Emily Brontë in the writing of this novel. The critic feels that Emily's "genius was entirely introspective" whereas Charlotte used models for her stories.

B300   Shunami, Gideon. "The Unreliable Narrator in *Wuthering Heights*." *Nineteenth Century Fiction*, 27 (1972), 449-468.

The two unreliable narrators reshape the story according to their biases. Nelly, the meddler, gives Lockwood a self-justifying account of events. Each undermines the reliability of the other, but together they augment the credibility of the inner story. They misunderstand the protagonists and force the reader to give a closer reading.

B301   Smith, Anne. "Introduction" in *The Art of Emily Brontë*. London: Vision Press, 1976.

The editor discusses *Wuthering Heights,* indicating that Nelly is a "mother figure" and concluding that the novel shows that "the supernatural and material worlds diverge."

B302   Smith, David. "The Panelled Bed and the Unrepressible Wish of *Wuthering Heights*." *Paunch,* 30 (1967), 40-47.

In reviewing chronologically the events in the novel related to the panelled bed, the critic presents "the fundamental connection between the childhood bedroom and its panelled-bed on one hand, and the grave and its coffins on the other." Smith explains that "the childhood sleeping arrangement represents an untensioned psychic wholeness" which, once severed, is not restored until Heathcliff joins Catherine in the grave.

B303   Solomon, Eric. "The Incest Theme in *Wuthering Heights*." *Nineteenth Century Fiction,* 14 (June 1959), 80-83.

This highly controversial article has been reprinted many times. It gives evidence that Catherine and Heathcliff could have been half-sister and half-brother. Such a reading heightens the tragedy and emotion and makes the dramatic separation inevitable.

B304   Sonstroem, David. "*Wuthering Heights* and the Limits of Vision."
        PMLA, 86 (Jan. 1971), 51-62.

        Emily Brontë does not limit her vision to the point of view
        of Heathcliff or Catherine (or any other character). *Wuthering Heights*
        is made of several patterns: genealogical symmetry, marriage triangles,
        and the arc from Hareton Earnshaw in 1500 to Hareton Earnshaw
        in 1802, for example. The critic senses that the characters'
        short-sightedness serves to illustrate the limited vision of all human
        beings.

B305   Stone, Roy de Montpensier."Re Wuthering Heights and ReThrushcross
        Grange: Case for the Opinion of Counsel." *BST,* 16 (1972),
        118-130.

        Applying practical knowledge to theoretical, a retired barrister
        prepares a case to be submitted to Counsel to advise on the title
        to the properties.

B306   Sucksmith, Harvey P. "The Theme of *Wuthering Heights*
        Reconsidered." *Dalhousie Review,* 54 (Autumn 1974), 418-428.

        In the light of the restricted Victorian views,*Wuthering Heights*
        stands out as a work of visionary art, revealing the tragedy of civilized
        man with regard to his instinctive life. The Catherine-Heathcliff
        relationship must be abandoned and that of Catherine-Edgar accepted
        in its place. The compromise of a Cathy-Hareton is suggested, one
        "which even now is scarcely realized" according to Sucksmith. He
        concludes that Emily Brontë's anguish is the anguish of her time.

B307   Sutcliffe, Halliwell. "The Spirit of the Moors." *BST,* 2 (Jan. 1903),
        174-190. Reprinted in *Charlotte Brontë: A Centenary Memorial.*
        London: T. Fisher Unwin, 1917.

        This early consideration of the novel concludes that the
        characters in *Wuthering Heights* could not live without their
        surroundings.

B308   Swinburne, Algernon Charles. "Emily Brontë." *Athenaeum,* June 16,
        1883, pp. 762-763. Reprinted in *Miscellanies.* London: Chatto
        and Windus, 1886.

This literary essay deals with the works of Emily Brontë in a wholly ornate style, with more concern for Swinburne's language than for content. He calls *Wuthering Heights* "a poem in the fullest and most positive sense of the term." Vol. also cited as B61.

B309   Symons, Arthur. "Emily Brontë." *The Nation,* 23 (Aug. 24, 1918), 546-547. Reprinted in *Living Age* (Oct. 12, 1918), 119-121.

This critic feels that *Wuthering Heights* is dominated by sheer chance. It is "one long outcry" from a woman of "passion without sensuousness." The novel is praised for the "mystery of its terrors," but is found to be, on the whole, not well-constructed.

B310   Thompson, Wade. "Infanticide and Sadism in *Wuthering Heights.*" *PMLA,* 78 (1963), 69-74.

The dark side of the novel is presented in this serious and unusual approach to *Wuthering Heights* which suggests that the central characters are perverse. In pointing out the underlying sadism, the critic declares that Heathcliff "deliberately wills his own death."

B311   Thomson, Patricia. "*Wuthering Heights* and *Mauprat.*" *Review of English Studies,* 24 (Fall 1973), 26-37.

Wuthering Heights is like George Sand's *Mauprat* (1837) in theme, characters, atmosphere, and the romanticism in the presentation of nature. There is evidence that Emily Brontë had read *Mauprat.* This critic feels that *Wuthering Heights* is the better novel of the two.

B312   Thurber, Barton Dennison. "Alter Ego: The Double in the English Novel." Unpublished doctoral dissertation, Harvard University, 1978.

His chapters seven and eight discuss two kinds of doubling in *Wuthering Heights,* the "absolute identity" of Catherine and Heathcliff, and the two-generation doubling of this pair with Cathy and Hareton. In this novel "duplication and resemblance . . . is of a piece with the division of self into two selves."

B313 Tombleson, Gary Earl. "Alpha and Omega Recast: The Rhetoric of Cosmic Unity in Poe, Brontë, and Hardy." Unpublished doctoral dissertation, University of California, San Diego, 1976. *DAI*, 37:2165.

This dissertation "examines the structure of 'cosmic unity' as it is manifested in various forms and degrees of fantastic art and literature. . . . The fourth chapter constructs an interpretation of *Wuthering Heights* . . . taking the question of the relationship of subject and object."

B314 Tough, A. J. "*Wuthering Heights* and *King Lear.*" *English*, 21 (Spring 1972), 1-5.

This article points out the parallel theme and language.

B315 Traversi, Derek. "The Brontë Sisters and *Wuthering Heights.*" *From Dickens to Hardy: A Guide to English Literature*. Ed. Boris Ford. *Pelican Guide to English Literature*, Vol. VI. Harmondsworth, Middlesex: Penguin, 1958.

In his discussion of the imaginative qualities of Charlotte and Emily Brontë, Traversi emphasizes the "spirit of concentration" in Emily Brontë's poems and in *Wuthering Heights*. In the latter, personal theme and social theme are seen symbolized in Wuthering Heights and Thrushcross Grange. The second part of the novel is like "*Wuthering Heights* after 100 years" (see B316). The strength of the work is in its "complete and consistent expression"; its weakness is seen as "a mixture of brutal melodrama and exaggerated sentiment."

B316 Traversi, Derek. "*Wuthering Heights* after a Hundred Years." *Dublin Review*, 222 (Spring 1949), 154-168.

Traversi suggests that *Wuthering Heights* may be seen as being based on a sequence of romantic melodramas, but full of dramatic intensity, morality, and mysticism. There are two main themes: one personal, one social.

B317 Trickett, Rachel. "*Wuthering Heights*: The Story of a Haunting." *BST*, 16 (1975), 338-347.

"Heathcliff, not Lockwood, is the truly haunted man of the novel. . . . He is possessed," according to this critic. *Wuthering Heights* is believable because of "Emily Brontë's profound simplicity of vision and also, more unexpectedly, the art by which she conveys it."

B318   Trilling, Diana. "The Liberated Heroine." *Times Literary Supplement,* Oct. 13, 1978, pp. 1163-1167.

In this article about the "fictional creation whose first concern is the exploration and realization of female selfhood," the critic omits any reference to Charlotte Brontë's characters and speaks in passing about the "spirited heroine" of *Wuthering Heights.* It is, however, an article to be included in any study of feminism in the nineteenth-century novel.

B319   Tristam, Philippa. "Divided Sources." *The Art of Emily Brontë.* Ed. Anne Smith. London: Vision Press, 1976.

The critic emphasizes that Emily Brontë's childhood experiences are the source and subject of *Wuthering Heights.*

B320   Turnell, Martin. *"Wuthering Heights." The Dublin Review,* 206 (Jan. 1940), 134-149.

In this social analysis of *Wuthering Heights,* Turnell declares that the novel is "one of the most tremendous indictments of contemporary civilizations" in all nineteenth-century literature. It vividly reveals the conflict between "two profoundly different ways of life."

B321   Twitchell, James. "Heathcliff as Monomaniac." *BST,* 16 (1975), 374-375.

Emily Brontë's use of the word "monomaniac" is discussed.

B322   Twitchell, James. "Heathcliff as Vampire." *Southern Humanities Review,* 11 (1977), 355-362.

Not quite presenting Heathcliff as an actual vampire, the critic suggests that Emily Brontë uses the vampire legend "as a metaphor"

163

to substantiate Heathcliff's actions and the attitude of the other characters.

B323 Vaisey, the Honorable Mr. Justice. "*Wuthering Heights:* A Note on Its Authorship." *BST,* 11 (1946), 14-15.

Here is another assertion that Branwell wrote part of *Wuthering Heights,* the first three chapters and the beginning of the fourth. We hear Branwell speaking "rather than Mr. Lockwood," according to this critic, who finds these early chapters different from the rest of the novel.

B324 Vancura, Zdenek. "The Stones of Wuthering Heights." *Philologica Pragensia,* 13 (1970), 1-15.

The influence of the ancient house, Wuthering Heights, is felt throughout the novel. It is the central stage where tragedy and "gloomy comedy" are performed.

B325 van de Laar, Elizabeth, Th.M. *The Inner Structure of Wuthering Heights.* The Hague and Paris: Mouton Press, 1969.

This analytic documentation traces "the language of the image," emphasizing the symbols of the elements, weather, dreams, and objects.

B326 Van Ghent, Dorothy. "The Window Figure and the Two-Children Figure in *Wuthering Heights.*" *Nineteenth Century Fiction,* 7 (Dec. 1952), 189-197. Reprinted in *The English Novel: Form and Function.* New York: Rinehart, 1953.

This outstanding myth-and-symbol interpretation of *Wuthering Heights* points out the window figure in the novel, the two-children figure in both the novel and poetry. The strangeness in *Wuthering Heights* results from the ethical attitudes, the level of experience and the great simplicity, what the critic calls a lack of the "web of civilized habits." Two "technical bulwarks" support this "uneasy tale": the credible, commonplace narrators and the double generations which allow the story to end with an emphasis on manners and morality.

B327   Vargish, Thomas. "Revenge and *Wuthering Heights*." *Studies in the Novel*, 111 (Spring 1971), 7-17.

In considering the theme of revenge, Vargish points out that Heathcliff attempts to structure his existence on revenge, but gives it up as it ties him to a world which has become meaningless.

B328   Viebrock, H. "Emily Brontë: *Wuthering Heights*" in *Der englische Roman im 19. Jahrhundert: Interpretationen.* Eds. P. Goetsch, H. Kosok, and K. Otten. Berlin: E. Schmidt, 1973. Vol. also listed as A133.

B329   Visick, Mary. *The Genesis of Wuthering Heights.* Hong Kong: Hong Kong University Press, 1958.

Stressing the point that Emily Brontë's novel arose "out of the same material as her poetry," this important critical work gives a thorough analysis of *Wuthering Heights* and the Gondal saga, with an appendix which shows parallels.

B330   Viswanathan, Jacqueline. "Point of View and Unreliability in Brontë's *Wuthering Heights,* Conrad's *Under Western Eyes,* and Mann's *Doktor Faustus.*" *Orbis Litterarum,* 29 (1974), 42-60.

The study analyzes the common features of the various narrators' positions and explains in what way the different authors manipulate the narrators to allow the reader to see beyond the obvious unreliability of the narrators.

B331   Vogler, Thomas A. "Introduction" in *Twentieth Century Interpretations of Wuthering Heights: A Collection of Critical Essays.* Englewood Cliffs, New Jersey: Prentice-Hall, 1968.

Vogler presents two contradictory ways of seeing *Wuthering Heights:* accepting (1) Nelly Dean and Lockwood's commonsense and empirical vision, or (2) Catherine and Heathcliff's vision which goes beyond the limits of reality. Perhaps the novel contrasts these visions, presenting the "impossibility of adopting decisively one or the other mode of vision."

B332   Vogler, Thomas A. "Story and History in *Wuthering Heights.*"
        *Twentieth Century Interpretations of Wuthering Heights: A
        Collection of Critical Essays.* Ed. Thomas A. Vogler. Englewood
        Cliffs, New Jersey: Prentice-Hall, 1968.

        The critic takes a look at Lockwood as a valid character, as
        well as examining the theme and structure. He finds that *Wuthering
        Heights* does not propose a resolution, in fact its theme emphasizes
        a series of contradictions. Vogler suggests that the "process of change"
        is the reality behind the events within the novel.

B333   Waddington-Feather, John. "Emily Brontë's Use of Dialect in
        Wuthering Heights." *BST,* 15 (1966), 12-19.

        Emily Brontë uses Yorkshire dialect on 15 occasions in
        Wuthering Heights to "create character and mood." Her use of
        dialectic expressions is quite accurate though inconsistent. The critic
        calls this variation "artistic use of dialect."

B334   Ward, Mrs. Humphry. "Introduction" in Emily Brontë. *Wuthering
        Heights.* London: Haworth Edition, 1899-1900. Reprinted in
        BST, 2 (1905).

        Mrs. Ward opposes Saintsbury (C114) and Leslie Stephen (B58)
        in claiming that the novel has still to take its proper place in English
        literature. In her judgment, one could wish for more "flowing unity"
        in the novel. It belongs to the "later romantic movement" and is
        influenced by German literature. Emily Brontë's genius has its source
        in her Celtic background.

B335   Watson, Melvin R. "Tempest in the Soul: The Theme and Structure
        of *Wuthering Heights.*" *Nineteenth Century Fiction,* 4 (Sept.
        1949), 243-263.

        In *Wuthering Heights,* Emily Brontë was attempting something
        "closely related to human experience." The work of a mature artist,
        it is "consciously organized like a five-act tragedy" with a prologue,
        in the tradition of Shakespeare. Heathcliff is a "Hamlet without
        Hamlet's fatal irresolution." The critic says simply, "Heathcliff *is* the
        story."

B336   Whitmore, Clara H. *Woman's Work in English Fiction.* New York: Putnam, 1910.

> *Wuthering Heights* and Emily Brontë's poetry are both discussed. In noting positive forces within the novel, the critic remarks that after three years of marriage to Edgar Linton, Catherine's "better nature triumphs." Heathcliff is shown to be "capable of love stronger than hate."

B337   Widdowson, Peter. "Emily Brontë: Romantic Novelist." *Moderna Sprak* (Stockholm), 66 (1972), 1-19.

> In identifying *Wuthering Heights* as a Romantic novel, Widdowson discusses Emily Brontë's "Romantic view of life": her love of nature, her view of childhood as "free from the taint of civilization," her use of country people, and her "great sense of rebellion against the values of 'social,' 'civilized' life." She represents the "opposition of Passion and Sense," using language "at once simple and poetic" and emphasizes the need for integrity to self. Widdowson believes that "*Wuthering Heights* is closer than any other to being a purely Romantic novel by an English author, the only fictional prose that approximates to 19th Century English Romantic poetry."

B338   Wilkins, Mary E. "Emily Brontë and *Wuthering Heights.*" *Booklover's Magazine,* 1 (May 1903), 514-519.

> Emily Brontë is intent upon truth; therefore, she handles brutality and coarseness "like another woman would a painted fan." *Wuthering Heights* has "the repulsiveness of power," according to this early reviewer.

B339   Williams, G. "The Problem of Passion in *Wuthering Heights.*" *Trivium,* 7 (1972), 41-53.

> A discussion of "the intensely sexual, vaguely perverse atmosphere of the novel." Williams relates Catherine's situation, which he feels is aggravated by the "Victorian denials of feminine passion."

B340   Willis, Irene Cooper. *The Authorship of Wuthering Heights.* London: Hogarth Press, 1936. Summarized in *The Trollopian,* 2 (Dec. 1947), 157-168.

In a stylistic analysis of *Wuthering Heights*, this astute critic answers Alice Law on the question of authorship. In Part I, Willis discusses *Wuthering Heights*, pointing out the value of Lockwood and the effect achieved by the double narrative. In Part II, she analyzes Branwell Brontë's writing, quoting him to prove that he could not have written *Wuthering Heights*.

B341   Willy, Margaret. *A Critical Commentary on Emily Brontë's Wuthering Heights.* London: Macmillan, 1966.

B342   Woodring, Carl. "The Narrators of *Wuthering Heights.*" *Nineteenth Century Fiction,* 12 (March 1957), 298-305.

In discussing the function of the double narrators, Woodring comments on the value of Lockwood, the stranger, and Nelly Dean, the intimate. Woodring's assessment is that Nelly adds warmth without interfering with the action.

B343   Worth, George. "Emily Brontë's Mr. Lockwood." *Nineteenth Century Fiction,* 13 (March 1958), 315-320.

The critic analyzes the narrator and comes to the conclusion that Lockwood deludes himself (but not the reader) about his personality and character. He is used by Emily Brontë as a foil for Heathcliff but also to give the point of view of an ordinary man so that the unusual events of the story will be acceptable.

B344   Wright, J.C. *The Story of the Brontës.* London: Leonard Parsons, 1925. Reissued, Folcroft, Pennsylvania: Folcroft, 1976.

The book discusses again J. Malham-Dembleby's claim that Charlotte Brontë wrote *Wuthering Heights.*

B345   Yskamp, Claire E. "Character and Voice: First-Person Narrators in *Tom Jones, Wuthering Heights,* and *Second Skin.*" Unpublished doctoral dissertation, Brandeis University, 1972. *DAI,* 32:6948.

"As examples of the diversity of handlings of narration," three novels are studied, among them *Wuthering Heights,* "to illustrate the interaction of the narrator's voice and the narrator's character. As a result of these examinations, one sees how a first-person narrator communicates the novelist's views to the reader."

Criticism of Poetry

B346   Akiho, Shinichi and Takashi Fujita. *Concordance to the Complete Poems of Emily Jane Brontë*. Tokyo: Shohakuska Publishing Company, 1976.

Noted but not inspected.

B347   Altick, Richard D. *Scholar Adventurers*. New York: Macmillan, 1950.

Altick refers to the manuscripts of Emily Brontë poems in their Gondal context. He briefly tells about the Wise doctoring of the juvenilia.

B348   Anon. "Pot-Shooting." *Times Literary Supplement*, April 30, 1949, p. 281.

This is an effort to stop the controversy of letters about "The Visionary," all of which must be based on conjecture.

B349   Anon. "An Unrecovered Poetess." *Times Literary Supplement*, June 10, 1915, p. 189. Reprinted in *Living Age*, 286 (July 24, 1915), 216-222.

During World War I, Emily Brontë's poems were thought to be timely. Here they are compared to those of William Blake. Emily Brontë is criticized for attempting to write "English" poetry, not knowing her true talents. She strove for the "conventional finish" for her poems.

B350   Benson, Arthur C. "Introduction" in *Brontë Poems*. New York: G. P. Putnam's Sons, 1915.

Benson believes that Emily Brontë's genius is "instantly apparent." As a poet, she is clearly superior to her sisters. The critic credits Reverend Brontë's writing of poetry and the books which the Brontës read.

B351   Blondel, Jacques. "Emily Brontë and Emily Dickinson: A Study in Contrasts." *Etudes Brontëennes*. Eds. Jacques Blondel and Jean-Pierre Petit. Paris: Edition Ophrys, 1970.

An article in English points out the differences and similarities in image and intention in the works of these two contemporaries.

B352 Blondel, Jacques. *Emily Brontë: experience spirituelle et création poétique.* [Publications de la Faculté l'Université de Clermont. Série 2, fasc. 3.] Paris: Presses Univérsitaires de France, 1955.

An excellent bibliography, a valid estimate of the Brontës' religious background, and a thorough and competent analysis of Emily Brontë's spiritual experience are combined by this excellent French critic. Her poetry is related to the European mystical tradition.

B353 Bridges, Robert. "The Poems of Emily Brontë." *Times Literary Supplement,* Jan. 12, 1911, pp. 9-11. Reprinted in *Collected Essays,* 9. London: Oxford University Press, 1932.

Here the late poet laureate gives an evaluation of the editions of Emily Brontë's poetry. He praises the poet enthusiastically.

B354 Brown, Helen and J. Mott. "The Gondal Saga." *BST,* 9 (1938), 155-172.

In this early pre-Ratchford study, the editors attempt to find a continuous story in Gondal. They point out that Gondal adventures have three heroines.

B355 Brown, Helen. "The Gondal Saga: Unpublished Verses by Emily Brontë." *Times Literary Supplement,* Feb. 19, 1938, p. 121.

A review of the facts concerning the two unpublished poems found in the Gondal notebook recently presented to the British Museum. She also notes variant forms of the published poems. (See also B356.)

B356 Brown, Helen and Joan Mott, eds. "Introduction" in *Gondal Poems by Emily Jane Brontë: Now Published from the MS. in the British Museum.* Oxford: Shakespeare Head Press, 1938.

The poems in this book are from the notebook presented to the British Museum in 1933, including verses not published prior to this date. The introduction explains the history of the manuscripts and the significance of this material.

B357 Carr, D. R. W. "The Sphinx of English Poetry." *Poetry Review*, 34 (March-April 1943), 85-90.

Carr points out that Emily Brontë was self-contained and was a mystic. Like Emily Dickinson, she was not concerned with publication or worried about posthumous fame.

B358 Chitham, Edward. "Emily Brontë and Shelley." *BST*, 17 (1978), 189-196.

In discussing the "Gondalisation" of all of Emily Brontë's poetry, primarily by Miss Fannie Ratchford, the critic focuses on the poems *not* in the so-called "Gondal Poems" notebook. Chitham concentrates on locating the man addressed in these non-Gondal poems and suggests that these references may indeed be to the poet Shelley. The critic searches out the possibility that Emily Brontë may have read enough about Shelley to feel romantically influenced by him.

B359 Cook, Davidson. "Emily Brontë's Poems: Some Textual Corrections and Unpublished Verses." *Nineteenth Century and After*, 100 (Aug. 1926), 248-262.

The author was allowed to examine the manuscript belonging to the Law collection and found "many differences and discrepancies" between the manuscript poems and the verses then in print. His conclusion: "the imperative need of another new edition of the poems of Emily Jane Brontë."

B360 Daniel-Rops, Henry (pseud. of Jules Charles Henri Petiot). *Where Angels Pass.* Trans. by Emma Crawford. London: Cassell, 1950.

This book, published in French in 1947 as *Où Passent des Anges*, includes a chapter on "Emily Brontë: Poetry and Solitude."

B361 Day-Lewis, C. "Emily Brontë." *Collected Poems.* London: Hogarth Press, 1954.

In his envisioning Emily Brontë, the poet writes: ". . . I roved the heather / Chained to a demon through the shrieking night."

B362   Day-Lewis, Cecil. "Emily Brontë and Freedom." *Notable Images of Virtue*. Toronto: Ryerson Press, 1954.

The poet laureate discusses Emily Brontë, George Meredith and W. B. Yeats, in this lecture. He finds Emily Brontë's poetry the "classic example of the way poetry moves from the particular to the universal."

B363   Day-Lewis, C. "The Poetry of Emily Brontë: A Passion for Freedom." *BST*, 13 (1957), 83-99.

This discussion of Emily Brontë's "passion for freedom" shows that her poetry is related to *Wuthering Heights* and reflects her religious background. Her struggle for freedom results in her use of images of prisoners and exiles. According to this article, "innocence and inspiration are the keynotes of Emily Brontë's best work."

B364   Deacon, Lois. *Poetic Fervour of Emily Brontë and Thomas Hardy*. No. 68, Monographs on the Life, Times and Works of Thomas Hardy. St. Peter Port, Guernsey: Toucan Press, 1971.

The similarities and differences apparent in the work of these two poets.

B365   Dingle, Herbert. "An Examination of Emily Brontë's Poetry from an Unaccustomed Angle." *BST*, 14 (1964), 5-10.

A study of the references to weather, time of day, time of year, and the light as it is described in the poems as compared with the "weather records and astronomical ephemerides" of the days of composition.

B366   Dobson, Mildred A. "Was Emily Brontë a Mystic?" *BST*, 11 (1948), 166-175.

After the critic defines a mystic, she determines that there is insufficient autobiography to support a conclusion about Emily Brontë. She then investigates the possible indications of mysticism within the poems.

B367 Dodds, Madeleine Hope. "Gondaliand." *Modern Language Review,* 18 (Jan. 1923), 9-21.

Written before there was much knowledge about the Gondal writings, this article offers a well-reasoned analysis. It is the first published attempt to link the poems with the Gondal saga. Both the Gondal and the non-Gondal poems are thought to contribute to the literary power which Emily Brontë later shows in *Wuthering Heights.*

B368 Dodds, Madeleine Hope. "The Gondal Poems and Emily Brontë." *Notes and Queries,* 188 (May 5, 1945), 189.

The critic questions Robert Bridges' interpretation of "Tell Me, Tell Me, Smiling Child" and "The Inspiring Music's Thrilling Sound" (B353). Dodds sees them as fragments of Gondal poems.

B369 Dodds, Madeleine Hope. "A Second Visit to Gondaliand." *Modern Language Review,* 21 (1926), 373-379. Revised, *Modern Language Review,* 22 (1927), 197-198.

Further speculations are offered by this critic on the same subject as B367. The second version corrects the attribution of some of the poems.

B370 Donoghue, Denis. "The Other Emily." *The Brontës: A Collection of Critical Essays.* Ed. Ian Gregor. Englewood Cliffs, New Jersey: Prentice-Hall, 1970.

Donoghue feels that in Emily Brontë's poetry every objective image is transformed into spirit. He finds the Gondal saga irrelevant, a smoke screen to cover the poet's real feelings.

B371 Drew, David P. "Emily Brontë and Emily Dickinson as Mystic Poets." *BST,* 15 (1968), 227-232.

The critic sees parallels in character, environment, and poetry of the two poets. The common theme for both poets is the expression of mystic experience.

B372   Eaubonne, Francoise d'. *Emily Brontë*. Paris: P. Seghers, 1964.

Part of the series "poètes d'aujourd'hui" (poets of today).

B373   Elton, Oliver. "Emily Brontë." *The English Muse.* London: Bell and Sons, 1933.

A brief analysis of Emily Brontë's poetry.

B374   Friesner, Donald N. "Ellis Bell and Israfel." *BST,* 14 (1964), 11-18.

This article compares the lives and poems of Emily Brontë and Poe.

B375   Garnett, R. "Commentary" in A. H. Miles. *Poets and Poetry of the Century.* London: Hutchinson and Company, 1891.

An early appraisal of some of Emily Brontë's poems.

B376   Grierson, H. J. C. and J. C. Smith. "Emily Brontë." *A Critical History of English Poetry.* New York: Oxford University Press, 1946.

This study looks at the poetry and talents of Emily Brontë and concludes that she is "more intense, if less variously accomplished than Mrs. Browning."

B377   Grove, Robin. "It Would Not Do: Emily Brontë as Poet." *The Art of Emily Brontë.* Ed. Anne Smith. London: Vision Press, 1976.

Grove proposes that the formulaic sufferings are in fact ways of allowing little access to the "real" self, a device for "sealing-off the self from the demands of the adult world." Emily Brontë believed that female power exists in passivity, "a figure resting but transfixed"; therefore, she is concerned with time, especially the past.

B378   Hartley, Leslie P. "Emily Brontë in Gondal and Gaaldine." *BST,* 14 (1965), 1-15. Reprinted in *The Novelist's Responsibility.* London: Hamish Hamilton, 1967.

Hartley suggests that *Wuthering Heights* presents "the dilemma of the soul." Some of the poems offer visions of lost happiness. The poet seems unhappy and possibly misanthropic.

B379   Hatfield, C. W. "Introduction" in *The Complete Poems of Emily Jane Brontë*. New York: Columbia University Press, 1941.

In introducing this definitive collection of poetry, the editor explains about the various manuscripts and the division of the material, as he sees it, into Gondal and non-Gondal subject matter. Vol. also listed as B15.

B380   Hatfield, C. W. "Preface" in *The Complete Poems of Emily Jane Brontë*. Ed. Clement Shorter. London: Hodder and Stoughton, 1923.

Not really the "complete" poems, but the most valuable collection at that time. Hatfield presents the poems, gives some detail about the ambiance in which they were written. Vol. also listed as B12.

B381   Henderson, Philip. "Introduction" in *Emily Brontë: Selected Poems*. London: Lawson and Dunn, 1947.

This inexpensive edition of the poems was very welcome at the time of publication. It includes explication of themes. The editor says that Emily Brontë's poetry "explores those regions known to readers of St. John of the Cross as the Dark Night of the Soul."

B382   Leavis, F. R. "Reality and Sincerity: An Exercise in Critical Comparison." *Scrutiny*, 19 (Winter 1952-1953), 90-98.

A comparison of "Cold in the Earth" with Hardy's "After the Journey." In speaking of the "great advantage in reality," Leavis concludes that "Emily Brontë's poem is a striking one, but . . . she is dramatizing herself in a situation such as she has clearly not known in actual experience: what she offers is betrayingly less real" than Hardy's poem.

B383   Lewis, Naomi. "Introduction" in *Emily Brontë: A Peculiar Music: Poems for Young Readers*. London: The Bodley Head, 1971.

175

In introducing these twenty-nine poems and diary letters, the editor suggests that there can be Gondal and non-Gondal messages, both in one poem.

B384   Maurer, K. W. "The Poetry of Emily Brontë." *Anglia*, 49 (June 1937), 442-448.

Maurer finds much of the poetry full of intense suffering caused by the closeness of Emily Brontë to Branwell. Some poems, however, barely escape "insipidity and flatness."

B385   Mew, Charlotte. "The Poems of Emily Brontë." *Temple Bar*, 130 (July 1904), 153-167.

Emily Brontë's poems (and *Wuthering Heights*) show what she might have become. *Wuthering Heights* shows her as a "great artist and a repulsive woman" while in her poetry "sweeter and lighter fancies" peer out.

B386   Miles, Rosalind. "A Baby-God: the Creative Dynamism of Emily Brontë's Poetry." *The Art of Emily Brontë*. Ed. Anne Smith. London: Vision Press, 1976.

This article touches on the quality of Emily Brontë's poems while maintaining that all the inhabitants of Emily Brontë's created world are aspects of herself.

B387   Moore, T. Sturge. "Beyond East and West: A Re-interpretation of Emily Brontë." *Asiatic Review*, 37 (Oct. 1941), 810-816.

An Eastern view of Emily Brontë is presented here with special attention given to her poetry. Moore compares her poetry to that of Blake.

B388   Morgan, Edwin. "Women and Poetry." *Cambridge Journal*, 3. (Aug. 1950), 643-673.

Emily Brontë is said to be the greatest of all women poets because she is not influenced by anyone in the literary world. Her physical isolation let her concentrate on her own inner world. Morgan discusses her poetry and its relation to the Gondal saga.

B389   Raine, Kathleen M. "Books in General." *New Statesman and Nation,* March 8, 1952, pp. 227-228.

What begins as a review of Philip Henderson's edition of *The Complete Poems of Emily Brontë* (Folio Society) continues as a clear view of Emily Brontë as poet. The critic sees the poet's greatness resulting from "two unique qualities – her total truthfulness and her capacity to imagine beyond her own experience."

B390   Ratchford, Fannie E. "The Gondal Story" in *The Complete Poems of Emily Jane Brontë.* Ed. C. W. Hatfield. New York: Columbia University Press, 1941.

Ratchford's is the strongest voice to declare that Emily Brontë's poems are not subjective; "the majority, perhaps all of them, pertain to . . . Gondal." We are presented here with the chronological outline of Gondal events. The poems are arranged as if they were all part of the epic of Gondal.

B391   Ratchford, Fannie E. *Gondal's Queen: A Novel in Verse by Emily Jane Brontë.* Austin: University of Texas Press, 1955.

Here Miss Ratchford attempts to create an epic from the fragmented literary remains of Gondal. Her hypothesis: all poems relate to Gondal. Here the plot is carried by the poems as Miss Ratchford arranges them, with her prose passages to maintain continuity. Her conclusion is that there is just one heroine in Gondal who goes by many names.

B392   Ratchford, Fannie E. *Two Poems* ("Love's Rebuke" and "Remembrance ") *by Emily Brontë: with the Gondal Background of her Poems and Novel.* Austin: Charles E. Martin Jr., 1934.

These two poems are seen as the key to all of Emily Brontë's works. They deal with the basis of the problem proposed: first the lover's accusation and then the sweetheart's response. They are the essence of Gondal, which was Emily Brontë's whole life. The poems which reveal this tale are closely related to *Wuthering Heights.*

177

B393 Ratchford, Fannie E. "War in Gondal: Emily Brontë's Last Poem."
      The Trollopian, 2 (Dec. 1947), 137-155.

      The war in Gondal shows Emily Brontë's hatred of war in the
      "vivid, gory imagery."

B394 Roseveare, Austin. "The Poetry of Emily Brontë." *Poetry Review*
      (London), 9 (Sept.-Oct. 1918), 257-267.

      Roseveare discusses the basic elements of Emily Brontë's poetry:
      its form and content, and the emotional response which it evokes.
      He feels that the poems are "natural," yet the sentences within the
      poems "lead one's thoughts literally towards infinity."

B395 Samaan, Angele Botros. "Themes of Emily Brontë's Poetry." *Cairo
      Studies in English.* Ed. Magdi Wahba, (1959), 118-134.

      According to this critic, all the poems, whether Gondal or
      non-Gondal in subject matter, have the "general feeling of desolation,
      loneliness, darkness, and gloom."

B396 Schmidt, Emily Tresselt. "From Highland to Lowland: Charlotte
      Brontë's Editorial Changes in Emily's Poems." *BST,* 15 (1968),
      221-226.

      When Charlotte Brontë edited the poetry for the 1846 *Poems*
      by the Bells, she made certain changes in Emily's poetry which they
      must have discussed and agreed upon. In 1850, however, after Emily's
      death, the changes Charlotte Brontë made were extensive and on her
      own authority. Charlotte was not the greater poet of the two. This
      critic mentions that one of the most apparent changes was the removal
      of references to Gondal. These changes resulted in making the poems
      tamer and more conventional.

B397 Sitwell, Edith in L. P. Hartley. "Emily Brontë in Gondal and
      Gaaldine." *BST,* 14 (1965), 1-15 (A348).

      Edith Sitwell states strongly how she feels about Emily Brontë:
      "I reverence that great woman, I genuflect at the mention of her
      name but I do not care for her poetry." She says she does not believe
      the emotions in "Cold in the Earth" are "genuine."

B398   Sonnino, Gorgina. "Il Pensiero Religioso di una Poetessa Inglese."
        Nuova Antologia (Roma), quarta serie, Jan.-Feb. 1904.

        A discussion of Emily Brontë's religious thoughts as they are
        evident in her poetry. Noted but not inspected.

B399   Spark, Muriel. "Introduction" in *A Selection of Poems by Emily Jane
        Brontë.* London: Grey Walls Press, 1952.

        This essay by the discerning Miss Spark is based on Swinburne's
        note concerning the three most important factors in Emily Brontë's
        poems: (1) her instinctiveness, (2) evidences of primitive
        nature-worship, and (3) the passion she voices.

B400   Spurgeon, Caroline. *Mysticism in English Literature.* Cambridge
        Manuals of Science and Literature. Cambridge: Cambridge
        University Press, 1913.

        It is the opinion of this critic that Emily Brontë might figure
        among the "intellectual mystics" of the world.

B401   Starzyk, Lawrence J. "Emily Brontë: Poetry in a Mingled Tone."
        Criticism, 14 (Spring 1972), 119-136.

        Starzyk believes that Emily Brontë's poetry must lead us to
        certain definite conclusions: that identity is not to be found in nature,
        God, love, or the soul, but that identity is established only in defiance
        of death. "The will to be is satisfied only in the moment of
        annihilation."

B402   Starzyk, Lawrence J. "The Faith of Emily Brontë's Immortality
        Creed." *Victorian Poetry,* 11 (1973), 295-305.

        The imortality of the soul is declared by Emily Brontë in "No
        Coward Soul is Mine," this critic feels. The remarkable poetic
        statement was made by the poet without traditional faith to support
        her and in full consciousness of the changing world in which she
        found herself.

B403   Symons, Arthur. "Introduction" in *Poems of Emily Brontë*. London: Heinemann, 1906.

Symons especially admires Emily Brontë's poetic intensity in expressing "a sense . . . of the pain and ineradicable sting of personal identity." He finds her to be a tragic poet whose "every poem is as if torn from her."

B404   Untermeyer, Louis. *Makers of the Modern World: The Lives of Ninety-Two Writers, Artists, Scientists, etc., and Other Creators Who Formed the Pattern of Our Century.* New York: Simon and Schuster, 1955.

The popularizer and poetic anthologizer gives praise to Emily Brontë by comparing her to Emily Dickinson in referring to the "inner knowledge" which they both have. He speculates about an unknown which must remain a question: how much of their writing is based on experience and how much on imagination?

B405   Vaynes Van Brakell Buys, Willem Rudolf de. *Drie dichteressen uit het Victoriaanse tijperk: Christina Rossetti, Emily Brontë, Elizabeth Barrett Browning.* Amsterdam: H. J. W. Becht, 1947.

A comparison of the three Victorian women poets, Christina Rossetti, Emily Brontë, and Elizabeth Barrett Browning.

B406   Vivante, Lello. *English Poetry and its Contribution to the Knowledge of a Creative Principle.* London: Faber and Faber, 1950.

A three-page chapter, "Emily Jane Brontë," discusses her seriousness in relation to the creative history of poetry. This volume has an introduction by T. S. Eliot.

B407   Willy, Margaret. "Emily Brontë, Poet and Mystic." *English*, 6 (Autumn 1946), 117-122.

One of the few serious studies of the tone and metaphysical content of Emily Brontë's poetry, this article offers evidence of the poet's mysticism. The critic feels that the influences on Emily

Brontë's poetry are easily discerned: the moors and the solitude of her life, the imaginative outlet in her juvenilia, and her devotion toward her brother Branwell. The critic points to the tension established in her poetry between an expressed death-wish and an apparent love-of-life.

B408   Willy, Margaret. "The Poetry of Emily Dickinson." *Essays and Studies 1957.* London: John Murray, 1957.

In her treatment of Emily Dickinson, the critic compares her with Emily Brontë. She is one of the early scholars to sense Emily Brontë's influence on Emily Dickinson. (See also B357 and B404.)

B409   Woodhouse, A. S. P. "Victorians" in *The Poet and His Faith.* Chicago: University of Chicago Press, 1965.

Noted but not inspected.

B410   Wordsworth, Jonathan. "Wordsworth and the Poetry of Emily Brontë." *BST,* 16 (1972), 85-100.

A Wordsworth family member speaks knowingly about the "affinities" between William Wordsworth and Emily Brontë. Both write about "passionately held beliefs" and "far-reaching assertions." The critic reminds us that poetic lines open up as they are read. He gives a close reading of "Why ask to know the date — the clime" and "The Prisoner." He approaches the poetry simply as the poet wrote it, giving it a serious Gondal reading, with no concession to any possible personal message.

181

Criticism of Other Writings

B411   Bracco, Edgar Jean. "Emily Brontë's Second Novel." *BST,* 15 (1966), 29-33.

   The author cites the evidence. Newby wrote to inquire about the progress of Ellis Bell's "second novel." Charlotte Brontë's letters refer to Ellis Bell's "second work" and comment that Emily is "too ill to occupy herself with writing."

B412   Isenberg, David R. "A Gondal Fragment." *BST,* 14 (1962), 24-26.

   A report of Emily Brontë's holographic fragment: a 4½" x 3½" note listing the heights and characteristics of Gondal characters. The article suggests that a comparison between these characters and those in *Wuthering Heights* may prove rewarding.

B413   Lane, Margaret. "The Mysterious Genius of Emily Brontë" in *Purely for Pleasure.* New York: Alfred A. Knopf, 1967.

   This extremely readable article discusses the five French essays recently published. The critic gives the locations of the manuscripts and discusses the content and meaning of the three most significant essays: "The Cat," "The Butterfly," and "The Palace of Death."

B414   Lemon, Charles. "Emily Brontë's Missing Novel." *Times Literary Supplement,* March 17, 1966, p. 223 (Letter to the Editor).

   This Brontë authority suggests that the Newby letter may very well have been a carelessness, as he may have addressed Ellis when he was actually intending to reach Acton Bell, who was then working on her second novel.

B415   Paden, William Doremus. *An Investigation of Gondal.* New York: Bookman Associates, 1958.

   A modern scholar looks into the relationship between Gondal and *Wuthering Heights,* finding the early narrative "extensive, elaborate, and mildly suggestive of the narrative pattern of *Wuthering Heights.*" He disagrees with some of Fannie Ratchford's beliefs, offering a genealogical diagram of the complex interrelationships.

B416   Ratchford, Fannie E. "Introduction and Notes" in Emily Jane Brontë. *Five Essays Written in French*. Translated, Lorine White Nagel. Austin: University of Texas Press, 1948.

Miss Ratchford points out that these essays are autobiographical, giving us a self-portrait by Emily Brontë. The introduction helps to explain when the essays were written and why they were written. Two of the original manuscripts are now in the Bonnell Collection in the Brontë Parsonage Museum, two in the Berg Collection in the New York Public Library, and one in the Stark Collection, University of Texas.

B417   Willson, Jo Anne A. "'The Butterfly' and *Wuthering Heights*: A Mystic's Eschatology." *Victorian Newsletter*, 33 (Spring 1968), 22-25.

The critic has made a careful comparison between Emily Brontë's essay and *Wuthering Heights*. She finds that both are based on perception, not reason. Both examine the forces of good and evil and try to discover the reason for evil on earth. Emily Brontë concludes that every evil has "the seed for that divine harvest." The critic approached this analysis in the hope "that the 'why' of *Wuthering Heights* may be found in one of the five seldom-discussed essays" from Emily Brontë's school days at the Heger Pensionnat in 1842.

B418   Abercrombie, Lascelles. "The Brontës Today." *BST,* 6 (1924), 179-200.

At this early day Abercrombie was certain of "the unquestionable supremacy of Emily Brontë." He particularly admires the "perfect coherence of purpose" of *Wuthering Heights.*

B419   Aiken, Ralph. "Wild-heart: An Appreciation of Emily Jane Brontë." *South Atlantic Quarterly,* 34 (April 1935), 202-210.

B420   Andrews, W. L. "Our Greatest Woman." *BST,* 10 (1945), 288-289. Reprinted in *The Brontës Then and Now.* Shipley: Outhwaite Brothers, 1947.

In commenting on Emily Brontë's reputation among men of letters, Andrews says that she was esteemed by Alexander Woollcott, who quoted James M. Barrie who once called her "our greatest woman."

B421   Anon. "Emily Brontë." *Times Literary Supplement,* (pre Jan. 30, 1909). Reprinted in *Living Age,* 260 (Jan. 30, 1909), 302-308.

In discussing the "enigma of Emily," this critic suggests that we are able to see her partially but accurately through her poetry. He suggests that the power of *Wuthering Heights* lies in the fact that the author gives us "threadbare truth unadorned by any 'romantic beauty' of landscape."

B422   Anon. "'The Splendid Isolation' of Emily Brontë." *Current Literature,* 40 (May 1906), 512.

A review of nineteenth-century criticism.

B423   Bald, Marjorie. *Women Writers of the Nineteenth Century.* Cambridge: Cambridge University Press, 1923.

Included in this discussion is an estimate of the effect of Emily Brontë's poetry and her novel on her readers.

B424   Bayne, Peter. *Essays in Biography and Criticism.* First Series. Boston: Gould and Lincoln, 1857.

This early biographer-critic declares that Emily Brontë is "one of the most extraordinary women that ever lived." He finds her to be much more talented than Charlotte Brontë. He considers *Wuthering Heights* "a work containing evidence of powers it were perhaps impossible to estimate." Her poetry is also impressive, "characterized by strength and freshness." In her poetry he found an altogether new quality, what he calls "power of melody, which be it wild or tender, or even harsh, was never heard before."

B425   Bell, Vereen M. "Character and Point of View in Representative Victorian Novels." Unpublished doctoral dissertation, Duke University, 1959. *DAI,* 20:3740.

Wuthering Heights is one of the six novels considered. It is said to be remarkable for Emily Brontë's "introspective method of presenting characters." Emily Brontë's style and approach to writing are considered. The critic remarks that the characters are known to the reader intellectually, but not through the senses.

B426   Blondel, Jacques. "Emily Brontë: Récentes Explorations." *Etudes anglaises,* 11 (Oct.-Dec. 1958), 323-330.

Professor Blondel, eminent Brontë scholar, here gives an overview of what had then been going on in Brontë scholarship.

B427   Bloomer, Nancy Hester. "Despair and Love in the Works of Emily Jane Brontë." Unpublished doctoral dissertation, State University of New York at Buffalo, 1976. *DAI,* 37:5135.

"This thesis is a study of Emily Brontë's passage through despair as revealed in her poetry and one novel *Wuthering Heights.* The profound spiritual dislocation which is at the center of her art has its roots in her concept of love and the theology of Eros."

B428   Bradby, Godfrey Fox. "Emily Brontë" in *Nineteenth Century Fiction,* 108 (Oct. 1930), 533-540. Reprinted in *The Brontës and Other Essays.* London: Oxford University Press, 1937.

Bradby believes that the Romantic poet who influenced Emily Brontë was Shelley. Not only her novel but primarily her poetry shows a yearning for an all-consuming love and speaks of the loneliness which she felt.

B429   Brown, Helen. "The Influence of Byron on Emily Brontë." *Modern Language Review,* 34 (1939), 374-381.

Helen Brown, an acknowledged authority on Emily Brontë's poetry, speaks here of the overall influence of Byron on Emily Brontë. Particularly in her poetry a reader can sense Byronic mood, cadence, and "movement of verse." Byron is thought to be responsible for her "tragic imaginings."

B430   Buchen, Irving H. "Emily Brontë and the Metaphysics of Childhood and Love." *Nineteenth Century Fiction,* 22 (June 1967), 63-70.

This critic finds *Wuthering Heights* to be a story of childhood and "paradise lost and regained." Incorporating a wholly Romantic vision of the innocence of childhood, Emily Brontë creates a new kind of novel. The critic suggests a valid approach to understanding *Wuthering Heights* by first reading "the poems in their own light" and then reading *"Wuthering Heights* in the light of the poems."

B431   Bullock, F. A. "The Genius of Emily Brontë." *BST,* 9 (1937), 115-128.

In the 'thirties, when psychological criticism was being unleashed on *Wuthering Heights,* this critic stated his objection to those who attempted to analyze Emily Brontë through her novel. He pleads for an objective approach to *Wuthering Heights,* which he says will then yield knowledge of "the structure of reality."

B432   Clarke, Isobel Constance. "The Enigma of Emily Brontë." *Fortnightly Review,* 124 (Aug. 1928), 195-202.

The critic attempts to shed some light on the complex personality and talents of Emily Brontë. Among other things, she proposes that Ruysbrocck, whose work Emily Brontë read in Brussels, should be considered as a possible source for *Wuthering Heights.*

B433   Cooper, Dorothy J. "The Romantics and Emily Brontë." *BST*, 12 (1952), 106-112.

Of all the writers Emily Brontë read, Byron had the greatest influence on her, according to Cooper. Emily Brontë was a "rebel against dependence." She was like Wordsworth in one way: she sensed and understood the power of nature. She had no dreams of the medieval past and lacked many other traits of the Romantics. Her ultimate tone was not Romanticism but a "genuine sadness of soul."

B434   Dingle, Herbert. *The Mind of Emily Brontë.* London: Martin Brian and O'Keefe, 1974.

In considering Emily Brontë as a novelist and a poet, the critic enumerates her qualities of mind: her conscientiousness, her application of energy and attention, her willingness to face truth and delineate it. In a novel which uses the moors as ambiance, they "are left almost entirely unpictured" while the reader learns in detail about the characters and their homes. Of the author's attitude toward the characters in *Wuthering Heights* the critic observes: "She herself stood outside and recorded their activities without censure or praise, portraying but not judging." Dingle also examines the poetry with attention to the weather on the date of composition. (See also B365.)

B435   Donoghue, Denis. "Emily Brontë: On the Latitude of Interpretation." *Harvard English Studies,* 1 (1970), 105-133.

Stressing the importance of identifying the genre of *Wuthering Heights*, the critic deals first with Emily Brontë's poetry, showing that the poet's imagination maintains itself "at the center of its circle" in these poems of soliloquy. He then discusses the latitude of interpretation by various critics over the years, concluding that in his analysis the novel-romance of Emily Brontë centers in the Catherine-Heathcliff alliance, as they "are leagued against all the other characters."

B436   Doyle, Louis F. "Of Something That Is Gone." *America,* 77 (June 14, 1947), 297-298.

This article points out that it was Emily Brontë's inexperience in the world which enabled her to write *Wuthering Heights.* The critic feels that she melts experience and imagination "in the crucible of the creative faculty until it is workable."

B437   Escoube, Lucienne. *Emily Brontë et ses démons.* Paris et Clermont: Fernand Serlot, 1941.

This French critic discusses "Emily Brontë and her demons."

B438   Evans, Margiad. "Byron and Emily Brontë: An Essay." *Life and Letters,* 47 (June 1948), 193-216.

Emily Brontë was a mystic like Byron – especially as he was just before he died. The critic compares various aspects of the poets: their poetry, philosophies, and religions and their diction. He finds that Manfred was like Heathcliff, though Byron's character seems to have more humanity. The critic suggests that the clue to Emily Brontë's life and writing is her "pacifism toward death." He speaks of her "reunion with the Absolute." The third section of the article is especially noteworthy.

B439   Fréchet, René. "Emily Brontë et son élan mystique." *Foi education,* 27 (1957), 95-103.

Here is a French critic's discussion of Blondel's "Emily Brontë . . . et ses experiences spirituelles" (B352).

B440   Haldane, R. B. "Emily Brontë's Place in Literature." *BST,* 2 (May 1901), 142-150.

Haldane declares that Emily was the real poet among the sisters: "Emily must be placed not only above Charlotte, but with Shakespeare and Milton." Such admiration for Emily was not common at the turn of the century.

B441   Hardy, Barbara. "The Lyricism of Emily Brontë." *The Art of Emily Brontë.* Ed. Anne Smith. London: Vision Press, 1976.

This eminent authority on the nineteenth century looks closely at the quality of Emily Brontë's expression, citing the lyric isolation, the exaggerated intensity, and the poet's frustrated movement toward knowledge. She speaks of Emily Brontë's use of "the enclosure and refusal to tell."

B442 Hawkes, Jacquetta. "Emily Brontë in the Natural Scene." *BST,* 12 (1953), 173-186.

This article points to the opposition of heredity and environment in Emily Brontë. Her Celtic heritage made her alien to the moors. Her poetry contrasts dark and light: this critic sees the dark as the moors.

B443 Hawkes, Jacquetta. "The Haworth Moors." *Spectator,* 190 (May 1953), 600.

Writing again about the negative force of the moors in Emily Brontë's writing (see B442), the critic discusses the setting of *Wuthering Heights* and the environment of the poetry. She sees a contrast between the moorlands and the light valley. (In answer to this, in the same issue of *Spectator,* B. Scholfield disagrees, pointing out the modern qualities of Haworth in the Brontë's time — with a daily newspaper and train to London — and suggesting instead: "let the moorlands stand for light.")

B444 Hewish, John. *Emily Brontë: a Critical and Biographical Study.* London: Macmillan, 1969.

A thoroughly researched study, this book covers Emily Brontë's life, her novel, and the response of her contemporaries as well as more recent scholars. It shows the climate of her environment, at home and in her brief ventures into the larger world.

B445 House, Roy T. "Emily Brontë." *The Nation,* 107 (Aug. 17, 1918), 169-170.

At the time of publication (one hundred years after Emily Brontë's birth on August 20, 1818), this article comments that *Jane Eyre* is widely read, *Wuthering Heights* "nearly forgotten." Emily Brontë was then considered, at least by this critic, to be a "poet turned novelist."

B446   Jaloux, Edmond. "Le Mystère d'Emily Brontë." *D'Eschyle à Giraudoux.* Paris: Librairie Universelle de France, 1947.

Another French critic looks into the "mystery" of Emily Brontë.

B447   Jennings, Elizabeth. "Introduction" in Emily Brontë. *Wuthering Heights and Selected Poems.* London: Pan Books, 1967.

Wuthering Heights, which "does almost all the forbidden things as far as nineteenth-century fiction is concerned," is brought off by the force of vision of its dynamic author. Jennings feels that the true nature of Emily Brontë is revealed through her poetry.

B448   Klingopulos, G. D. "The Literary Scene" in *From Dickens to Hardy.* Vol. 6 of *The Pelican Guide to English Literature.* Ed. Boris Ford. Harmondsworth, Middlesex: Penguin, 1958.

Emily Brontë's poetry is based on "the stress of personal experience." She "wrote some things," according to this critic, "which set her quite above the range of other Victorian poets." She is further discussed in considering her position among Romantic and Victorian writers as Klingopulos gives a general sweep through the whole literary scene.

B449   Lane, Margaret. "Introduction" in Emily Brontë. *Wuthering Heights with Selected Poems.* Ed. Philip Henderson. London: J. M. Dent and Sons, 1957.

Although this Brontë authority admits that most of Emily Brontë's poems are of no great worth, she declares that a few are as beautiful as any in our language. Furthermore, *Wuthering Heights* is one "long intoxicating poem." It is this critic's belief that the power in the novel lies in the love of Catherine and Heathcliff. Vol. also listed as B207.

B450   Leavis, F. R. *The Common Pursuit.* Harmondsworth, Middlesex: Penguin, 1952.

Leavis, one of the *Scrutiny* critics, offers this excellent evaluation of such writers as Jane Austen, George Eliot, James, Conrad, Lawrence — all praised for their "form and method." It is a comment indeed that he merely mentions Emily Brontë in a brief note.

B451   Levin, Harry. "Janes and Emilies, Or the Novelist as Heroine."
        Southern Review (Baton Rouge, Louisiana), n.s. 1 (Oct. 1965),
        735-753.

        A discussion of women authors versus men authors, in which
        Emily Brontë is said to have identified herself with Heathcliff.

B452   MacCarthy, B. G. "Emily Brontë." *Studies: An Irish Quarterly
        Review,* 39 (March 1950), 15-30.

        This "appreciation" of the author avoids analysis or scholarship,
        but voices approval of this "poet-mystic of the natural order."

B453   Mirsky, Prince D. S. "Emily Brontë." *London Mercury,* 7 (Jan. 1923),
        266-272.

        Prince Mirsky contrasts Emily Brontë and Charlotte Brontë,
        considering their personality and first novels. It is the "spiritual
        intensity" and "artistic efficiency" of *Wuthering Heights* which
        distinguish it from other novels.

B454   Moers, Ellen. *Literary Women: the Great Writers.* Garden City, New
        York: Doubleday, 1976; London: W. H. Allen, 1977.

        Emily Brontë, who does not fit the usual pattern of feminist
        writers, is referred to as a writer for whom "women's literature has
        mattered hardly at all." Moers sees *Wuthering Heights* as a novel about
        "a girl's childhood and the adult woman's tragic yearning to return
        to it." Vol. also listed as A314.

B455   Morgan, Charles. "Emily Brontë" in the *Times Literary Supplement,*
        (pre-1932). Reprinted in *Great Victorians.* Eds. H. J. Massingham
        and Hugh Massingham. London: Nicholson and Watson, 1932.

        This objective discussion of Emily Brontë gives little biography,
        but a conjectural musing about her. Morgan discusses the two phases
        of her life: the domestic, known to Charlotte Brontë and revealed
        by her, and the mystic, which we sense in her poetry and in *Wuthering
        Heights.*

B456   Neufeldt, Victor. "Emily Brontë and the Responsible Imagination."
        Victorian Newsletter, 43 (Spring 1973), 15-21.

> Neufeldt has come to a conclusion about the relationship
> between the Gondal saga and *Wuthering Heights.* The earlier writing
> represents ten years of escapism. In a supreme effort to face up to
> the "responsible imagination," Emily Brontë abandoned the security
> of fantasy and wrote *Wuthering Heights* in an effort to come to terms
> with reality.

B457   Ocampo, Victoria. *Emily Brontë: Terra Incognita.* Buenos Aires: Sur,
        1938.

> Noted but not inspected.

B458   Ohmann, Carol. "Emily Brontë in the Hands of Male Critics." *College
        English,* 32 (May 1971), 906-913.

> Ms. Ohmann suggests that the earlier critics and present-day male
> critics such as Schorer and Moser see what they see in *Wutheirng
> Heights* because of what they assume or know about the author's
> sex.

B459   Oram, Eanne. "Emily and F. D. Maurice: Some Parallels of Thought."
        BST, 13 (1957), 131-140.

> Oram points out the similarities between Maurice's philosophy
> and that expressed by Emily Brontë in her poetry and in *Wuthering
> Heights.*

B460   Petit, Jean-Pierre. "Emily Brontë: la vision et les thèmes."
        Unpublished doctoral dissertation, University of
        Clermont-Ferrand, March 8, 1975.

> This dissertation covers both *Wuthering Heights* and the poetry
> of Emily Brontë.

B461   Petit, Jean-Pierre. "Preface" in *Emily Brontë: A Critical Anthology.*
        Harmondsworth, Middlesex: Penguin, 1973.

In discussing the shift in criticism over the years, Petit points to the contrast of appreciation, indicating that the power of *Wuthering Heights* has always been acknowledged but that contemporaneous critics rejected the novel "on grounds of taste and ethics."

B462 Powys, John Cowper. "Emily Brontë: *Wuthering Heights*" in *Suspended Judgments: Essays on Books and Sensations.* New York: G. Arnold Shaw, 1916. Reprinted in *Essays on Emily Brontë and Henry James.* Girard, Kansas: Haldeman-Julius, 1923.

B463 Ratchford, Fannie E. "Biography" in Emily Brontë. *Wuthering Heights.* New York: Harper and Row, 1965.

After a brief biography of the Brontë family, Miss Ratchford discusses the novels, stating that *Jane Eyre* grew out of Angria and *Wuthering Heights* grew out of Gondal. She also gives the history of the publication of *Wuthering Heights* and Emily Brontë's poems, and names the major critics of the novel.

B464 Rébora, Victoria. "Emily Brontë." *I Libri del Giorno.* (Nov. 1926).

Noted but not inspected.

B465 Sinclair, May. "Introduction" in Emily Brontë. *Wuthering Heights.* London: J. M. Dent and Sons, 1921.

In this introduction, Emily Brontë is compared with Charlotte Brontë as to personality, fame, and authorship. This Brontë enthusiast then states that Emily Brontë's poems are the precursors of *Wuthering Heights*: the "vision of life as she wished it."

B466 Smith, J. C. "Emily Brontë: a Reconstruction." *Essays and Studies by Members of the English Association.* Ed. O. Elton. Oxford: Clarendon Press, 1914.

A new understanding of Emily Brontë's underlying impetus is reached by Smith through an analysis of the 1910 edition of her *Complete Poems* which, he feels, clarifies the Gondal saga. He believes that when she wrote "A Farewell to Gondal" she was signaling an

end to fantasy and a readiness to face reality in *Wuthering Heights.*
He comments favorably on the mystic qualities of the novel.

B467   Spark, Muriel, and Derek Stanford. *Emily Brontë: Her Life and Work.*
London: Peter Owen, 1953.

A two-part study separates biography from criticism. In Part I,
Spark presents a biography in which she tries to distinguish between
fact and legend. Among the "facts" is the suggestion that Emily
Brontë was mentally unbalanced by 1847. Part II gives a review of
criticism up to that date, including material on the novel, poetry,
and on Emily Brontë herself.

B468   Steen, Ellisiv. "Problemet Emily Brontë." *Edda* (Oslo), 49 (1949).

Noted but not inspected.

B469   Stephens, Margaret Adele West. "Mysticism in the Works of Emily
Jane Brontë." Unpublished doctoral dissertation, Case Western
Reserve University, 1970. *DAI,* 31:2890.

"Both in the poetry and the novel, there is an intense drive
to complete the self outside the self, either in another person or
in God as in Emily's mystical quest through much of her life. Her
works are a detailed description of her pursuit of the spiritual life,
often to the exclusion of the material world."

B470   Veges, G."Emily Brontë." *L'Information Littéraire,* 19 (1968), 68-70.

B471   Williams, A. M. "Emily Brontë." *Our Early Female Novelists and
Other Essays.* Glasgow: J. MacLehose and Sons, 1904.

This early critic of Emily Brontë discusses the writer as a person
as well as commenting on her works. He believes that her early
association with such story-tellers as her father, Aunt Branwell, and
Tabby helped form her writing, as did her feelings toward the moors.
Emily Brontë's poetry, while often formless and gloomy, is full of
a grandeur of thought. The characters in *Wuthering Heights* make
it memorable, as this critic is repulsed by the story. Her feeling for
nature and her pensiveness give quality to her work.

194

B472   Wilson, David. "Emily Brontë, First of the Moderns." *Modern Quarterly Miscellany,* 1 (1947).

Here is a 1947 presentation of the style and theme of Emily Brontë's writing which indicate the modern nature of her approach. Heathcliff is shown as a member of the working class and Catherine is shown to be a sympathizer with his cause.

Textual Criticism

B473   Anon. "A First Edition of *Wuthering Heights.*" *BST,* 14 (1964), 50.

This article describes a copy of Newby's 1847 edition of *Wuthering Heights* with penciled corrections in the first volume. These corrections are believed to be Charlotte Brontë's. The book was sold at auction in July of 1964.

B474   Cook, Davidson. "Brontë Manuscripts in the Law Collection." *The Bookman* (London), 69 (Nov. 1925), 100-104.

Here is a discussion of this collection which has Emily Brontë's poems and her 1841 "diary," a collection which Cook was invited to inspect.

B475   Kite, J. F. *"Wuthering Heights"* (Letter to the Editor). *Times Literary Supplement,* March 16, 1951, p. 165.

The owner of a first edition of *Wuthering Heights* with penciled corrections states that the handwriting has been identified by Thomas J. Wise as being that of Emily Brontë. These corrections were not adhered to by Charlotte Brontë in her preparation of the 1850 edition. Kite was later quoted in *Sunday Times* (Sept. 26, 1954) as believing that this copy was used by Shorter in preparing *Wuthering Heights* (B4).

B476   Marsden, Hilda and Ian Jack. "Introduction" in Emily Brontë. *Wuthering Heights.* London: Oxford University Press, 1976.

The editors, in explaining their own textual problems, give a descriptive list of the editions published between 1847 and 1857.

B477   Parrish, M. L. "Adventures in Reading and Collecting Victorian Fiction." *Princeton University Library Chronicle,* 3 (Feb. 1942), 33-44.

This article, intended for book collectors, points out that *Wuthering Heights* is "one of the scarcest books in Victorian fiction."

Biography
Emily Brontë as a Person

B478   A., W. L. [W. L. Andrews?] "An Emily Brontë Excursion, 1968." *BST*, 15 (1968), 262.

The article describes a Brontë Society visit to Law Hill House, to Shibden Hall (suggested as the model for Thrushcross Grange) and to the site of High Sunderland Hall (possibly the model for Wuthering Heights), destroyed in 1950.

B479   Allen, H. Merian. "Emily Brontë — One Hundred Years After." *Education*, 39 (Dec. 1918), 225-230.

The author suggests that a loveless childhood helped to produce *Wuthering Heights*.

B480   Anon. "Emily Brontë: 1818-1848" in Emily Brontë. *Wuthering Heights*. Boston: Houghton Mifflin, 1965.

This brief biographical introduction suggests the intense emotion in Emily Brontë which may have been caused by the tuberculosis which she suffered.

B481   Barker, Ernest. "The Inspiration of Emily Brontë." *BST*, 12 (1951), 3-9.

The critic proposes that Emily Brontë's inspiration came from her Celtic blood, the Yorkshire environment, her "mental diet," and the books she read.

B482   Brash, W. Bardsley. "Emily Brontë." *London Quarterly and Holborn Review*, 160 (Oct. 1935), 521-523.

This discussion of G. Elsie Harrison's book (C164) identifies the tone of *Wuthering Heights* with the fanaticism of the Methodist William Grimshaw.

B483   Chadwick, Esther Alice. "Emily Brontë." *Nineteenth Century*, 86 (Oct. 1919), 677-687.

This biographer identifies Charlotte Brontë's Shirley Keeldar in *Shirley* as a portrait of Emily Brontë. The article quotes from many critics to try to help the reader envision Emily Brontë's personality.

B484   Chadwick, Esther Alice. *In the Footsteps of the Brontës.* London: Sir I. Pitman and Sons, 1914.

This early biographical study introduces the spurious idea that Emily Brontë loved M. Heger, the Belgian schoolmaster. The critic is responding to a proposal by M. H. Spielmann in the *Times* relating to the love letters from Charlotte Brontë to Heger. Mrs. Chadwick believes that "Emily was not so visionary and introspective as she has been described."

B485   Chitham, Edward. "Almost Like Twins." *BST,* 16 (1975), 365-373.

In writing about Emily Brontë in *Scribner's Monthly,* May, 1871, Ellen Nussey reports, "She and Anne were almost like twins — inseparable companions, and in the very closest sympathy, which never had any interruption." She is discussing the period around 1833. By 1845, Anne had become bored with Gondal (she was 25, Emily 27). By 1846, all the sisters were writing novels, but the dissimilarity between *Wuthering Heights* and *The Tenant of Wildfell Hall* shows how the sisters had grown apart. After this, Emily was isolated.

B486   Clarke, Isabel Constance. *Haworth Parsonage: a Picture of the Brontë Family.* London: Hutchinson and Company, 1927.

One more inquirer looks into Emily Brontë's personal life, trying to find a biographical source for her understanding of passion. This biographer suggests a love affair between Emily Brontë and her father's curate William Weightman (see B509). The book also discusses Emily Brontë's mysticism.

B487   Crandall, Norma. *Emily Brontë: A Psychological Portrait.* Rindge, New Hampshire: Richard R. Smith, 1957. Reprinted, Millwood, New York: Kraus, 1976.

This unreliable critic draws some unusual conclusions based on psychological suppositions.

B488   Cunliffe, W. R. "Emily Brontë: A Clue to Her Appearance." *BST,* 13 (1959), 363.

Cunliffe discusses a letter from Charlotte Brontë in which she says that Emily looks like George Henry Lewes.

B489   Débû-Bridel, Jacques. *Le Secret d'Emily Brontë.* Paris: Ferenczi, 1950.

The secret is that Emily Brontë had a childhood playmate who became a farm servant like Heathcliff.

B490   Dooley, Lucille. "Psychoanalysis of the Character and Genius of Emily Brontë." *Psychoanalytic Review,* 17 (April 1930), 208-239. Reprinted in *The Literary Imagination.* Ed. H. M. Ruitenbeck. Chicago: Quadrangle Books, 1965.

Since a close family circle "intensifies family relationships and conserves the emotions of infancy," Emily Brontë saw herself as "the doomed child," according to this presentation. Her attitude can be seen in *Wuthering Heights* and her poetry. Nature became her "adopted mother." Her acknowledged love of liberty is shown to be rebellion against her father.

B491   Durrell, Lawrence. Quoted in "Dylan Thomas and Emily Brontë: The Only Woman I've Ever Loved." *BST,* 14 (1963), 36. Reprinted from *Dylan Thomas: The Legend and the Poet.* Ed. E. W. Tedlock. London: Heinemann, 1960.

In one paragraph the unusual information is passed on that Emily Brontë's physical characteristics and her handwriting resembled those of Dylan Thomas.

B492   Fleming, Edward V. [Letter to the Editor]. "Emily Brontë and 'Louis Parensell.'" *Poetry Review,* 34 (May-June 1943), 190.

The then-current confusion over Virginia Moore's misidentification of "Louis Parensell" (see B501) is explained by Fleming in answer to a letter, in the January 1943 issue of this magazine, suggesting that Emily Brontë might have met (the non-existent) "Parensell" at Branwell's studio in Bradford.

B493   Gardam, Jane. *The Summer After the Funeral*. London: Hamish Hamilton, 1973.

In this juvenile fiction the heroine identifies herself with Emily Brontë and thereby offers young readers a highly romanticized version of biography.

B494   Gérin, Winifred. *Emily Brontë*. Oxford: Clarendon Press, 1971.

A modern reconsideration of the earlier biographies, this study, written in popular style, reveals interesting incidents, but seems to rely greatly on secondary sources and supposition as there remains so little documented evidence as to the author's life or — the area which interests Miss Gérin in this biography — Emily Brontë's interior life.

B495   Gleave, J. J. *Emily Brontë: An Appreciation*. Manchester: Marsden, 1904.

B496   Hanson, T. W. "Emily Brontë's Footprints." *Municipal Libraries Readers' Guide*, Feb. 1910.

B497   Hatfield, C. W. (Letter to the Editor.) "Emily Brontë's 'Lost Love.'" *Times Literary Supplement*, Aug. 29, 1936, p. 697.

The Brontë authority, C. W. Hatfield, is drawn into a discussion of Virginia Moore's *Life and Eager Death* (B501), in answer to a review entitled "Emily Brontë's Lost Love."

B498   Hervey-Bathurst, P. *An Account of Emily Brontë*. Brontë Booklet No. 2. Stanbury, Yorkshire: Brontë Booklets, 1971.

A local publication giving facts about Emily Brontë's life.

B499   Mackay, Angus M. "On the Interpretation of Emily Brontë." *Westminster Review*, 100 (Aug. 1898), 213-218.

This early Brontë biographer tries to separate fact from fantasy in this and his other articles.

B500   Moore, Virginia. "Emily Brontë." *Distinguished Women Writers*. New York: E. P. Dutton, 1934.

The book gives dramatic treatment of the traditional biography in sequential chapters on Charlotte and Emily Brontë.

B501   Moore, Virginia. *The Life and Eager Death of Emily Brontë: A Biography*. London: Rich and Cowan, 1936.

One of the truly strange approaches to understanding Emily Brontë: as the Gondal poems are masculine in tone, the voice of a man bereaved of his love, therefore Emily Brontë must be homosexual and Heathcliff must be a projection of this male image of herself. Guilt drives her to will her own death. The critic also misreads Emily Brontë's handwriting and sees "Love's Farewell" as the name of a possible lover "Louis Parensell."

B502   Nicoll, William Robertson. "Introductory Essay" in Emily Brontë. *Complete Works*. Ed. C. K. Shorter. London: Hodder and Stoughton, 1910-1911.

A simple condensed biography is supported by snippings from letters and diaries. Nicoll reviews *Wuthering Heights,* discusses its criticism and considers its sources. In discussing Emily Brontë's genius, Nicoll questions her "personal faith or unfaith."

B503   Ralli, Augustus J. "Emily Brontë: The Problem of Personality." *North American Review,* 221 (March 1925), 495-507. Reprinted in *Critiques.* New York: Longmans, Green, 1927.

Here is a biography which relates to the author's work: Ralli shows Emily Brontë in *Wuthering Heights.* He finds the characters psychologically real as they are as self-conscious "as Shakespeare's characters are." He believes that Emily Brontë was a mystic, at peace with nature but not with man, depicting "the soul" and "eternity."

B504   Read, Herbert. "The Writer and His Region." *The Tenth Muse: Essays in Criticism.* London: Wyman and Sons, 1957.

Sir Herbert cites *Wuthering Heights* and Emily Brontë's use of the moors as examples of a writer's use of his region to prove universal truths.

B505   Robinson, A. Mary F. *The Life of Emily Brontë*. Eminent Women Series. London: Allen, 1883.

Commissioned to write this biography, the biographer attempted the first full-length study of Emily Brontë. As Robinson (later Mme. Duclaux) knew Ellen Nussey, she had an intimate view of the family and relied heavily on her vivid imagination to fill in the details. Her interest in Patrick Branwell Brontë dominated her writing and caused her to press the idea that he invented the legend of *Wuthering Heights*. She presents Emily Brontë as revolting from "the narrow prejudices of the Calvinists at Haworth."

B506   Shorter, Clement. "A Biographical Note" in *The Complete Works of Emily Jane Brontë*. Vol. I. *Poetry*. London: Hodder and Stoughton, 1910.

A note to tell the uninformed about the lives of the Brontës, as an introduction to their poetry.

B507   Simpson, Charles Walter. *Emily Brontë*. London: Country Life, 1929. Reissued, Folcroft, Pennsylvania: Folcroft Library Editions, 1977.

One of the best biographers, Simpson discusses local scenery and history, tells about the possibility of a romance at Law Hill, and describes Emily Brontë's life as it may have been. He is level-headed throughout. The book was long out of print.

B508   Sitwell, Edith. *English Women*. London: William Collins, 1942.

A very brief biography of Emily Brontë (six paragraphs) in which the critic remarks that a local person described the Brontës: "distrait and distant, large of nose, small of figure, red of hair, prominent of spectacles; showing great intellectual ability, but with eyes constantly cast down, very silent, painfully retiring."

B509 Snowden, J. Keighley. "The Enigma of Emily Brontë." *Fortnightly Review*, 124 (Aug. 1928), 195-202.

Snowden believes that Emily Brontë knew love, passion, and pain. For sources of *Wuthering Heights* he suggests Ruysbrocck's *The Heavenly Espousals.* He also postulates that Emily Brontë and William Weightman had a love affair, attributing three poems to this attachment. (See also B486.)

B510 Thomas, Edward. "Emily Brontë." *A Literary Pilgrim in England.* London: Methuen, 1917.

The article discusses the Haworth area and Emily Brontë's love for it, using Charlotte Brontë's words to support the theory. The critic also comments on the moorland in Emily Brontë's poetry and in *Wuthering Heights.*

B511 Wilson, Romer (Florence Romer Muir Wilson O'Brien). *All Alone: the Life and Private History of Emily Jane Brontë.* London: Chatto and Windus, 1928.

This wholly speculative presentation of Emily Brontë's psychological "case history" is based entirely on secondary evidence found in her novel and on the lively imagination of the biographer. Conjectural in nature, the study condemns the influence of the moor and the Brontë family, speculates on "some episode of imprisonment" in Emily Brontë's childhood, and attributes *Wuthering Heights* and its author's early death to neurotic tensions, guilt over envy of her brother, and projection of herself on the image of Heathcliff whose death rehearsed her own.

B512 Wyzewa, T. de. "Emily Brontë 1818 – 19th Dec. 1848." Translated by Effie Brown. *BST,* 17 (1976), 30.

As though to introduce Emily Brontë to the reader, the biographer gives her own personal comments about experiencing the ambiance of the village of Haworth.

C. THE BRONTË FAMILY

PRIMARY MATERIAL

Joint Authorship of Brontë Family Members
Listed in Chronological Order

C1   *Poems by Currer, Ellis, and Acton Bell.* London: Aylott and Jones, 1846. Vol. also listed as A7 and B7.

C2   *Poems by Currer, Ellis and Acton Bell.* London: Smith, Elder, 1848. Reissue of the earlier volume.

C3   Brontë, Charlotte, Emily, and Anne. *Works.* London: Smith, Elder, 1872-1873.

       First collection of all Brontë novels, reprinted without comment.

C4   Brontë, Charlotte, Emily, and Anne. *Works.* London: Temple Edition, 1893.

       Twelve volumes in this first critical edition, edited by F. J. S. (unidentified). Reprinted 1901 and 1905 with Introduction by May Sinclair.

C5   Brontë, Charlotte, Emily, and Anne. *Life and Works of the Sisters Brontë.* London: Haworth Edition, 1899-1903. Preface by Mrs. Humphry Ward and annotations to Mrs. Gaskell's *Life of Charlotte Brontë* by C. K. Shorter.

       Before the recent Clarendon Editions, this edition was "still the best," according to Lionel Stevenson (1964).

C6   Brontë, Charlotte, Emily, and Anne. *Works.* 12 vols. London: Thornton Edition, 1901. Ed. by Temple Scott, with Mrs. Gaskell's *Life of Charlotte Brontë,* Vol. 12, edited by B. W. Willett.

C7   *The Shakespeare Head Brontë.* Ed. T. J. Wise and J. A. Symington. 19 vols. Oxford: Newly printed for the Shakespeare Head Press and published for the press by Blackwell, 1931-1938.

Twenty volumes were proposed: novels, 11 vols.; life and letters, 4 vols.; miscellaneous and unpublished writings, 2 vols.; poems, 2 vols.; and bibliography, 1 vol. The last volume never appeared. Recognized from the beginning as being neither definitive nor complete, this edition is now noticed to be full of inaccuracies.

C8   Brontë, Charlotte, Emily, and Anne. *Works.* Ed. Phyllis Bentley. London: Collins New Classics, 1947-1954.

In her introduction, the late Dr. Bentley gives a helpful analysis of the structure of the novels in one of her first major publications on the Brontës.

C9   Brontë, Charlotte, Emily, and Anne. *Works.* Ed. Phyllis Bentley. Heather Edition. London: A. Wingate, 1949.

In this collection of six novels, the Angrian tales, and poetry, the editor gives details of the lives of the Brontë sisters to help readers understand the environment which produced this work.

C10   Spark, Muriel, ed. *The Brontë Letters.* London: Nevill, 1954; Norman, Oklahoma: University of Oklahoma, 1954 as *Letters of the Brontës.*

The editor gives the background of the letters. The book also includes a fragment of Emily Brontë's journal, two "birthday notes" and one letter from Emily to Ellen Nussey.

C11   Brontë, Charlotte and Emily. "French Essays by Charlotte and Emily Brontë: Translated by Margaret Lane." *BST,* 12 (1954), 273.

C12   Davies, Stevie, ed. *The Brontë Sisters — Selected Poems of Charlotte, Emily and Anne Brontë.* Cheadle, Cheshire: Carcanet Press, 1976.

Anne Brontë
Listed in Chronological Order

C13   *Agnes Grey.* Vol. 3 with Emily Brontë, *Wuthering Heights.* London: Thomas C. Newby, 1847.

The manuscript of this novel has disappeared.

C14   *The Tenant of Wildfell Hall.* 3 vols. London: Thomas C. Newby, 1848.

The manuscript of this novel has disappeared.

C15   *Agnes Grey.* With Emily Brontë. *Wuthering Heights, together with a selection of Poems by Ellis and Acton Bell. Prefixed with a Biographical Memoir of the authors by Currer Bell.* London: Smith, Elder, 1850. Vol. also listed as B2.

Patrick Branwell Brontë
Listed in Chronological Order

C16   *And the Weary Are at Rest.* Eds. T. J. Wise and C. W. Hatfield. Privately printed, 1924.

This is the fragment of a novel privately printed in a limited edition, taken from Wise's *Shakespeare Head Brontë.*

C17   "Unpublished Letters: Sir Edward A. Brotherton's Collection." *BST,* 6 (1925), 278.

C18   "Unpublished Poems." Ed. C. W. Hatfield. *BST,* 7 (1927), 71.

The Reverend Patrick Brontë
Listed in Chronological Order

C19   *Cottage Poems: A Miscellany of Descriptive Poems.* Halifax, 1811. Reprinted in Bradford, 1859 in *Brontëana: The Reverend Patrick Brontë: His Collected Works and Life.* Ed. J. Horsfall Turner, 1898. Reprinted, New York: Garland Publishing, 1977.

The Reverend Brontë came to Bradford in 1809. He had West Riding booksellers publish privately: two books of verse, two prose tales, three pamphlets, and two sermons.

C20   *The Rural Minstrel: A Miscellany of Descriptive Poems.* Halifax, Yorks.: 1813. Reprinted in *Brontëana: The Reverend Patrick*

Brontë: His Collected Works and Life. Ed. J. Horsfall Turner, 1898. Vol. also listed as C19.

C21   *The Cottage in the Wood.* Halifax, 1815, in *Brontëana: The Reverend Patrick Brontë: His Collected Works and Life.* Ed. J. Horsfall Turner, 1898. Vol. also listed as C19.

C22   *The Maid of Killarney.* Halifax, 1818, in *Brontëana: The Reverend Patrick Brontë: His Collected Works and Life.* Ed. J. Horsfall Turner, 1898. Vol. also listed as C19.

C23   Letters in *Leeds Intelligencer.* (Jan. and Feb. 1829), cited by Frank Beckwith, "The Reverend Patrick Brontë's Letters to the Leeds Intelligencer." *BST,* 13 (1960), 433.

The Reverend Brontë gives his Tory opinion about Roman Catholic Emancipation, asserting that "our limited Monarchy . . . affords the most rational liberty" to be found and is "as near to perfect as anything can be. . . ."

SECONDARY MATERIAL

Poems of Currer, Ellis, and Acton Bell
Nineteenth-Century Reviews
Listed in Chronological Order

C24　[Dobell, Sydney]. "Poetry of the Million." *Athenaeum*, 975 (July 4, 1846), 682.

　　　One of the first three published reviews of poems by Charlotte, Emily and Anne Brontë. He speaks of "a family in whom appears to run the instinct of song" though in varying proportions. He praises Ellis Bell above the others.

C25　Anon. A review of *Poems by Currer, Ellis, and Acton Bell. Critic,* (July 1846).

　　　One of the three published reviews of the poems which the Brontës read, according to T. J. Wise and J. A. Symington, *The Brontës: Their Lives, Friendships and Correspondence.* Vol. 2, p. 102. Oxford: The Shakespeare Head Press, 1932-1938. The reviewer comments that "in these compositions" the alert reader will recognize "more genius than it was supposed this utilitarian age had devoted to the loftier exercise of the intellect. . . ."

C26　Butler, William Archer. "Evenings With Our Younger Poets." A review of *Poems by Currer, Ellis, and Acton Bell. Dublin University Magazine,* 28 (Oct. 1846).

　　　One of the three published reviews (of the poems) reported to have been read by the Brontës. The reviewer, as Charlotte Brontë says in a letter (see Gaskell, A386), "conjectured that the *soi-disant* three personages were in reality but one. . . ."

C27　Anon. A review of *Poems by Currer, Ellis, and Acton Bell. Spectator,* Nov. 11, 1846, pp. 1094-1095.

　　　Noted but not read. Listed in Parkison, D17.

C28   Anon. A review of *Poems by Acton, Currer, and Ellis Bell. Spectator,*
        Nov. 18, 1848, pp. 1094-1095.

        As Charlotte Brontë reports in a letter to Mr. William of Smith,
        Elder (the publisher of the second edition of the poems in Oct.
        1848, C2): "The *Spectator* consistently maintains the tone it first assumed
        regarding the Bells."

Agnes Grey - Nineteenth-Century Reviews
Listed in Chronological Order

C29   Anon. A review of *Agnes Grey* (and *Wuthering Heights*). *Examiner,*
        Dec. 21, 1850, p. 815.

        An argument concerning the critics' attitude toward the Brontës.

C30   Anon. "Our Library Table." A review of *Agnes Grey* (and *Wuthering
        Heights*). *Athenaeum,* Dec. 25, 1847, pp. 1324-1325.

        Critic thinks all Brontë novels are written by one writer.

C31   [Lewes, George H.] A review of *Agnes Grey* (and *Wuthering Heights*).
        Leader, Dec. 28, 1850, p. 953.

        Lewes finds Anne Brontë weaker in humanity and intellect than
        Charlotte Brontë.

C32   Anon. A review of *Agnes Grey* (and *Wuthering Heights*). *Britannia,*
        Jan. 15, 1848, pp. 42-43.

        The critic thinks that all Brontë novels come from one family,
        if not from one writer. He finds them artistically crude.

C33   Anon. A review of *Agnes Grey* (and *Wuthering Heights*). *Atlas,* Jan.
        22, 1948, p. 59.

        Comparison of *Agnes Grey* with the work of Charlotte Brontë,
        which the critic prefers.

C34   Anon. A review of *Agnes Grey* (and *Wuthering Heights*). *Douglas Jerrold's Weekly Newspaper*, Jan. 15, 1848, p. 77.

The reviewer prefers Charlotte Brontë's work. He finds this work unconventional.

C35   Anon. A review of *Agnes Grey* (and *Wuthering Heights*). *Athenaeum*, Dec. 28, 1850, pp. 1368-1369.

The critic finds women writers in general to be inventive.

C36   Anon. A review of *Agnes Grey* (and *Wuthering Heights*). *Economist*, Jan. 4, 1851, p. 15.

Emphasis on the Yorkshire quality of the novels.

The Tenant of Wildfell Hall: Nineteenth-Century Reviews Listed in Chronological Order

C37   Anon. A review of *The Tenant of Wildfell Hall. Examiner*, July 29, 1848, pp. 483-484.

A positive review which compares the Brontës' handling of reality with the shallowness of their contemporaries. The book was negatively received by most reviewers. Reviews appeared in many magazines such as: *Holden's Dollar Magazine*, 2 (Sept. 1848), 566-567; *Literary World*, 3 (12 June 1848), 544-546; and *Peterson's*, 14 (Sept. 1848), 112.

C38   Anon. A review of *The Tenant of Wildfell Hall. Spectator* (July 1848).

The reviewer says that "there is power, effect, and even nature," but the writer has a "morbid love of the coarse, not to say the brutal."

C39   Whipple, Edwin Percy. A review of *Jane Eyre, Wuthering Heights* and *The Tenant of Wildfell Hall. North American Review*, 67(Oct. 1848), 354-360. Vol. also listed as A62.

Whipple comments, "The truth is, that the whole firm of Bell & Company seem to have a sense of the depravity of human nature peculiarly their own. It is the yahoo, not the demon, that they select for representation; their Pandemonium is of mud rather than fire."

C40   P., W. P. *Jottings on Currer, Ellis, and Acton Bell.* London: Longman, Brown, Green, and Longmans, 1856.

Still unidentified, this contemporary of the Brontës prefers Charlotte to Emily, but feels that they both are excellent writers.

C41   Delafield, E. M. (pseudonym of Edmée E. M. de la Pasture). *The Brontës: Their Lives Recorded by Their Contemporaries.* London: Hogarth Press, 1935.

Excerpts from nineteenth-century reviews are presented in chronological order to give a feeling of the contemporary response to the novelists.

C42   Weir, Edith M. "Contemporary Reviews of the First Brontë Novels." *BST,* 11 (1947), 89-96.

This article quotes fully from the contemporary reviews of the Brontë novels, beginning with Sydney Dobell's lyric praise and including many lesser reviews and some passages from Charlotte Brontë's letters in reference to the reviews.

C43   Fielding, K. J. "The Brontës and 'The North American Review.'" *BST,* 13 (1956), 14.

C44   Van Arsdel, Rosemary Thorstenson. "The Westminster Review, 1824-1857: with Special Emphasis on Literary Attitudes." Unpublished doctoral dissertation, Columbia University, 1960.

The periodical is reviewed and analyzed, suggesting the possibility of its influence on the Brontës during their productive years.

C45   Nelson, Jane Gray. "First American Review of the Brontë Novels." *BST,* 14 (1964), 39-44.

C46 Pollin, Burton. "The Brontës in the American Periodical Press of their Day." *BST*, 16 (1975), 383-399. Vol. also listed as B74.

Here is a listing, with brief annotations, of 193 reviews and comments, mostly unsigned, appearing between 1848 and 1857. The comprehension of this list demonstrates tireless research.

Criticism of *Jane Eyre* and *Wuthering Heights* or of Both Charlotte Brontë and Emily Brontë

C47   Allen, Walter. *The English Novel*. New York: E. P. Dutton, 1955.

Allen suggests that the double narrator forces a role on the reader and thus anticipates Conrad. He sees *Wuthering Heights* as an "intensely individual apprehension of the nature of man and life" and Heathcliff as a "primordial figure of energy." His opinion of *Wuthering Heights* is that it is "the most remarkable novel in England." He sees Charlotte Brontë's novels as a working out of the fundamental "pupil-master" relationship, with close affinities to the Cinderella story. He says, of *Jane Eyre,* "As to structure, it is artless."

C48   Allott, Miriam. *Novelists on the Novel*. London: Routledge and Kegan Paul, 1959.

In "a discussion about the nature and craft of fiction by novelists," Dr. Allott includes Charlotte and Emily Brontë. She contrasts their inspiration and creative process, the structural problems of their novels, the handling of time, as well as the general areas of characterization, dialogue, and style. She gives an overview of what novelists have been thinking about the novel, from the eighteenth century to the present.

C49   Baker, Donald Whitelaw. "Themes of Terror in Nineteenth Century English Fiction: The Shift to the Internal." Unpublished doctoral dissertation, Brown University, 1955. *DAI,* 16:1, 118.

Baker shows the influence of Gothicism on novelists, including the Brontës. He describes this genre as using psychopathological materials treated subjectively: sadism, masochism, madness, neuroses, and psychoses in nineteenth-century fiction.

C50   Baker, Ernest A. *History of the English Novel*. Vol. 8. London: H. F. and G. Witherby, 1937.

This classic literary history gives a good primary approach to *Wuthering Heights*. Of especial interest is note 1 on page 72, concerning Methodism and the possible sources of Methodist-Anglo controversy. He raises the question again: is Branwell part author of *Wuthering Heights*? Baker feels that the Brontës mark the "revival of imagination in the novel, the entry of romance" as Charlotte Brontë replaced a "literature of manners" with a "literature of the spirit." Of *Wuthering Heights* he says, "If it was clumsy to take the last events first, it was assuredly the clumsiness of genius."

C51   Basch, Francoise. *Relative Creatures: Victorian Women in Society and the Novel: 1837-1867.* Translated by Anthony Rudolf. London: Allen Lane, 1974.

The chapter "Revolt and Duty in the Brontës" appeared originally as the critic's doctoral dissertation. It merges criticism with biography.

C52   Batho, Edith C. and Bonamy Dobrée. *The Victorians and After.* New York: Dover Publications, 1950.

In a study of Victorian writers the authors evaluate the Brontë sisters and conclude that "Charlotte was a very considerable artist, Emily a supreme one."

C53   Bayne, Peter. *Two Great Englishwomen: Mrs. Browning and Charlotte Brontë.* London: James Clarke, 1881.

Part II: Charlotte Brontë and her Sisters. These essays, which appeared earlier in *The Literary World,* have been "carefully revised, greatly modified, and considerably extended." The style is literary and gossipy. On the question much discussed at this time, he supports the belief that *Wuthering Heights* "was produced by Emily Brontë, and by her alone." Bayne feels that Charlotte Brontë "errs in *Jane Eyre* by casting too great a charm over Rochester."

C54   Bell, Mackensie. "Charlotte Brontë and Emily Brontë." *Half Hours with Representative Novelists of the Nineteenth Century,* Vol. 1. London: George Routledge and Sons, 1927.

The critic offers biographies of the Brontës, excerpts from the novels of the sisters, along with summaries of the plots.

C55   Bentley, Phyllis. "A Novelist Looks at the Brontë Novels." *BST,* 11 (1948), 139-151.

This novelist sets up her own criteria: a consideration of the "kind . . . and degree of impression they make." In judging whether or not the Brontës produced masterpieces, Dr. Bentley concludes that the greatest among them are *Jane Eyre, Wuthering Heights,* and part of *Villette.*

C56   Bowen, Elizabeth. *English Novelists.* London: Collins, 1942.

Among the novels which this novelist considers, *Wuthering Heights* is judged to be a book of "fire and ice" with no feminine stamp about its style; and in contrast the protagonist in *Jane Eyre* "gains force by being a woman from beginning to end."

C57   Cazamian, Louis. "Charlotte and Emily Brontë" in George Bellais. *A History of English Literature, Modern Times, 1660-1950.* Translated by W. D. MacInnes and the author. New York: Macmillan, 1957.

Charlotte and Emily Brontë are considered along with all the major British writers.

C58   Cecil, Lord David. *Early Victorian Novelists.* London: Constable, 1934; Chicago: University of Chicago Press, 1935.

This close analysis of Charlotte Brontë as a writer is destructive in tone and biased in attitude. Cecil finds Charlotte Brontë novels "formless, improbable, humorless, exaggerated, uncertain in their handling of characters" and her genius "childish naïveté, rigid Puritanism, fiery passion." On the other hand, he declares that "Emily Brontë's imagination is the most extraordinary that ever applied itself to English fiction." Cecil introduces the idea of "storm and calm" in comparing the dichotomies within the novel.

C59   Cecil, Lord David. "Early Victorian Novelists: As they Look to the Reader." *Victorian Literature: Modern Essays in Criticism.* Ed. Austin Wright. New York: Oxford University Press, 1961.

This is Cecil's purely personal reaction to the writers he discusses.

C60   Cecil, Lord David. "Fresh Thoughts on the Brontës." *BST,* 16 (1973), 169-176.

On second thought, almost 40 years later, the critic believes that he was "too harsh" in his earlier appraisal. But about the storm and calm symbolism in *Wuthering Heights,* this respected critic reaffirms his early statements. He adds that he too believes in the theory that Heathcliff was Catherine's half-brother.

C61   Chapman, Raymond. "The Brontës" in *The Victorian Debate: English Literature and Society, 1832-1901.* London: Weidenfeld and Nicholson; New York: Basic Books, 1968.

The "popular image of them remains somewhat vague and inaccurate," this critic believes. He stresses background and resources of the writers and their part "in the history of female emancipation." After a brief analysis of the works of each, Chapman states that "Emily Brontë has some claim to be the best woman poet of Victorian literature."

C62   Chase, Richard. "The Brontës: A Centennial Observance (Reconsiderations VIII)." *Kenyon Review,* 9 (Autumn 1947), 487-506. Reprinted as "The Brontës, or Myth Domesticated" in *Forms of Modern Fiction.* Ed. William Van O'Connor. Bloomington, Indiana: Indiana University Press, 1954.

Chase accepts uncritically Rosamund Langbridge's theories (A401) as well as adding conclusions from an approach based on Jung and Toynbee. The study, considered by some to be highly overrated, is an interesting one. In it Chase declares that *Jane Eyre* and *Wuthering Heights* "translated the social customs of the time into forms of mythical art." Both Emily and Charlotte Brontë see the universe as an embodiment of masculine sexual and intellectual energy. The heroes are godlike and satanic, in fact Heathcliff is a "dazzling sexual and intellectual force."

C63   Chesterton, Gilbert Keith. *Twelve Types.* London: Arthur L. Humphreys, 1902.

Chesterton points out the essential "truth to life" quality of the Brontë novels.

C64   Chesterton, Gilbert Keith. *Victorian Age in Literature.* London: Williams and Norgate; New York: Henry Holt, 1913.

Chesterton suggests that what the Brontës brought to fiction was "the blast of mysticism of the North." He accuses both Emily and Charlotte of having a "false view of men." His analysis, while not exhaustive, is of interest for its point of view.

C65   Church, Richard. *The Growth of the English Novel.* London: Methuen, 1951.

Church presents a short and not unusual passage on *Wuthering Heights* and *Jane Eyre.* He adds that Emily Brontë's poems are as "stark" as Blake's.

C66   Cooke, John Daniel and Lionel Stevenson. *English Literature of the Victorian Period.* New York: Appleton-Century-Crofts, 1949.

In this chronological coverage of British literature written between 1830 and 1900, these experts refer to the Brontës as "the most remarkable family of geniuses in literary history." The writers give a brief biography, then summary statements on the novels.

C67   Copley, J. "*Wuthering Heights* and *Shirley* – A Parallel." *Notes and Queries,* 3 (Nov. 1956), 499-500.

This note points out that in both of these novels the ending refers to ghosts.

C68   Craik, Wendy Ann. *The Brontë Novels.* London: Methuen, 1968.

In a thorough analysis of Brontë novels, Dr. Craik gives a separate chapter to each of the seven novels, Anne's as well as her sisters'. Objecting to biographical readings of the novels, the critic proposes serious stylistic considerations,with attention to imagery and rhetoric. She comments on the "brutal datelessness" of Emily's prose.

C69   Crompton, D. W. "The New Criticism: a Caveat." *Essays in Criticism,* 10 (1960), 359-364.

The critic warns us: don't look for *Wuthering Heights'* structural complexities in *Jane Eyre.*

221

C70   Cruse, Amy. *The Victorians and Their Reading.* New York: Houghton Mifflin, 1935.

The critic tells something about Charlotte Brontë's reaction to current reading (as expressed in her letters) and a good deal about how her novels were received. Cruse comments that "the strange, wild genius of *Wuthering Heights* went for a time almost unrecognized."

C71   Daiches, David. *A Critical History of English Literature.* Vol. 2. New York: Ronald Press, 1960.

Daiches gives fifty pages to the Victorian novel, only two of them to the Brontës. He remarks that the Brontës "shared an imaginative as well as a physical life." Emily's "lonely power of the imagination" produced *Wuthering Heights.* He finds Charlotte Brontë "sensitive, passionate, and sensuous."

C72   de Selincourt, E. "The Genius of the Brontës" in *BST,* 2 (1906), 234-255.

An appreciative paper expresses de Selincourt's admiration of the style and imagination of the Brontë sisters. Emily and Charlotte's novels are considered together, distinct from other nineteenth-century novels. The critic praises the "haunting presence" and the "poetic atmosphere."

C73   Dexant, B. "Originalité de *Jane Eyre* et des *Hauts de Hurlevent* par rapport au roman féminin anglais dans la première moitié du XIXe siècle." *Annales du Centre d'Enseignement Supérieur de Brazyaville,* 4 (1968), 13-22.

C74   Dimnet, Ernest. *Les Soeurs Brontë.* Paris: Blond, 1910. Reprinted as *The Brontë Sisters.* Translated, Louise Morgan Sill. London: J. Cope, 1927.

The eminent Phyllis Bentley called this "the most important foreign study" of the Brontës. It is scholarly, perceptive, and sympathetic.

C75   Drabble, Margaret. "The Writer as Recluse: the Theme of Solitude in the Works of the Brontës." *BST*, 16 (1974), 259-269.

The Brontës "present themselves as archetypal figures. Their situation was an archetype of the romantic writers' imagined solitude," according to this critic. "They write in and about a great solitude." Anne and Charlotte wrote of loneliness; Emily wrote of solitude. All three sisters were fascinated by the Byronic hero.

C76   Eagleton, Terry. *Myths of Power: A Marxist Study of the Brontës.* London: Macmillan, 1975.

To read *Wuthering Heights* and *Jane Eyre* as expressions of class struggle has required a particularly partisan view on the part of this critic. He is also able to see the life stories of the Brontës as substantiating those capitalistic principles revealed in the novels.

C77   Elliott, Reverend W. Thompson. "Atmosphere in the Brontës' Works." *BST*, 7 (1928), 119-136.

The vicar of Leeds discusses the imagination of the Brontës and the atmosphere which they create in their novels. His analysis is that they created from "tragic genius." He particularly points out Emily Brontë's mystic personality.

C78   Evans, Ifor. *English Literature: Values and Traditions.* London: George Allen and Unwin, 1962.

Sir Ifor gives a two-sentence summary of Brontë writing: in *Wuthering Heights*, Emily Brontë "raised the novel to a product of pure imagination by a uniqueness of vision," and Charlotte's *Jane Eyre* "holds the mind and the senses by the strength of its impact."

C79   Evans, Ifor. *A Short History of English Literature.* Harmondsworth, Middlesex: Penguin, 1940.

Sir Ifor speaks more fully on the Brontës. He finds Rochester to be "a Montoni" from Mrs. Radcliffe's *Mysteries of Udolpho* "modified into a middle-class setting." *Jane Eyre* is "grounded in realism" but goes into wish fulfillment. "Charlotte Brontë's power," he remarks, is "the creation of an atmosphere of terror without departing from a middle-class setting." He claims that *Wuthering Heights* is the result of stimulation from a "strange source." Like *Lear's* storm scenes, *Wuthering Heights* offers "wild and cruel reality." This novel, he feels, is "original beyond any other novel in the century."

C80   Ewbank, Inga-Stina. *Their Proper Sphere: A Study of the Brontë Sisters as Early Victorian Novelists.* Cambridge, Massachusetts: Harvard University Press, 1966.

This unemotional study attempts to avoid a biographical approach and examines the literary aims of the Brontës in relation to the "proper sphere" for female writers of the 1840's. The author points out that the Brontës went beyond this sphere by exhibiting "coarseness" and by expressing passion and intellect. About their role as women writers, Ewbank makes certain statements. Of the three sisters, only Charlotte Brontë considered writing her career and cared about woman's role in society. She helped the cause as can be seen in the public attitude toward woman writers. In 1800 there was general hostility toward them. By 1850 they were acceptable. The Brontë novels, however, were considered to be "immoral and subverted" because they were not like other women's novels. Charlotte was truly a feminist as she dealt with the "emotional and intellectual needs of a woman." In fact, "her art is the expression of a personal vision of those needs."

C81   Flahiff, Frederick Thomas Colum. "Formative Ideas in the Novels of Charlotte and Emily Jane Brontë." Unpublished doctoral dissertation, University of Toronto, 1965. *DAI,* 27:746.

Flahiff writes about the technical problems which Charlotte Brontë struggled with and Emily Brontë solved. He believes that *Wuthering Heights* balances involvement against detachment. His conclusion: *Wuthering Heights* is not like Charlotte Brontë's novels.

C82   Forster, E. M. "Prophecy" in *Aspects of the Novel.* New York: Harcourt, Brace, 1927.

About *Wuthering Heights,* Forster says: after constructing *Wuthering Heights* on a time chart and genealogical table, Emily

Brontë introduced "muddle, chaos, and tempest" because she was prophetess "and what is implied is more important to her than what is said." He is pleased to say that Charlotte Brontë created "round characters."

C83   Friedman, Alan. *The Turn of the Novel: The Transition to Modern Fiction.* London: Oxford University Press, 1966.

Of the two major Brontë novels, *Wuthering Heights* is an "explosive" structure, in which the "centrifugal force of its moral savagery" is hemmed in by the "counterpace, the conventional force, of its narrators' viewpoints." He speaks of the "containment of the expanding stream of conscience" in *Jane Eyre*'s marriage ending.

C84   Gérin, Winifred. "Byron's Influence on the Brontës." *Keats-Shelley Memorial Bulletin* (Rome), 17 (1966), 1-19.

The critic discusses the four general characteristics of Byron's poetry which cause it to sound like *Wuthering Heights* and *Jane Eyre.* After a broad appraisal of the poetry, the critic compares Heathcliff with Byron's Manfred.

C85   Gerould, Gordon Hall. *Patterns of English and American Fiction.* Boston: Little, Brown, 1942.

The author suggests that *Shirley* is less important than Charlotte Brontë's other novels and that *Villette* has some of her "finest work." He finds *Wuthering Heights* clumsy in structure, with technical defects. Nelly Dean keeps it rational, but the mad characters are hard to believe.

C86   Halperin, John and Janet Kunert. *Plots and Characters in the Fiction of Jane Austen, the Brontës, and George Eliot.* Hamden, Connecticut: Archon Books, Shoe String Press; Folkestone: William Dawson, 1976.

In a resource book for student use, the authors give plot summaries and character listings. In the introduction they name Jane Austen, George Eliot, and Charlotte Brontë among the 20 greatest writers of the last 300 years.

C87   Heilbrun, Carolyn G. *Toward Androgyny: Aspects of Male and Female in Literature.* London: Victor Gollancz, 1973.

Here Heilbrun, in discussing the emerging image of the androgynous figure in literature, uses *Jane Eyre* and *Wuthering Heights* as examples of a feminist novel and an androgynous novel respectively. The critic notes that *Jane Eyre* exerts "the moral strength necessary to demand an equal rights bill and dignity for all." *Wuthering Heights,* on the other hand, "is an androgynous novel; the sense of waste, of lost spiritual and sexual power, of equality of worth between the sexes, is presented with no specific cry for revolution, but with a sense of a world deformed."

C88   Hopewell, Donald. "The Misses Brontë – Victorians." *BST,* 10 (1940), 3-11.

Hopewell tries to explain how "Victorian" the Brontës were. Then he goes on to say that *Wuthering Heights* is the only "perfectly constructed" Brontë novel. Charlotte Brontë, in life and writing, was unable to construct. Charlotte and Emily both had a "tendency to crude moralizing," Victorian in "their range of character, their delight in melodrama, their effort at pathos, their preference for a happy ending."

C89   Houghton, W. E. *The Victorian Frame of Mind.* New Haven: Yale University Press, 1957.

Here the attitude of the Victorian is examined, particularly the question of pretense and hypocrisy.

C90   Karl, Frederick. "The Brontës: The Outsider as Protagonist." *An Age of Fiction: the Nineteenth Century British Novel.* New York: Farrar, Straus and Giroux, 1964.

Karl points out that the protagonists in the Brontë novels are all outcasts or placeless persons in a society that is alien and threatening. Exile is a dominant motif. *Wuthering Heights* is without hero or heroine, held together by doubling of structure and character, and a counterpoint of themes. He also considers the other Brontë novels, comparing Charlotte Brontë with Jane Austen.

C91   Karl, Frederick R. "The Brontës: The Self Defined, Redefined, and Refined" in Richard Levine. *Victorian Experience*. Columbus, Ohio: Ohio University Press, 1976.

Karl feels that the Brontë novels "impinge upon us for their insistence on the intensity of their inner lives and their almost mythical reconstruction of a self." The critic confuses the issues by referring to "the Brontës" yet taking major examples from Charlotte Brontë. Once, he says, "only Heathcliff fails to alter his assumptions," but all other references are to characters in Charlotte's novels.

C92   Kenton, Edna. "Forgotten Creator of Ghosts; Joseph Sheridan Le Fanu, Possible Inspirer of the Brontës." *Bookman* (New York), 69 (July 1929), 528-534.

Kenton feels that Le Fanu's *The Purcell Papers* and other "Irish" and "ghostly" tales with their occult overtones influenced Emily Brontë in her creation of Heathcliff. *Jane Eyre* seems to the critic to be an outgrowth of Le Fanu's "A Chapter in the History of the Tyrone Family."

C93   Kinkead-Weekes, Mark. "The Place of Love in *Jane Eyre* and *Wuthering Heights*" in *The Brontës: A Collection of Critical Essays*. Englewood Cliffs, New Jersey: Prentice-Hall, 1970.

Charlotte Brontë tried to "break through the public and social" to "free the personal selfhood" of Jane; so says this writer. Therefore *Jane Eyre* is a novel of the heart in which each house serves as a metaphor of the "condition of the private heart." In *Wuthering Heights* "individual selfhood" is broken through to "liberate a mode of being and loving beyond personality, beyond life, beyond death." The double narrative speaks in two languages; therefore there can be two readings of the book. When Heathcliff gives up his vengeance, seeing its futility, he recaptures the vision of Catherine.

C94   Knight, Grant C. *The Novel in England*. New York: Richard E. Smith, 1931.

Calling both Brontës "the unorthodox Victorians," the author mentions the biographical elements in *Jane Eyre* and little else.

227

C95   Lambert, Diana Elizabeth Downing. "The Shaping Spirit: A Study
        of the Novels of Emily and Charlotte Brontë." Unpublished
        doctoral dissertation, Stanford University, 1967. *DAI*, 28:4634.

C96   Littell, Philip. "Books and Things." *New Republic*, 16 (Aug. 31,
        1918), 142.

        In this discussion of Charlotte and Emily Brontë, the reviewer
        claims that the inaccessibility to facts about Emily has added to her
        fame.

C97   Lovett, R. M. and Helen S. Hughes. *The History of the Novel in
        England*. Boston: Houghton Mifflin, 1932.

        This biographical and literary treatment of the Brontës discusses
        the conflicting elements of realism and romanticism in their work.

C98   MacCarthy, Desmond. "The Brontës in Their Books." *BST*, 10 (1945),
        263-264.

        Here is a plea that the works should be considered outside Brontë
        biography. Especially with Emily there is an "enormous gap between
        what little is known and what is conjectured about her."

C99   McCurdy, Harold Grier. "A Study of the Novels of Charlotte and
        Emily Brontë as an Expression of Their Personalities." *Journal
        of Personality*, 16 (Dec. 1947), 109-152.

        In this psychological dissection of *Wuthering Heights* and
        Charlotte Brontë's four novels, the characters are examined and
        compared. The result: Charlotte Brontë is considered to be defensive,
        Emily Brontë aggressive. This "scientific" conclusion is then
        corroborated by biographical information. Emily Brontë's personality,
        we are told, was "organized at the level of a child's." The two sisters
        are reasoned to have had a great influence on each other.

C100   Masefield, Muriel. *Women Novelists, from Fanny Burney to George
        Eliot*. London: Ivor Nicholson and Watson, 1934.

        This writer stresses the importance of Mrs. Gaskell's *Life of
        Charlotte Brontë* in understanding the Brontës.

C101   Meynell, Alice. "Charlotte and Emily Brontë." *Hearts of Controversy.*
London: Burns and Oates; New York: Scribner's, 1917.

The lady poet searches out some possible sources of the poetic
passages in *Wuthering Heights* in an article first appearing in the
Dublin Review, April, 1911. The same article, revised, was reprinted
in Meynell's *Essays of Today and Yesterday,* London: George G.
Harrap, 1926.

C102   Mirsky, Prince D.S. "Through Foreign Eyes." *BST,* 6 (1923), 147-152.
Reprinted in *The Brontës Then and Now.* Shipley: Outhwaite
Brothers, 1947.

In a lighthearted and personal way, the Prince gives his "foreign"
view of the Brontës. He compares Rochester and Heathcliff and
decides that the later and his creator Emily were both "outside
nature."

C103   Miyoshi, Masao. *The Divided Self: A Perspective on the Literature
of the Victorians.* New York: New York University Press, 1969.

In this study of conflict, Miyoshi points out the tension between
nature and civilization in *Wuthering Heights.* "*Wuthering Heights*
carries the Brontëan self-division of reason and feeling to an
uncompromising extreme." Of *Jane Eyre* the critic claims that Jane's
self-discovery asserts the author's moral vision. The novel is based
on contrast: "where Rochester is Gothic, St. John is classic . . .
where he is fire, St. John is ice . . . where Rochester is all passion,
St. John is reason itself."

C104   Moore, Charles L. "Another Literary Mare's-nest." *The Dial,* 53 (Oct.
16, 1912), 277-278.

Moore attacks the non-conformist views: Leyland's (that
Branwell wrote *Wuthering Heights*) and Malham-Dembleby's (that
Charlotte did). The later he is especially indignant about. He asserts
that Emily and Charlotte Brontë differ in poetry, style, and
characters. (See C333 and A309.)

C105   Neill, S. Diana. *A Short History of the English Novel.* London:
Jarrolds, 1951; New York: Macmillan, 1952.

In her chapter "Passion Spins the Plot," the author speaks of Charlotte Brontë's imagination ("she did not attempt to discipline its fiery force") and interweaves biographical information about the Brontës' lives. She emphasizes the "romantic daydream" quality of Charlotte Brontë's work. She further explains that Emily Brontë saw evil as energy misdirected. In *Wuthering Heights*, note the symbolism: two houses, one of passion, one of reason.

C106   Oldfield, Jenny. *Jane Eyre and Wuthering Heights: A Study Guide.* London: Heinemann Educational Books, 1976.

A helpful publication for students approaching these novels for the first time.

C107   O'Neill, Judith (ed.). "Introduction" in *Critics on Charlotte and Emily Brontë: Readings in Literary Criticism.* London: George Allen and Unwin; Coral Gables, Florida: University of Miami Press, 1968.

The editor points out the variety of criticism included in this work, giving a brief summary of the critical history of the novels.

C108   Parkinson, E. M. "The Brontës' Domestic Servant Problem." *Saturday Review* (London), 150 (Aug. 16, 1930), 196-197.

This critic notes that in the novels Charlotte and Emily had "no mercy on their servants." For example: in *Wuthering Heights* poor Nelly Dean is "lady's maid, nurse, housekeeper, fruit-picker, companion, seamstress."

C109   Parrot, Thomas Marc and Robert Bernard Martin. *A Companion to Victorian Literature.* New York: Charles Scribner's Sons, 1955.

A very brief biography of the Brontës is included with a survey of the social background and "history of the age." *Wuthering Heights* and *Jane Eyre* are said to have "brought to the novel an introspection and an intense concentration on the inner life of emotion" which before were found only in poetry.

C110   Paul, David. "The Novel Art. II." *Twentieth Century,* 154 (Oct. 1953), 294-301.

Wuthering Heights and *Jane Eyre* are both thought to be their authors' wish-fulfillment. Such psychological motivation is essential to any novelist.

C111   Petit, Jean-Pierre. "Temps et Récit dans *Jane Eyre* et *Wuthering Heights.*" Actes du Congrès de Dijon (1968) in *Formes du roman anglais du XVIé au XXè siècle.* Paris: Marcel Didier, 1972.

C112   Read, Herbert. "Charlotte and Emily Brontë." *Yale Review,* 14 (July 1925), 720-738. Reprinted in *Reason and Romanticism.* London: Faber and Gwyer, 1926.

This Jungian interpretation shows the relationship between neuroses and art. The critic considers heredity, environment, childhood influences and education. He believes that M. Heger was probably a "master of the art of writing." Read finds that *Wuthering Heights* evokes pity and terror with "dignity of classic tragedy" and also has the spirit of Romanticism. He sees an "amazing quality of innocence" in Emily Brontë. He believes that Charlotte's "longing for a lost mother" is the psychological basis for her plots.

C113   Saintsbury, George. *The English Novel.* New York: E. P. Dutton, 1913.

Saintsbury believes that the Brontës joined romance proper (Scott) to the novel proper (Austen): a "union of realism and dream in the English novel." For him *Wuthering Heights* is one of those books "rather ornament than essential parts in novel history." Charlotte and Emily Brontë's main contribution is that they kept the novel and romance together.

C114   Saintsbury, George. "The Position of the Brontës as Origins in the History of the English Novel." *BST,* 2 (1899), 18-30.

This evaluative study of the Brontës attempts to place them in literary history. The article has been reprinted many times. In it the critic finds Emily Brontë "rather a poet than a novelist."

C115   Sale, William, Jr. "Preface" in Emily Brontë. *Wuthering Heights.* New York: W. W. Norton, 1963.

In this brief preface the editor discusses the conflict which has arisen over Charlotte Brontë's editorial changes in Emily's use of dialect.

C116   Sherry, Norman. *Charlotte and Emily Brontë.* Literature in Perspective. London: Evans Brothers, 1969.

A basic book for beginners, this succinct account gives the contrasts and comparisons which bring the Brontës and their work to life.

C117   Skilton, D. *The English Novel.* London: Barnes and Noble, 1977.

A chapter on "Victorian Views of the Individual" includes some discussion of the Brontës.

C118   Simon, Irene. *Formes du roman anglais de Dickens à Joyce.* Liège: 1949.

C119   Simpson, Jacqueline. "The Function of Folklore in *Jane Eyre* and *Wuthering Heights.*" *Folklore,* 85 (Spring 1974), 47-61.

In an effort to explain the use of folklore in these novels by the Brontë sisters, the critic first identifies the nature of the love which appealed to them. Emily Brontë had a dark view of life and saw the darkness in the folklore which she used. In *Jane Eyre,* however, the relationship of Jane and Rochester is based on a folkloric spiritual affinity.

C120   Slattery, Eugene E. M. "The Brontës: Refined Gothic." *Unisia,* 12 (Sept. 1974), 24-27.

In *Jane Eyre,* Charlotte Brontë reshapes the Gothic genre by using symbolism which "calls for a mature and complicated response." In *Wuthering Heights,* Emily Brontë uses two main narrators and other lesser ones who play parts in the action. Charlotte Brontë is more conventional and her characters remain consistent as they mature within the novel.

C121   Smith, David J. "The Arrested Heart: Familial Love and Psychic Conflict in Five Mid-Victorian Novels." Unpublished doctoral dissertation, University of Washington, 1966. *DAI*, 27:1839.

This Freudian reading of *Jane Eyre* and *Wuthering Heights* (as well as other novels) shows that the principal characters are motivated by the basic unconscious conflict: the incest wish versus incest taboo.

C122   Spacks, Patricia Meyer. *The Female Imagination*. New York: Alfred A. Knopf, 1975.

Wuthering Heights is a novel "detailing the education of the heart." This critic feels that "passion . . . dictates the plot of *Wuthering Heights*." She attempts a psychoanalysis of Catherine and finds that she is narcissistic. The critic compares the novel to Plath's *The Bell Jar*. Charlotte Brontë's heroine, on the other hand, is an "admirable woman" who "will think correctly and claim to be guided by reflection; but she believes in the privacy of feeling and the virtue of impulse, believes, finally, emotional capacity an index of worth." The book gets side-tracked into a discussion of the classroom reactions of Dr. Spacks' Wellesley students whom she quotes with a good teacher's subjective appreciation.

C123   Stevenson, Lionel. *The English Novel: A Panorama*. Boston: Houghton Mifflin, 1960.

Stevenson speaks of Charlotte Brontë's strength in creating atmosphere, in asserting women's rights, and in contributing to the novels of social consciousness. He emphasizes the importance of the double narrative in *Wuthering Heights*. As one of the most knowledgeable authorities on the Victorian period, he speaks of *Wuthering Heights* as "a symbolic embodiment of elemental forces" and a "belated masterpiece of romanticism."

C124   Tillotson, Geoffrey. "Charlotte and Emily Brontë." *A View of Victorian Literature*. Oxford: Clarendon Press, 1978.

A posthumous work of material to have been published in the Oxford History of English Literature offers new thoughts on the Brontës. Of Charlotte Brontë he writes mostly on novels other than

Jane Eyre. Her tone is "constantly urgent." Her principles of description are based on an accumulation of detail, ordered, sparse, selective. Her dialogue he finds abrupt, terse, and real. The "strangeness" of her writing "comes from the inner life." Emily Brontë's prime quality, according to Dr. Tillotson, is her self-sufficiency derived from her writing. "*Wuthering Heights* is the only English novel that stands within hailing distance of *King Lear* and *Macbeth.*" The truthfulness in her handling of people is valid because "she saw that people are largely explained by heredity and training." In explaining Charlotte Brontë's "Preface," Dr. Tillotson feels that the purpose was to win for Emily's genius due response from an unresponsive public.

C125   Tillotson, Kathleen. *Novels of the Eighteen-Forties.* Oxford: Clarendon Press, 1954.

In one of the remarkable books of its time, this critic concentrates on the dramatic and stylistic qualities of the novels. In selecting the works to study, Tillotson chose novels "which are essentially 'of' the forties as well as 'for all time.' With that intention I was precluded from choosing . . . *Wuthering Heights.* This novel, which speaks so clearly to our generation, hardly spoke at all to its own." She further remarks on "the courage of its passion" and "its elaboration of structure." Its post-dating or post-setting produces "aesthetic distance" which controls the reader's attitude toward Nelly and Lockwood. *Jane Eyre* is the least related to its time of all the novels she studies fully. It is "a novel of inner life, not of man in his social relations; it maps a private world." It is related to its time in some ways: it expresses "the convictions of many creedless Christians of the eighteen-forties." Also the master-influence is voiced by Jane telling Rochester: "We are born to strive and endure." *Jane Eyre* is not really feminist. Had Jane yielded to Rochester, the author would have been "striking a blow for insurgent feminism, the anarchy of passion, and the reform of divorce laws." But that would have violated the novel's own moral pattern.

C126   Vaughan, C. E. "Charlotte and Emily Brontë: A Comparison and a Contrast." *BST,* 4 (April 1912), 217-235.

Charlotte Brontë's "errors" in depicting scenes in her novels arose from her strayings into "a field that was not hers." He suggests that she was the first English novelist to bring in the familiar French figure of the *femme incomprise*. He speaks with admiration of Emily and suggests that the sisters had in common: passion, lyricism, and revolt. Emily was more intense; Charlotte had more humor.

C127   Vogele, Hermann. "Aufbau und Sprache in Charlotte Brontës 'Jane Eyre' und Emily Brontës 'Wuthering Heights': ein Vergleich." Unpublished doctoral dissertation, University of Freiburg, 1954.

This dissertation is a Germanic study of construction and diction in these novels.

C128   Waidner, Maralee L. "From Reason to Romance: A Progression from an Emphasis on Neoclassic Rationality to Romantic Intuition in Three English Woman Novelists." Unpublished doctoral dissertation, University of Tulsa, 1973. *DAI*, 34:1259.

Discusses the tension between reason and romance which characterizes the early years of the nineteenth century. "In this study the conflicts brought on by the mixing of these elements at the beginning of the nineteenth century are examined in four novels by three women novelists: *Emma* (1813) and *Persuasion* (1818) by Jane Austen, *Jane Eyre* (1847) by Charlotte Brontë, and *Wuthering Heights* (1847) by Emily Brontë."

C129   Walker, Hugh. "The Brontës." *Literature of the Victorian Era.* Cambridge: University Press, 1910.

Charlotte Brontë is superior to Emily Brontë as an artist, Walker believes. He finds that Emily Brontë's *Wuthering Heights* is marred by the "excess of the qualities which made her great."

C130   Watson, Melvin R. "Form and Substance in the Brontë Novels" in *From Jane Austen to Joseph Conrad: Essays Collected in Memory of James T. Hillhouse.* Ed. by Robert C. Rathburn and Martin Steinmann, Jr. Minneapolis: University of Minnesota Press, 1958.

Here is a novel-by-novel plot summary and a rudimentary study of structure — not profound but suggestive. *Jane Eyre* and *Wuthering*

Heights survive as classics because their form and substance are welded together (in other novels this is not so). *Wuthering Heights* is trimmed of all that is extraneous and the timing is remarkable. Watson says *Wuthering Heights* is the greatest Brontë novel, but he writes mainly about the others.

C131   Watt, Ian. *The Rise of the Novel*. Berkeley: University of California Press, 1957.

In his primary discussion of Defoe, Richardson, and Fielding, the literary historian uses Heathcliff and Rochester as examples of "perpetual imminence of attacks on pure womanhood" and "as a stereotype of the male as a combination of terrifying animality and diabolic intellect which is equally pathological."

C132   Wellek, Rene and Austin Warren. *The Theory of Literature*. New York: Harcourt, Brace, 1949.

In this reference work there is a brief use of *Jane Eyre* and *Wuthering Heights* to support their theories. They warn of the dangers of biographical readings, citing Romer Wilson (B511), V. Moore (B501), and Edith E. Kinsley (C332).

C133   Wells, Augustin-Lewis. "Les Soeurs Brontë et l'étranger: étude des influences européennes sur leur pensée et sur leur oeuvre." Doctoral dissertation, Université de Paris, 1937. Published privately, Paris: L. Rodstein, 1937.

European influences on the writings and thought of the Brontës are discussed in this lengthy treatment. The dissertation includes a complete bibliography.

C134   West, Rebecca. "The Role of Fantasy in the Works of the Brontës," *BST*, 12 (1954), 255-267.

In this discussion of the imaginative process by which the Brontës created real people, as opposed to girlish day-dreams, Miss West emphasizes *Wuthering Heights* but includes some treatment of *Jane Eyre*. Literary technique in *Wuthering Heights*, she feels, has triple significance: (1) truth is told about the characters, (2) English society is exposed through Lockwood, and (3) the poetic aspects of the work interpret the universal. Miss West condemns Charlotte Brontë for her fantasy, her day dreaming, and the suppression of truth.

C135   Weygandt, Cornelius. "The Spectacle of the Brontës." *A Century of the English Novel*. New York: Century, 1925.

Jane Eyre and *Wuthering Heights* are distinguished by the intensity of emotion in them. The critic knows that *Wuthering Heights'* survival is assured despite its "burden of absurdities." He praises the lyricism in the novel and recognizes the need to overlook the brutalities.

C136   Willcocks, M. P. "Charlotte and Emily Brontë." *Between the Old World and the New*. London: Allen and Unwin, 1925.

Though writing about both Brontës, the critic emphasizes Emily Brontë, describing her as being absolutely independent of the Victorian world and its creeds. She merely escapes to an inner world, a strongly mystic inner world.

C137   Williams, Harold. "The Brontë Sisters." *Two Centuries of the English Novel*. London: Smith, Elder, 1911.

Again the critic speaks more clearly on the subject of Emily Brontë, "pagan in temperament and creed," an independent being who felt "neither hope nor optimism."

C138   Williams, Raymond. "Charlotte and Emily Brontë." *The English Novel from Dickens to Lawrence*. London: Chatto and Windus, 1970.

The novels are viewed in historical perspective with attention to their sociological implications.

C139   Willis, Irene Cooper. *The Brontës*. London: Duckworth, 1933. Reissued, New York: Haskell House, 1977.

This well-known Brontë authority views the family members with an eye to their differences. The novels are considered after the author gives a short history of the Brontës.

C140   Wilson, Angus. "Evil in the English Novel." *Kenyon Review*, 29 (March 1967), 167-194.

After giving brief consideration to Rochester, the critic analyzes Emily Brontë's vision of Heathcliff as a fallen angel. His beginning was in the Gothic novel. Rochester is redeemed by Jane's love, but Heathcliff is not by Catherine's love. However, Catherine and Heathcliff's love transcends the events in the rest of the book.

C141   Wilson, F. A. C. "The Primrose Wreath: The Heroes of the Brontë Novels." *Nineteenth Century Fiction*, 29 (June 1974), 40-57.

In both Emily and Charlotte Brontë's work, the characters, events, and situations reject convention. The relationship is always the dominant male imposing his will on the submissive female. In Charlotte's novels there is an androgynous hero (masculine but with gentle sensibility) and a determined heroine (who also represents dual urges). Anne and Emily learned from Charlotte. In the beginning of *Wuthering Heights,* Catherine's choice is between brutal Heathcliff and effeminate Edgar. At the end, Hareton is the androgynous figure.

C142   Winnifrith, Tom J. *The Brontës.* London: Macmillan, 1977.

Lacking the objectivity of some of the other critics, Winnifrith states his judgments: the "juvenilia is bad"; has "a romantic and pathetic air." His objection to biographic criticism causes him to lose his perspective in order to fulfill his purpose: "to show that the lives of the Brontës are different from their books." He has devoted himself to the effort of undermining the Brontës "mythology."

C143   Winnifrith, Tom J. *The Brontës and Their Background: Romance and Reality.* London: Macmillan, 1973.

The myth of the Brontë family is compared with such substantiated evidence as is available. The work contains an excellent evaluation of the Brontë attitude toward religion. He attempts to relate the Brontës to the Yorkshire society of their day. He suggests that they were very class-conscious. He feels that Anne Brontë's novels are almost wholly sociological. *Wuthering Heights* seems to blend anti-capitalism with broader views of the universe. Charlotte Brontë is more novelist than sociologist, but her message is blurred. She believes in the aristocracy of intellect over the aristocracy of class and wealth — but she is inconsistent and ignorant.

C144 Wood, Butler. "Influence of the Moorlands on Charlotte and Emily Brontë." *BST*, 6 (1922), 79-87. Reprinted in *The Brontës Then and Now*. Shipley: Outhwaite Brothers, 1947.

Much is said about the strong-hold of nature on the Brontës. Emily Brontë's nature-worship is reflected in *Wuthering Heights*.

C145 Woodberry, George E. "The Brontë Novels." *Studies of a Litterateur*. New York: Harcourt Brace, 1921.

The Brontës considered in a broad view. Their "reputation remains side by side with Jane Austen's."

C146 Woolf, Virginia. *The Common Reader*. London: The Hogarth Press, 1925.

The critic discusses the intensity of Charlotte Brontë's style and refers to *Villette* as her "finest novel." She is analyzed as having an "ardent love of nature" and as having, in common with Hardy, a power of personality and a narrowness of vision. Woolf feels that Emily Brontë "could free life from its dependence on facts." According to Woolf, *Wuthering Heights* says "'we, the whole human race' and 'you, the eternal powers . . .' the sentence remains unfinished." Commenting on the poetic qualities of both Brontës, she observes an "untamed ferocity perpetually at war with the accepted order of things" and senses a "desire to create instantly rather than observe patiently." She feels that they are allied with "their more inarticulate passions." In fact, "we read Charlotte Brontë not for exquisite observation of character . . . not for comedy . . . not for philosophic view of life . . . but for her poetry."

C147   Allott, Miriam (ed.). *The Brontës: The Critical Heritage.* London: Routledge and Kegan Paul, 1974.

Following a perceptive introduction, the book is divided into three parts: (1) "The critical reputation of the brothers Bell, 1846-1853," (2) "The Brontës in the 1850's," and (3) "Judgements and Opinions, 1859-1899." While presenting a good selection of criticism, the editor concludes that *Wuthering Heights* has attracted more interest than *Jane Eyre.*

C148   Andrews, W. L. "Ups and Downs of Celebrity." *The Brontës Then and Now.* Shipley: Outhwaite Brothers, 1947.

An informal article about the reputation of the Brontës.

C149   Anon. *The Brontës Then and Now.* Shipley: Outhwaite Brothers, 1947.

This collection of eleven articles, mostly reprinted from earlier issues of *BST,* includes Butler Wood's "The Influence of the Moorland on Charlotte and Emily Brontë" (C144) and C. Mabel Edgerley's "Causes of Death in The Brontë Family" (C261). Most of the articles are biographical or personal notes of appreciation by the authors.

C150   Bennett, Joseph T. "The Critical Reception of the English Novel: 1830-1880." Unpublished doctoral dissertation, New York University, 1969. *DAI,* 30:272.

This study "deals with the relationship between the development of the nineteenth century English novel and the periodical criticism of fiction from the 1830's through the 1870's."

C151   Bentley, Phyllis. "The Daydream Writings of the Brontës." *The Listener,* Jan. 27, 1949, pp. 145-146.

This article, based on a talk given by Dr. Bentley on the Third Programme of the BBC, contains pertinent thoughts on the childhood world of the Brontës. "Yes; while outwardly the young Brontës looked insignificant, quiet, demurely Christian children of the

Parsonage," she told her audience, "Inwardly they were making speeches in Parliament, leading armies, dealing with State papers, wielding arrogant power or tenderest love." The juvenilia shed light on family relations. Branwell's "rebel complex" shows through, and even "an instinctive fear of ending his pleasure by approaching reality" as he wrote of one of his characters. Charlotte's "Angria is a sex-wish-fulfillment world if there ever was one," while Emily's Gondal poems seem "sometimes" to reveal "her own emotions."

C152   Bentley, Phyllis. "Dr. Phyllis Bentley on the Brontës and Methodism." *BST*, 11 (1949), 270.

A reprint of Dr. Bentley's letters to the editor explains the influence of Methodism on the creative output of the Brontës.

C153   Chew, Samuel C. "The Nineteenth Century and After" in *A Literary History of England*. Ed. Albert C. Baugh. New York: Appleton-Century-Crofts, 1948.

A standard, evaluative, and concise statement about the Brontës with an excellent bibliography of the major texts of the first hundred years of criticism.

C154   Christian, Mildred G. "The Brontës." *Victorian Newsletter*, 13 (Spring 1958), 19.

A comment by this most responsible bibliographer of the Brontës.

C155   Colby, Vineta. *The Singular Anomaly: Women Novelists in the 19th Century*. New York: New York University Press, 1970.

The critic mentions the Brontës only in passing, but she gives a fair view of the state of things for "Women Novelists in the Nineteenth Century."

C156   Craik, Wendy Ann. "The Brontës." *The Victorians*. Ed. A. Pollard. Vol. 6 of *The Sphere History of Literature in the English Language*. London: Cresset, 1969.

The author of *The Brontë Novels* (C68) gives due consideration to the place of the Brontës in the literary history of their time.

C157   Cunningham, Valentine. *Everywhere Spoken Against: Dissent in the Victorian Novel.* Oxford: Clarendon Press, 1975.

Although there is only a short section on the Brontës, this book deals with a pertinent area: non-conformity in Methodism and its influence. The author asks that unoriginal question: how could three spinsters living in obscurity record such passion?

C158   Gérin, Winifred. *The Brontës: II. The Creative Work.* Writers and Their Work Series. Ed. Ian Scott-Kilvert. Harlow: Longman for the British Council, 1974.

With *The Formative Years* (C266), a biographical volume, this study of the Brontës serves to give a complete picture of their lives and works. This volume summarizes each of the novels with analysis as well as plot, and quotations from the poetry of Charlotte and Anne. See also Gérin on the influence of environment on the Brontës (C224).

C159   Gorsky, Susan R. "Old Maids and New Women." *Journal of Popular Culture,* 7 (1973), 68-85.

This article presents alternatives to marriage in Englishwomen's novels, 1847-1915. The Brontë novels are included in the discussion.

C160   Hannah, Barbara. *Striving Toward Wholeness.* New York: G. P. Putnam's Sons, 1971.

This Jungian critic and literary analyst studies the biography and literary works of five writers: Robert Louis Stevenson, Mary Webb, Charlotte, Emily, and Anne Brontë with something added about Branwell. Both the juvenilia and *Wuthering Heights* are examined closely from a Jungian point of view. The critic concentrates mainly on two symbolic images: the archetype of four (potential totality) and the archetype of the four rivers of paradise. As children "the Brontës saw the most extraordinary images in the collective unconscious" but "they had no idea what they were seeing." The

242

critic finds *Jane Eyre* "a woman's self-revelation." She feels that Emily's "complete surrender to the creative spirit" gives a representation "of the process of individuation."

C161   Hannah, Barbara. *Victims of the Creative Spirit: Contributions to the Psychology of the Brontës from the Jungian Point of View.* London: Guild of Pastoral Psychology, 1951.

Admitting that in titling the work "I might just as well have said: 'Rescued by the Creative Spirit,'" this Jungian critic stresses the duality of the creative experience. She further suggests that the Brontës "were all in a situation where the sea of the unconscious might close over them at any time." This lecture was originally given before the Guild of Pastoral Psychology on July 21, 1950.

C162   Harrison, Grace Elizabeth. *The Clue to the Brontës.* London: Methuen, 1948.

Wesleyan Methodism is the "clue" in what has been called this "gleefully malicious" study. The patron of the Reverend Brontë in Ireland, Thomas Tighe, drew the Wesley's traveling preachers to him, thus influencing the young Patrick. Mrs. Harrison feels that this influence is transferred to Emily Brontë, and *Wuthering Heights* is based on Methodist lore.

C163   Harrison, Grace E. *Haworth Parsonage: A Study of Wesley and the Brontës.* London: Theeworth Press, 1937.

This is a printed version of Lecture No. 3 of the Wesley Historical Society Lectures, delivered at Haworth, July 16, 1937. In it the speaker suggests that the influence of Aunt Branwell's Methodism was one of the strong forces in molding the Brontës' characters. It is of interest to learn that an entry in John Wesley's journal mentions Lockwood, Grimshaw, and Sutcliffe.

C164   Harrison, Grace E. *Methodist Good Companions.* London: Epworth Press, 1935.

Mrs. Harrison believes that "Methodism was Emily Brontë's nursery . . . her university also." In this highly respected book,

243

Chapter Five covers what must have been the center of tension, "Reactions in Haworth Parsonage." For an Anglican Parsonage, the atmosphere was hardly conventional.

C165   Hopewell, Donald. "The Brontës in Our Thoughts Today" in *The Enduring Brontës*. Ed. Linton Andrews. Shipley: Outhwaite Brothers, 1951. Reissued, New York: Folcroft, 1974.

The same year that he wrote the article "New Treasures at Haworth," *BST,* 12 (1951), 18, the later president of the Brontë Society appeared with other Brontë authorities in this tribute to the novelists.

C166   Howe, Bea. *A Galaxy of Governesses.* London: Derek Verschoyle, 1954.

Under the heading of "A Triumvirate of Governesses," the author discusses briefly the role of the governess in the lives and works of the Brontës.

C167   James, Louis. *Fiction for the Working Man: 1830-1850.* London: Oxford University Press, 1963.

This study of the "literature produced for the working classes in early Victorian urban England" is more biographical than critical.

C168   Johnson, James W. "Nightmare and Reality in *Wuthering Heights*" in Emily Brontë. *Wuthering Heights.* Boston: Houghton Mifflin, 1965.

Writing about both Emily and Charlotte Brontë, the critic deals first with the structure of *Wuthering Heights* in which he sees the characters as the central nucleus. Continuity is achieved through weather, landscape, family lines, and repeated events. Emily's use of irrational emotions, shown through dreams and ghosts, has a relationship to Charlotte's use of the supernatural in *Villette.* This unreality of ghosts is identified with Lucy's "private world of fantasy." For her, emotion and reason are reconciled in her love for M. Paul.

C169   Kellett, E. E. "New Light on the Brontës." *London Quarterly and Holborn Review*, 160 (Oct. 1935), 591-621.

Another scholar forty years ago tries to bring light to the problem of the influence of Methodism on the Brontës.

C170   Lane, Margaret. "The Drug-Like Brontë Dreams." *BST*, 12 (1952), 79-87.

The four Brontës, even as young adults, escaped into the dream world which they had made up as children. Charlotte Brontë broke out of it, but Emily Brontë stayed caught in it. From this unreality emerged her novel and her poetry.

C171   Leeming, Glenda. *Who's Who in Jane Austen and the Brontës*. London: Hamish Hamilton, 1974.

Here are thumbnail sketches of all the main characters in all the novels of all three Brontës. The entries are alphabetically arranged, giving the name of the novel each appeared in, his identity, physical description, and his part in the plot. As much as possible, the author's own words are used.

C172   Lord, Walter F. "The Brontë Novels." *Nineteenth Century*, 53 (March 1903), 484-495.

In this unusual and dated criticism of all the Brontë novels we are told: "one yawns over *Wuthering Heights*." Emily Brontë was not a great artist, according to the critic, but Anne Brontë's *Agnes Grey* "makes a great impression."

C173   Marks, William Sowell, II. "The Novel as Puritan Romance: A Comparative Study of Samuel Richardson, the Brontës, Thomas Hardy, and D. H. Lawrence." Unpublished doctoral dissertation, Stanford University, 1964. *DAI*, 25:1214.

In discussing Puritan ideals of love and marriage, Marks says that the Brontës had "greater sympathy with the demonic" than with the Puritanic. They criticized society which repressed the demonic. *Wuthering Heights* is compared to Blake's songs and prophecies.

245

C174   Mews, Hazel. *Frail Vessels: Woman's Role in Women's Novels from Fanny Burney to George Eliot*. London: Athlone Press, 1969.

In an overview of the role of women in the novels of eight major (and several minor) women writers in the nineteenth century, the critic examines "Women Awaiting Marriage," "Women as Wives," "Women as Mothers," and "Women Standing Alone." The characters in the Brontë novels are used as examples in all these categories. Of all three Brontë sisters the critic says, "The early Victorian Brontës wrenched the view of women in the novel to a different level by the power of their own emotions." She is particularly interested in Charlotte Brontë's part in the development of the theme. "Charlotte Brontë cried out against the waste of women's intellectual and emotional powers in mid-nineteenth-century England," she says.

C175   Miles, Rosalind. *The Fiction of Sex: Themes and Functions of Sex Difference in the Modern Novel*. London: Vision Press, 1974.

Seeing the work of women writers divided between the "honorary male" mode (of George Eliot, for example) and the "feminine" mode initiated by Charlotte Brontë, the critic credits Charlotte Brontë with being "feminine, not feminist." She writes of a "woman in search of her identity" and, particularly in Lucy Snowe, of the importance of work in establishing "even a tenuous self-esteem." In her work women carry the thematic burden; for the author, the position of the female is central in her thoughts. The critic comments on Emily Brontë, emphasizing her importance as one of the few women poets.

C176   Nicoll, William Robertson and Thomas Seccombe. "The Brontës." *A History of English Literature*. New York: Dodd Mead, 1907.

This early criticism by two knowledgeable men of letters presents *Wuthering Heights* as a unique book "by reason of its sincerity, its freedom from affectation, triviality or verbiage." Despite imperfection or the suggestion that it is embryonic art, the critics speak more vigorously about *Wuthering Heights* than about any of the other Brontë novels.

246

C177   Odom, Keith Conrad. "The Brontës and Romantic Views of Personality." Unpublished doctoral dissertation, University of Wisconsin, 1961. *DAI,* 22:2004.

The author investigates the attitudes of Charlotte, Emily, and Anne Brontë toward the beliefs of the Romantics (their attitude toward childhood, organicism, emotion and passion, Byronism, and religious thought and feeling) in an attempt to establish them as Romantic writers. As they all see good in nature (a Romantic concept), their good characters speak for a unity of nature.

C178   Parrish, M. L. "The Brontë Sisters." *Victorian Lady Novelists: George Eliot, Mrs. Gaskell, The Brontë Sisters.* London: Constable, 1933.

In presenting the ideas of what it was like to be a Victorian lady who was also a Victorian author, the critic gives factual information about problems and rewards.

C179   Pinion, F. B. *A Brontë Companion.* London: Macmillan, 1975.

Here are all the facts needed to have a good comprehension of the Brontës. The second section discusses each of the known works — from Angria and Gondal, through all the novels, poems and known fragments. The appendices add support concerning the Gondal saga. An extremely informative volume. Vol. also listed as C288.

C180   Platt, Carolyn V. "The Female Quest in the Works of Anne, Charlotte, and Emily Brontë." Unpublished doctoral dissertation, University of Illinois at Urbana-Champaign, 1974. *DAI,* 35:4450.

"Discussions in the Brontë works of the active, questing heroine, who strives for independence and self-development in a society in which women are encouraged to remain passive."

C181   Quertermous, Harry M. "The Byronic Hero in the Writings of the Brontës." Unpublished doctoral dissertation, University of Texas at Austin, 1960. *DAI,* 21:191.

The Byronic hero is present in all the early works of all four Brontës but "reaches its greatest realization" in *Wuthering Heights,* in Catherine as well as in Heathcliff.

C182   Ratchford, Fannie E. *The Brontës' Web of Childhood.* New York: Columbia University Press, 1941.

This is the most formidable of all authoritative analyses of the Brontës' childhood play and its influence on later writings of the novelists. Miss Ratchford had many examples of Charlotte and Branwell's version of Angria, but she was called upon to use her ingenuity in the reconstruction of Gondal. She views *Wuthering Heights* "as an adaptation of a purely imaginary creation to the demands of realism," and sees throughout the adult work of all the Brontës the memory of the sagas of childhood.

C183   Ratchford, Fannie E. "The Brontës' Web of Dreams." *Yale Review,* 21 (Autumn 1931), 139-157.

In this article Miss Ratchford gives a hint, in the account of the Brontës' childhood plays, of the unusual study she is in the process of preparing.

C184   Ratchford, Fannie E. "Family of Scribblers." *Saturday Review of Literature,* 36 (June 20, 1953), 21.

A brief intimation of the potential in the young Brontës.

C185   Showalter, Elaine. "Women Writers and the Double Standard" in *Woman in Sexist Society: Studies in Power and Powerlessness.* Eds. Vivian Gornick and Barbara K. Moran. New York: New American Library, 1971.

Using the Brontës' problems as examples of those of Victorian women writers, the critic points out the difficulties women have faced in trying to be considered as "writers" instead of "women writers." She reminds us that "women novelists were both fearful and defiant of the critics; they expected a certain amount of derision and hostility; they took precautions against personal attack if they could; but they had a keen sense of professional and artistic responsibilities, and where these were involved, they would not make concessions or ask for favors."

C186   Stedman, Jane W. "The Genesis of the Genii." *BST,* 14 (1965), 16-19.

This critic feels that it was not so much *Arabian Nights* as the *Tales of the Genii* by James Ridley which influenced the young Brontës in their childhood sagas.

C187   Stevenson, W. H. *Emily and Anne Brontë.* Profiles in Literature Series. London: Routledge and Kegan Paul, 1968.

This concise informative volume gives a selection of writings by the two sisters, a brief biography of the family, some commentary and analysis, and a bibliography.

C188   Stuart, J. A. Erskine. "The Brontë Nomenclature." *BST,* 1:3 (1895), 14-18.

Using a great deal of conjecture, this critic assumes certain facts about the choice of Brontë as the family name. He then speculates on the origin of "Currer Bell." After that he gives the source of place names and proper names in all the Brontë novels.

C189   Thomson, Patricia. *The Victorian Heroine: A Changing Ideal, 1837-1873.* London: Oxford University Press, 1956.

The Brontë governess-novels may be viewed as part of a sub-genre which revealed something of the social structure of Victorian England.

C190   Thorburn, Donald B. "The Effects of the Wesleyan Movement on the Brontë Sisters, as Evidenced by an Examination of Certain of their Novels." Unpublished doctoral dissertation, New York University, 1947. *DAI,* 8:109.

A further study of the influence of Methodism on the Brontës. The dissertation examines the religious principles revealed in the novels: the attitude against liquor, improper dress, Sabbatarianism, Catholicism, the High Church. They stress sanctity of daily work, use of the Bible for daily guidance, humanitarianism, salvation through free choice, and worth of the common man. The Brontës are referred to as "spiritual children of Methodism."

C191   Wagenknecht, Edward. "Fire Over Yorkshire" in *Cavalcade of the English Novel.* New York: Holt, 1943; second edition, 1954.

A summary of the lives and works of the Brontës includes: how it all began, Charlotte Brontë relives Angria, the greatness of *Wuthering Heights*, Anne Brontë's novels, what the Brontës mean. The critic also includes a bibliography to the date of the second edition.

C192   Weir, Edith M. "New Brontë Material Comes to Light." *BST*, 11 (1949), 249.

A comment on the reappearance of hitherto unknown manuscripts of the juvenilia, including a picture attributed to Emily Brontë and letters from the Hegers.

Criticism of Poetry
of the Brontës

C193   Childe, Wilfred Rowland. "The Brontës as Poets" in *The Enduring Brontës*. Ed. Linton Andrews. Shipley: Outhwaite Brothers, 1951.

One of the few articles which treats the poetry of the three sisters, while recognizing that these poets are not of equal talents.

C194   Drinkwater, John. "The Brontës as Poets" in *Prose Papers*. London: Mathews, 1917.

An authority on poets and poetry declares that Emily Brontë is a genius. He says that she carries the "dead weight" of Charlotte, Anne, and Branwell's poetry. Drinkwater separates the poems for consideration and analyzes them.

C195   Livingston, Luther S. "Prefatory Note" in *Poems by Charlotte, Emily and Anne Brontë Now for the First Time Printed*. New York: Dodd, Mead, 1902.

In explaining about the poems selected, the editor notes that most are by Emily Brontë. All are presented as written, not edited. Some are from the juvenilia.

C196   Rainwater, Mary Janice. "Emily Dickinson and Six Contemporary Writers: Her Poetry in Relation to her Reading." Unpublished doctoral dissertation, Northwestern University, 1975. *DAI*, 36:4479.

Both Emily and Charlotte Brontë are considered as contemporary authors who influenced the American poet.

C197   Tinker, Chauncey Brewster. "The Poetry of the Brontës." *Saturday Review of Literature*, 1 (Jan. 10, 1925), 441-442. Reprinted in *Essays in Retrospect: Collected Articles and Addresses.* New Haven: Yale University Press, 1948.

Professor Tinker gives a thorough analysis of the poetry. All of the Brontës, he says, lack discipline in their poetry. Even Emily Brontë can "strike a false note," but she is the poetic genius of the family. He admires her "unchastened emotionalism . . . emphasis on freedom" and "intense self-confidence."

C198   Wise, Thomas J. "Preface" in *The Poems of Emily Jane Brontë and Anne Brontë.* Oxford: Shakespeare Head Press, 1934.

This editor and businessman gives a factual history of the publication of the poems.

C199   Wyatt, Edith. "Brontë Poems" in *Great Companions.* New York: Appleton-Century, 1917.

In discussing the relationship between the Brontës' lives and works, Wyatt claims that the poems show that art does not depend on experience.

Criticism of Writings
Anne Brontë

C200   Andrews, W. L. "A Challenge by Anne Brontë." *BST*, 14:5 (1965), 25-30.

Although Andrews admits that *The Tenant of Wildfell Hall* was written with a "transparently conscientious purpose," he feels that it shouldn't be condemned for this reason. The novel offers "sharp challenge to the conventions of Anne's day." It is certainly a "novel of purpose."

C201   Bell, A. Craig. *Anne Brontë: The Tenant of Wildfell Hall: A Study and Reappraisal.* Ilkley: Emeril Publications, 1974.

A stated attempt to "try to vindicate a genuine minority opinion" by turning the reader away from "unthinking, repetitive, generally accepted canons." The critic's wish to suggest new depths to be found in this least appreciated Brontë work is based on his belief that Anne Brontë's second novel was her attempt to efface the earlier criticism of *Agnes Grey* in which the *Atlas* critic stated that the novel "leaves no impression" on the mind of the reader.

C202   Hargreaves, G. D. "Further Omissions in *The Tenant of Wildfell Hall.*" *BST,* 17 (1977), 115-121.

In his second study (see also C203) this critic reports that there are many disturbing omissions, from one word to almost an entire chapter. Short omissions made have been made for propriety. Longer omissions have usually been made to shorten the work when one-volume editions have been prepared.

C203   Hargreaves, G. D. "Incomplete Texts of *The Tenant of Wildfell Hall.*" *BST,* 16 (1972), 113-117.

Hargreaves discloses that the majority of the British editions omit the opening section which was written to precede chapter one. The chapter headings are also frequently omitted.

C204   Harrison, Ada May and Derek Stanford. *Anne Brontë: Her Life and Work.* London: Methuen, 1959.

Here two Brontë scholars treat Anne as a serious writer. The first section, on her poetry, covers love poems, didactic poems, and religious poems, and then discusses the verbal texture. The second section, on her novels, discusses each and then points out that Anne is our first realist woman author, audacious in her manner of presentation and intellectually daring.

C205   Le Guern, Joseph. *Anne Brontë 1820-1849: La Vie et l'oeuvre.* Paris: Librairie Honoré Champion, 1977.

A serious scholarly treatment of this writer, whom the critic feels must be considered for herself alone and whose writing must be judged on its own merits. The first volume presents Anne Brontë's life and character, based on all the known facts. The second volume contains a perceptive analysis of her works, both fiction and poetry.

C206   McKneely, Lewis Marvin. "Anne Brontë: Novelist of Reform." Unpublished doctoral dissertation, Emory University, 1956. *DAI,* 19:2954.

The author attempts to determine "whether Anne's suggestions for reform were innovations or whether they were reflections of the general humanitarian tendencies of the age."

C207   Meier, T. K. *"The Tenant of Wildfell Hall:* Morality as Act." *Revue des Langues Vivantes,* 39 (1973), 59-62.

This study draws parallels between characters in the novel in an attempt to find Anne Brontë's definition of ideal marriage.

C208   Moore, George in E. Gosse, *Conversations in Ebury Street.* London: Heinemann, 1924.

Here George Moore praises Anne's *Agnes Grey* as the "most perfect prose narrative in English letters." Moore thought that Charlotte's depreciation of Anne caused critics to look down on her.

C209   Sholto-Douglas, Nora I. *Synopsis of English Fiction.* London: George G. Harrap, 1926.

Both *Agnes Grey* and *The Tenant of Wildfell Hall* are discussed, primarily to give the plots rather than criticize.

C210   Visick, Mary. "Anne Brontë's Last Poem." *BST,* 13 (1959), 352.

This Brontë authority (see B329) examines the final outpouring of this introspective yet didactic poet.

C211   Drinkwater, John. *A Book for Bookmen: Being Edited Manuscripts and Marginalia with Essays on Several Occasions.* London: Dulau, 1926.

One of the rare occasions on which a serious critic discusses Branwell Brontë, in a chapter called "Patrick Branwell Brontë and his 'Horace.'"

C212   Gérin, Winifred. "The Authorship of *Wuthering Heights*" in *Branwell Brontë.* London: T. Nelson, 1961.

Through close investigation, Gérin concludes that Branwell Brontë could not have written *Wuthering Heights.* The biographer analyzes Branwell's character and cites examples from his prose and poetry to prove her contention.

C213   Hatfield, C. W. "Unpublished Poems by Patrick Branwell Brontë." *BST,* 7 (1927), 71-96.

In an effort to make Branwell's talents and thought process clearer, Hatfield presents some material not available to scholars prior to that time.

C214   Law, Alice. *Patrick Branwell Brontë.* London: A. M. Philpot, 1923. Reissued, New York: Richard West, 1974.

This discussion of Branwell's life centers on the critic's belief that Branwell, not Emily, wrote *Wuthering Heights.* (See also B212.) Vol· also listed as B213.

C215   Hargreaves, G. D. "The Publishing of *Poems by Currer, Ellis, and Acton Bell.*" *BST,* 15:4 (1969), 294-300. Reprinted in *Library Review,* 22:7 (Autumn 1970), 353-356.

Hargreaves gives a picture of the literary scene in 1846 – a bad time for publishing poetry. Charlotte Brontë contracted with Aylott and Jones to produce probably a thousand copies "on the author's account," completed by May 1846 to be sold at four shillings each. Fourteen complimentary copies were sent out for reviewing; both the *Critic* and the *Athenaeum* printed favorable reviews. Two copies of the book were sold; in September of 1848 Smith, Elder (publisher of *Jane Eyre*) bought the remaining 961 and reissued the book.

C216   Larken, Geoffrey. "The Shuffling Scamp." *BST,* 15:5 (1970), 400-407.

This forthright description of Thomas C. Newby, original publisher of *Wuthering Heights, Agnes Grey,* and *The Tenant of Wildfell Hall,* says bluntly: "He was shifting, elusive and evasive, a rogue and a rascal, and thoroughly deserved to be dubbed by Charlotte a 'shuffling scamp.'"

C217   Partington, Wilfred. *Forging Ahead: The True Story of the Upward Progress of Thomas James Wise, Prince of Book Collectors, Bibliographer Extraordinary and Otherwise.* New York: G. P. Putnam's Sons, 1939.

According to Robertson Nicoll, Clement Shorter bought the literary estate of Charlotte Brontë – manuscripts and letters – from the Reverend Arthur Bell Nicholls. Shorter in turn sold them to Thomas Wise, but kept the copyright. This was only one of the many complications of the T. J. Wise editorial activities.

C218   Reid, Stuart J. *Memoirs of Sir Wemyss Reid, 1842-1885.* London: Cassell, 1905.

Here is a review of Sir Wemyss Reid's contribution to the interpretation of British literature, including his Brontë scholarship.

C219   Sadleir, Michael. *Nineteenth Century Fiction.* Vol. I and II. New York: Cooper Square Publishers, 1969.

   In volume one, Sadleir describes particular volumes of the Brontë first editions.

C220   Stephens, Fran Carlock. "Hartley Coleridge and the Brontës." *Times Literary Supplement,* May 14, 1970, p. 544.

   A discussion of three letters from the Coleridge collection, one between Hartley Coleridge and Branwell, one between Charlotte and H. Coleridge, and the letter sent out with the *Poems* in 1846.

C221   Stevens, Joan. "Woozles in Brontëland: A Cautionary Tale." *Studies in Bibliography,* 24 (1971), 99-108.

   Stevens shows that the errors in Clement Shorter's publication of the Brontë letters (C298) were carried forward by Wise and Symington in the *Shakespeare Head Brontë* in 1932. This idea is verified by an analysis of Charlotte Brontë's letter describing her visit to Smith, Elder (her publisher) on September 4, 1848.

C222   Sutherland, J. A. *Victorian Novelists and Publishers.* London: Athlone Press, 1976.

   The history of the publishing of the Brontë novels is clearly stated. *Jane Eyre* was rejected nine times, *Wuthering Heights* six. It took Newby six months to produce an "execrable edition" of *Wuthering Heights* and *Agnes Grey.* Just six weeks after Smith, Elder read the manuscript of *Jane Eyre,* they had it for sale in shop windows. The first edition was produced in October 1847, the second January 1848, and the third in April 1848.

C223   Taylor, Robert H. "The Singular Anomalies." *Princeton University Library Chronicle,* 17 (Winter 1956), 71-76.

   This discussion of the Parrish Collection describes the early editions of *Wuthering Heights* and *Poems by Currer, Ellis, and Acton Bell.*

Biography
Charlotte and Emily Brontë Considered Together

C224 Gérin, Winifred. "The Effects of Environment on the Brontë Writings." *Essays by Divers Hands: Transactions of the Royal Society of Literature,* 36 (1972), 67-83.

This Brontë authority, who lives in Haworth and understands the ambiance, shows how the writers were influenced by their way of life.

C225 Grimshaw, Beatrice. "First Love: A Glory That is Never Forgotten." *John O'London's Weekly,* Oct. 4, 1924, p. 4.

A sentimental investigation which includes Charlotte Brontë and Emily Brontë. The biographer feels that Emily knew love as proved in her poem, "Cold in the Earth."

C226 Hinkley, Laura L. *The Brontës: Charlotte and Emily.* New York: Hastings House, 1945.

Here is a once-popular rendering of the Brontë life story, showing the moving experiences of their personal lives. The biographer suggests that Heathcliff could be modeled on Joshua Taylor. She recognizes twenty non-Gondal poems. She attempts to reconstruct the sagas of childhood.

C227 James, Henry. "The Art of Fiction" in *The Future of the Novel.* New York: Vintage Books, 1956.

Speaking out against the problems created by biographical readings, James has only a few things to say, here, about the Brontës. He feels that the Romantic tradition of the Brontës is reinforced by "the attendant image of their dreary, their tragic history, their loneliness and poverty of life." This feeling about them leads to an "intellectual muddle" in which we "confound the cause with the results."

C228 James, Henry. From "The Lesson of Balzac." Reprinted in *The House of Fiction: Essays on the Novel.* London: R. Hart-Davis, 1957.

Again James suggests that the biography of the Brontës "covers and supplants" the works, causing a "complete intellectual muddle." He feels that the case of the Brontës represents "the high-water mark of sentimental judgement."

C229 Lawrence, Margaret. "Brontë Sisters Who Wrestled with Romance." *School of Feminity.* New York: Stokes, 1936. Reprinted in *We Write as Women.* London: Michael Joseph, 1937.

A simplistic approach to the Brontë sisters' lives attributes romantic attachment between each of them and all the men they knew.

C130 Zeman, Anthea. *Presumptuous Girls: Women and their World in the Serious Woman's Novel.* London: Weidenfeld and Nicolson, 1977.

In a larger view of "serious" women writers, the Brontës are included as examples of "nineteenth-century middle-class . . . liberation."

Biography
Brontë Family

C231 Anon. [The Honorable Lady Barbara Wilson]. "The Brontës as Governesses." *BST,* 9 (1939), 217-235.

Here is a discussion of the Brontës when they left home to "earn a living in a profession which was abhorrent to them" during the years from 1835 to 1844.

C232 Arnold, Matthew. "Haworth Churchyard: April, 1855." *Fraser's Magazine,* (May 1855), reprinted in *Poetical Works.* London: Macmillan, 1907.

The moving description includes these lines:
There, on its slope, is built
The moorland town. But the church
Stands on the crest of the hill,
Lonely and bleak; at its side
The parsonage-house and the graves.

C233 Auerbach, N. "Elizabeth Gaskell's Sly Javelins: Governing Women in Cranford and Haworth." *Modern Language Quarterly,* 38 (Summer 1977), 276-291.

An interesting addition to the study of Charlotte Brontë's biographer and her attitude toward the family she portrayed. The critic sees Haworth as the origin of Cranford and identifies Charlotte Brontë as the person on whom Miss Matty is based.

C234 Baillie, Dr. J. B. "Religion and the Brontës." *BST,* 7 (1927), 59-69.

The Vice-Chancellor of Leeds University draws his own conclusions about the Brontës' religion. Among his beliefs: Emily's poems reveal her to be a regularly religious person.

C235 Benson, E. F. "The Brontës" in *The English Novelists.* Ed. Derek Verschoyle. New York: Harcourt Brace, 1934.

Here an informed and respected biographer tells the traditional story in his own way.

C236 Bentley, Phyllis. *The Brontës.* London: Home and Van Thal, 1947.

One of the most respected short critical biographies. A clear approach to Angrian and Gondal material accompanies a sympathetic treatment of the personal relationships within the family. She touches on all the novels and discusses Emily's poetry. She mentions "the struggle of integrity to hold its own in a difficult world." To explain the Brontë genius, Dr. Bentley credits heredity, environment, education, and influences within the family.

C237 Bentley, Phyllis E. *The Brontës and Their World.* London: Thames and Hudson, 1969.

Rich with 140 photographs and art reproductions, this easily read work gives a sense of atmosphere and environment of the life in Haworth.

C238 Bentley, Phyllis. *The Brontës: Creators of Wuthering Heights, Jane Eyre, Villette, The Tenant of Wildfell Hall.* Jackdaws Series 116. London: Jackdaws Publications, 1971.

A charming and reliable collection of replicas brings a feeling of the Brontës to the student, young or old. The kit includes reproductions of portraits, samples of letters, and a facsimile of one of the miniature books from the childhood play.

C239   Bentley, Phyllis. *The Brontë Sisters* in Writers and Their Works Series. British Council and National Book League. London: Longmans Green, 1950.

Dr. Bentley presents a short clear introduction to the writers, a factual account of their lives which stresses the importance of the Irish strain. She is especially good on *Villette*, which she refers to as "a study of a woman's loneliness." Around the core circle three other groups, she explains, "their inter-relations rather too neatly and skillfully arranged."

C240   Bentley, Phyllis. "The Lives and Writings of the Brontës" in *The Brontës*. Heather Edition. Ed. Phyllis Bentley. London: A. Wingate, 1949.

After a review of the biography, the critic places major emphasis on the "day-dream" writing and its significance.

C241   Bentley, Phyllis. "Love Among the Brontës." *Contemporary Review*, 217 (Nov. 1970), 225-230.

Dr. Bentley discusses the various kinds of love which the Brontës knew: attitudes toward each other, toward their father, and Charlotte's marriage attitude. The two puzzles for all biographers — Charlotte's feeling for M. Heger and Branwell's problem at the Robinsons — are covered. In the case of the latter, the critic suggests that Branwell's "affair" may have been used as a cover-up for something more serious in the relationship between him and his pupil.

C242   Bentley, Phyllis. "The Significance of Haworth." *The Trollopian*, 2 (Dec. 1947), 127-136.

This is an expansion of a chapter from her book *The Brontës* (C236) in which the critic discusses, on the one hand, the landscape and ideology of Haworth, and on the other, the Celtic heritage of the family.

C243   Bentley, Phyllis. "Yorkshire and the Novelist." *Essays by Divers Hands: Being the Transactions of the Royal Society of Literature*, 33 (1963), 145-157. Later bound and published, London: Oxford University Press, 1965.

In this article the critic tells of the significance of setting in the case of several writers, including the Brontës. Discussion covers the general ambiance, the landscape, and the character of the inhabitants.

C244   Bentley, Phyllis. *The Young Brontës*. London: Max Parrish, 1960.

The respected Brontë critic offers a fictional biography of the young Brontës.

C245   Blackburn, Ruth M., ed. *The Brontë Sisters: Selected Source Material for College Research Papers*. Boston: D. C. Heath, 1964.

This fragmented collection of material, by the Brontës and about them, might possibly be useful for freshman theme writing, but has neither bibliography nor critical evaluation.

C246   Bradby, Godfrey Fox. "Brontë Legends" in *The Brontës and Other Essays*. London: Oxford University Press, 1932.

In this article, the Brontë scholar questions some legends which were reported by A. Mary Robinson in her biography of Emily Brontë written in 1883 (B505).

C247   Braithwaite, William Stanley. *The Bewitched Parsonage: the Story of the Brontës*. New York: Coward-McCann, 1950.

In spite of its fanciful title this is a factual yet sensitive account of the lives of the Brontë family.

C248   Brown, T. J. "English Literary Autographs, No. 17: The Brontës." *Book Collector*, 5 (Spring 1956), 55-56.

In this unusual approach to a study of the Brontës as living human beings, Brown shows through facsimiles and analytic

261

description the "microscopic" handwriting which all four Brontës used as well as their normal script.

C249 Butterfield, Herbert. "Charlotte Brontë and her Sisters in the Crucial Year." *BST,* 14 (1963), 3-17.

In the year 1845 the Brontë sisters and Branwell came together after having been separated by various occupations. Emily's creative period had begun the previous year and all of the others had reached an important point in their lives.

C250 Butterfield, Mary. "Face to Face with the Brontës." *Sunday Times Magazine* (London), Oct. 17, 1976, 64-68.

In the Cliffe Castle Museum in Keighley, the author claims to have seen a picture of three men, identified on the back of the photo as Branwell Brontë, the Reverend Nicholls, and Mr. Brown the sexton. Ms. Butterfield also talks about the picture in Brian Wilks' book, *The Brontës* (C313), of six figures, two men and four ladies, whom she identifies as the three Brontë sisters, Ellen Nussey, Branwell Brontë and one other. She dates the picture 1844 or 1845. However, there is serious doubt that this identification is valid, as the picture is said to have been taken by Jackson Brothers of Oldham in 1861, and one lady has been recognized as being Martha Hopkinson.

C251 Chadwick, Esther Alice. "The Haworth Parsonage: The Home of The Brontës." *Nineteenth Century Fiction,* 103 (Jan. 1928), 133-144.

This article was published just when the Parsonage was to be converted into the Brontë Museum. The Reverend William Grimshaw had lived there before the Brontës and other parsonage families had followed them. Mrs. Chadwick describes the building, the relics and the manuscripts.

C252 Chadwick, Esther Alice. *In the Footsteps of the Brontës.* London: Sir I. Pitman and Sons, 1914.

One of the classic studies of the Brontës within their own environment, by a biographer who gives her version of the world through which the Brontës moved. Vol. also listed as B484.

C253   Chernaik, J. "All Roads Lead to the Moor: Haworth Parsonage." *Saturday Review,* 1 (Jan. 1973), 62-63.

A modern critic gives a feeling of the moorland world surrounding the Haworth Parsonage. "The museum may be tame," Chernaik admits, "but outdoors the Brontë spirits reign."

C254   Collins, Norman. "The Independent Brontës." *The Facts of Fiction.* London: Gollancz, 1932.

This biography tries to show that the Brontës' books and their life stories must be viewed together. His critical comments about *Wuthering Heights* tell us that it is "childlike" and "leaps like a frog."

C255   Crandall, Norma. "Charlotte, Emily and Branwell Brontë." *American Book Collector,* 13 (Feb. 1963), 21-22.

As before, Crandall offers an opinion which differs from the usual approach. Here she remarks on the Brontës' "eccentric childhood" and concludes that psychological disability combined with innate gifts leads to "real and marvelous achievement."

C256   Dawson, William J. "The Brontës." *The Makers of English Fiction.* New York: Revell, 1905.

Dawson considers both heredity and environment as contributing to the genius of the Brontës. He admits that it is difficult to judge their work: (1) because so much of their personal lives is in their work, and (2) because the art of fiction writing has progressed so much since their time. This article was written in 1905, at which time the critic felt that *Wuthering Heights* was still not understood.

C257   Delafield, E. M. (pseudonym of Edmée Elizabeth Monica de la Pasture). *Ladies and Gentlemen of Victorian Fiction.* New York: Harper and Brothers, 1937.

A popular survey of the writers of the nineteenth century, with special attention given to the biography of the Brontës.

C258   Dupont, V. "Trois notes sur les Brontës." *Etudes Anglaises,* 6 (Feb. 1953), 1-27.

M. Dupont shows the importance of the Brontës' reading of the *Leeds Intelligencer* and *Leeds Mercury*. He also mentions the influence of the religion of their childhood.

C259   Earle, Kathleen. "Haworth, Home of the Brontës." *Queen's Quarterly*, 75 (1968), 340-346.

The author describes the village of Haworth, which she tells us means "High Farm," and then tells about the parsonage as it is now, a museum and memorial.

C260   Edgerley, C. Mabel. "The Brontës and Haworth" in *Brontë Papers*. Shipley: Outhwaite Brothers, 1951.

A paper read to the Royal Society of Literature on Nov. 10, 1937, called "The Brontës and Haworth," is included in this memorial tribute published by the Brontë Society. It also includes reprints of two articles, "The Eyesight of the Brontës" and "Causes of Death in the Brontë Family."

C261   Edgerley, C. Mabel. "Causes of Death in the Brontë Family." *The Brontës Then and Now*. Shipley: Outhwaite Brothers, 1947.

This Brontë enthusiast has prepared a consideration of the medical history of the Brontës, with the conclusion that consumption was at the base of almost all the deaths in the family.

C262   Edgerley, C. Mabel. "The Eyesight of the Brontës." *British Medical Journal*, Feb. 7, 1931, pp. 21-23.

This Brontë authority deals with a problem of great interest to biographers, considering the myopia of Charlotte Brontë and the production of the juvenile books in minuscule script. This article is reprinted in *Brontë Papers* (C260).

C263   Fry, Christopher. *The Brontës of Haworth*. London: Davis-Poynter, 1975.

Television script of biographical presentation in 1973.

C264   Fry, Christopher. "Genius, Talent and Failure." *BST*, 17 (1976), 1-14.

The illustrious Mr. Fry discusses Emily as genius, Charlotte as talent, and Anne as failure. Of Emily's work he admits, "*Wuthering Heights* is a book I always think most highly of when I'm not actually reading it." He feels that Charlotte must be partly responsible for our attitude toward Anne because Charlotte "snubbed her." He also gives the details of the Brontës' life as he sees it.

C265   Fry, Christopher. "The Parson's Gifted Four." *Daily Telegraph Magazine*, Oct. 5, 1973, pp. 19-20, 22.

In preparing background material for those about to watch the television series, Fry explains much that is worth knowing about the "Gifted Four."

C266   Gérin, Winifred. *The Brontës: I, The Formative Years.* Writers and Their Work Series. Ed. Ian Scott-Kilvert. Harlow: Longman for the British Council, 1973.

The early years of the Brontë children is presented as biography with generous use of illustrations. (For Part II, see C158.)

C267   Green, Julien. "Charlotte Brontë and Her Sisters." *Virginia Quarterly Review*, 5 (1929), 42-58.

This popular writer gives further information in English about the Brontë biography. (See C268 for earlier work in French.)

C268   Green, Julien. *Suite anglaise.* Paris: Les Cahiers de Paris, 1927.

In a book about several earlier British writers (Charles Lamb, Samuel Johnson, and William Blake), Green gives his personal response to the life story of the Brontë family. (In French. See C267 for later article in English.)

C269   Hadow, Sir E. A. "Education as Treated by the Brontës." *BST*, 6 (1925), 261-275.

This article discusses the various aspects of education – in schools and by governess and tutor – which appear in the Brontë novels. (See also Muriel Spark, "The Brontës as Teachers," C302.) The critic is also interested in the education which the Brontës received, particularly at Cowan Bridge School, from the Reverend Brontë and from their independent reading.

C270   Haldane, Elizabeth S. "The Brontës and Their Biographers." *Nineteenth Century*, 112 (Dec. 1932), 752-764.

Here is a discussion of Mrs. Gaskell (A386) and E. F. Benson (A364), the two major biographers up to the time of this article.

C271   Haley, William. "Three Sisters." *BST*, 11 (1947), 73-80. Reprinted in *The Brontës Then and Now*. Shipley: Outhwaite Brothers, 1947.

Haley treats Emily, Charlotte, and Anne as three distinguishable and remarkable personalities. He then compares them with Chekov's Olga, Irina, and Masha Prozorov in *The Three Sisters*.

C272   Hanson, Lawrence and E. M. *The Four Brontës: The Lives and Works of Charlotte, Branwell, Emily, and Anne Brontë*. New York: Oxford University Press, 1950. (First published 1949, second impression revised.)

In this remarkable biography the lives of the four Brontës are examined, especially their effect on one another. The Hansons feel that the rejection of Branwell's romanticizing led Emily to mysticism: her conclusion, that contentment of the soul is not found on earth. The biographers give a romantic reading of the writers' lives as reflected in their work. The Hansons assume that Branwell is Heathcliff. The biography is generally based on fact, but it becomes full of conjecture concerning Emily's reaction to Branwell after the Robinson issue.

C273   Hardwick, E. *Seduction and Betrayal: Women and Literature*. New York: Random House; London: Weidenfeld and Nicolson, 1974.

In this group of essays from the *New York Review of Books,* Hardwick includes the lecture "The Brontës," given earlier at Princeton. The critic touches on biography, seeing the origin of Heathcliff in Branwell. An examination of the sexual overtones in the novels reveals the works as reflecting "the worries that affected genteel impoverished women in the nineteenth century." The weakness in the essay is that the author states as true what can only be assumed.

C274   Henneman, John B. "The Brontë Sisters." *Sewanee Review,* 9 (April 1901), 220-234.

Here is a turn-of-the-century study which states that environment is more influential than heredity in the development of the young Brontës. Tabby affected them in childhood, both by her Yorkshire character and by the folklore which she transmitted on to them. They were also influenced by their unusual association with their unusual father.

C275   Hinkley, Laura L. *Ladies of Literature.* New York: Hastings House, 1946.

In this study of the Brontës, the biographer raises the question of Branwell's influence on his sisters. Hinkley feels that Lockwood is modeled on Branwell.

C276   Hirst, J. C. "The Burial Place of the Brontës." *BST,* 9 (1938), 181-185. Reprinted in *The Brontës Then and Now.* Shipley: Outhwaite Brothers, 1947.

The Rector of Haworth gives a factual account of the burial place.

C277   Kellett, Jocelyn. *Haworth Parsonage: The Home of the Brontës.* Keighley: The Brontë Society, 1977.

This Brontë Society publication gives a graphic history of the parsonage to mark the bi-centenary of the Reverend Patrick Brontë. It was prepared as a tribute to the former president, Dr. Donald Hopewell.

C278   Mackay, Angus Mason. *The Brontës, Fact and Fiction.* London: Service and Paton, 1897.

In this volume expanded from his article "A Crop of Brontë Myths" in the *Westminster Review*, Oct. 1895, the Brontë authority attempts to remove the myth from Brontë biography.

C279   Mackay, Angus. "The Brontës: Their Fascination and Genius." *The Bookman* (London), 27 (Oct. 1904), 9-17.

Another early presentation of the personalities and problems of the Brontë family, written by a knowledgeable Brontë scholar.

C280   Masson, Flora. *The Brontës.* London: T. C. and E. C. Jack, 1912. Reissued, Port Washington, New York: Kennikat Press, 1970.

This biography is mostly on Charlotte Brontë, giving her history chronologically from the meeting of her parents through to her own death.

C281   Matthews, Thomas S. *The Brontës: A Study.* Dawlesh: Channing Press, 1934.

This study concentrates on the story of the Brontë children, up to the time when Charlotte and Emily went to Brussels. This is a logical break in the pattern of their lives.

C282   Maurat, Charlotte. *Le Secret des Brontës: ou Charlotte Brontë d'après les Juvenilia, ses lettres, et ceux qui l'ont connus.* Paris: Editions Buchet-Chastel, 1967. Reissued as *The Brontës' Secret.* Translated by Margaret Meldrum. London: Constable, 1969.

The familiar story is prepared for a French audience. The supporting material is taken directly from primary sources.

C283   Midgley, Wilson. "Sunshine on Haworth Moor." *BST,* 11 (1950), 309-326.

Here is Brontë family history mixed with a description of local scenery and material on Yorkshire customs and character.

C284 Morrison, Nancy Brysson. *Haworth Harvest: The Story of the Brontës.* London: J. M. Dent; New York: Vanguard Press, 1969.

Divided into three sections: seed-time, hay-time, yield-time, this is a biography with no literary criticism. The author uses Brontë letters as the authority to substantiate what she has to say.

C285 Newton, A. Edward. "Brontë Country; My First Visit" and "Brontë Country; My Second Visit" in *Derby Day and the Other Adventures.* Boston: Little, Brown, 1934.

These are first-person narratives in a popular style of his reaction to the transfer of the Bonnell Collection to the Brontë Society and the setting up of the Brontë Museum. He also tells of his personal feelings on learning about the Brontës. The volume also contains an Angrian story from the juvenilia. Vol. also listed as A31, since a pocket within the book contains a facsimile of a Charlotte Brontë manuscript.

C286 Oram, Eanne. "Brief for Miss Branwell." *BST,* 14 (1964), 28-38.

Oram presents the life story of the Brontës' Aunt Branwell whose task it was to oversee the young Brontë clan.

C287 Peters, Maureen. *An Enigma of Brontës.* New York: St. Martin's Press, 1974.

This story of the family, which is generally considered to be closer to historical fiction than to biography, gives the feeling of a psychological interest on the part of the author. There are photographs to illustrate which help to lend historicity to the presentation.

C288 Pinion, F. B. *A Brontë Companion: Literary Assessment, Background, and Reference.* London: Macmillan Press, 1975.

Here is a real Brontë companion: a biography of all the Brontës, with special attention to the problem areas disputed among biographers and critics; a guide to the geographic surroundings, with maps and illustrations; details of family history and Brontë legend and myth. All well substantiated and approached with a scholarly attitude. Vol. also listed as C179.

C289   Quennell, Peter. "The Brontës" in *Casanova in London.* New York: Stein and Day, 1971.

This short essay gives the usual material but stresses that familiar issue: how could three sisters living in obscurity create their fictional characters?

C290   Raymond, Ernest. "The Brontë Legend, Its Cause and Treatment." *Essays by Divers Hands: Being the Transactions of the Royal Society of Literature of the United Kingdom,* 26 (1953), 127-141.

The critic takes on the defense of those whom biographers have maligned: the Reverend Brontë, Aunt Branwell, and M. and Mme. Heger, among others. He has attempted to move Brontë biography out of legend and into fact.

C291   Raymond, Ernest. *In the Steps of the Brontës.* London: Rich and Cowan, 1948.

The critic here devotes himself to the relationship between the Brontës and their physical surrounding. He also considers earlier biography as to its accuracy. He believes that Emily got the idea for *Wuthering Heights* from a family legend she heard while she was at Law Hill.

C292   Rhodes, Philip. "A Medical Appraisal of the Brontës." *BST,* 16 (1972), 101-109.

Here a physician attemps to overcome traditional and amateur medical theories concerning the Brontës. He acknowledges the presence of tuberculosis and recognizable neuroses. "It is precisely because of the isolation and seclusion of the inhabitants of the Parsonage and the neuroticism which, with bereavements, it engendered that the genius flourished so marvellously."

C293   Robertson, Charles G. "The Brontës 'Experience of Life.'" *BST,* 9 (1936), 37-47.

It is Robertson's belief that familiarity with the biography of a writer can mislead those reading his novel. It is a mistake, he feels, to allow such knowledge to interfere with literary criticism.

C294   Romieu, Emilie and Georges. *La Vie des Deux Soeurs Brontë.* Paris: Gallimard, 1929. Reissued as *Three Virgins of Haworth: Being an Account of the Brontë Sisters.* Translated, Roberts Tapley. New York: E. P. Dutton and Company, 1930.

Fascinating but inaccurate, this is one of the classic studies of the lives of the Brontë sisters, as seen from a French point of view. It is emotional and sentimental with the underlying message that the Brontës were unable to love because as children they had been deprived of their mother.

C295   Sharp, William. "The Brontë Country." *Literary Geography.* London: Pall Mall Publication, 1904.

A description of the Yorkshire countryside is supported by quotations from *Wuthering Heights* and Charlotte Brontë's novels.

C296   Shorter, Clement K. *The Brontës and Their Circle.* New York: E. P. Dutton, 1914.

The material presented here is reworked from his earlier biographies (C267, C269, and C270).

C297   Shorter, Clement K. *The Brontës: Life and Letters.* 2 vols. London: Hodder and Stoughton; New York: C. Scribner's Sons, 1908.

Somewhat more accurate than the similar volumes in the *Shakespeare Head Brontë*, this biography uses Mrs. Gaskell's *Life of Charlotte Brontë* and also "numerous hitherto unpublished manuscripts and letters." It is still very early for objective biography, and Shorter is not without bias.

C298   Shorter, Clement K. *Charlotte Brontë and Her Circle.* London: Hodder and Stoughton; New York: Dodd Mead, 1896.

Here Shorter speaks for Ellen Nussey, giving us the reaction of one who knew the family.

C299   Shorter, Clement K. *Charlotte Brontë and Her Sisters.* London: Hodder and Stoughton; New York: Charles Scribner's Sons, 1905.

An investigation of the Brontës is made by one who knew those close to them, including letters not available to Mrs. Gaskell.

C300   Sinclair, May. *The Three Brontës.* London: Hutchinson, 1912; Boston: Houghton Mifflin, 1912 as *The Brontë Sisters.*

The biographer presents a romanticized life in the parsonage with much to say about Emily Brontë based on the attitudes of Charlotte Brontë, Ellen Nussey, and the servants. She agrees with Maeterlinck's conception of Emily Brontë: her "experience took place in her heart if not in her life." Sinclair feels that *Wuthering Heights* was important in Charlotte's artistic development, while the Heger affair was unimportant. The biographer sees the germ of *Wuthering Heights* in the Gondal poems, as both function on a mystic plane. This material first appeared as "The Three Brontës" in the Modern Biography series.

C301   Southwart, Elizabeth. *Brontë Moors and Villages from Thornton to Haworth.* London: John Lane, 1923.

A guide book to the countryside.

C302   Spark, Muriel. "The Brontës as Teachers." *The New Yorker,* 41 (Jan. 22, 1966), 30-33.

This spirited review of the experiences of the Brontës in the teaching world is summed up by the critic: "Branwell's conduct was unprofessional, to say the least. Charlotte was not, to say the least, proof against those states of mind that the most protected upbringing will not protect. Anne's reaction was to hoard her resentment. Emily's way, by far the most successful, was to get out of the predicament with all speed. . . ."

C303   Stead, J. J. "A Chronology of the Principal Events in the Lives of the Brontë Family." *BST,* 1 (1897), 1-11.

One of the first attempts to set forth a reliable and factual presentation of events and dates in the lives of the Brontës.

C304   Strachan, Pearl. "Across the Moors." *Christian Science Monitor*, May 24, 1947, p. 10.

Another writer gives her reaction to the setting of the Brontë home.

C305   Sugden, K. A. R. *A Short History of the Brontës.* London: Oxford University Press, 1929.

An earnest attempt to replace legend with truth about the Brontës. This is part of the Oxford Bookshelf series.

C306   Traz, Robert de. "L'Enfance des Brontës." *Revue de Paris*, 45 (1938), 579-605.

C307   Traz, Robert de. *La Famille Brontë.* Paris: A Michel, 1938.

C308   Walker, Janie. "The Brontës." *Stories of the Victorian Writers.* Cambridge: University Press, 1922.

A retelling of the traditional story of the family, mentioning the novels but brief on Emily Brontë's poetry. Of interest is the suggestion of a possible source for *Wuthering Heights.* The author relates an old Irish story told about Hugh Prunty's adoption of a Welsh orphan boy.

C309   Walters, J. Cuming. *The Spell of Yorkshire.* London: Methuen, 1931.

Walters finds Yorkshire a gloomy geographical area and consequently gives a depressing view of the Brontës' lives.

C310   White, W. Bertram. *The Miracle of Haworth: A Brontë Study.* London: University of London Press, 1937. Reissued as *Studies in the Brontës.* No. 64. New York: Haskell, 1974.

This unusual study of the family presents the idea that Emily Brontë's whole life was altered by the death of the young curate William Weightman. The biographer believes that Emily began reading mystics in Brussels. He also feels that Branwell's influence was very strong.

273

C311   Whitehead, Phyllis. *The Brontës Came Here*. Halifax: Fawcett, Greenwood, 1965.

Here is a guide to north-country places associated with the Brontës.

C312   Whone, Clifford. "Where the Brontës Borrowed Books: The Keighley Mechanics Institute." *BST*, 11 (1950), 344-358.

The author presents a list of the holdings of the library in 1841. The institute was not really for workers. Of the seventy-one members, six of them were clergymen. Most of the others were millowners and businessmen. Among the members were two whose names are of especial interest: Miss Frances Mary Richardson *Currer* and William *Ellis*.

C313   Wilks, Brian. *The Brontës*. London: Hamlyn, 1975.

This illustrated book includes the picture (seen by M. Butterfield) said to be of Branwell Brontë, Reverend Nicholls, and Brown (Sexton) and the picture of six figures in the Haworth churchyard. See C250 for rejoinder.

C314   Wilks, Brian. "Through the Eyes of the Brontës." *Sunday Times Magazine* (London), March 14, 1976, pp. 32-41.

Drawings and paintings by the Brontë children give a new view of their creativity.

C315   Wise, Thomas James and J. A. Symington. "Preface " in *The Brontës: Their Lives, Friendships, and Correspondence*. 4 vols. in *The Shakespeare Head Brontë*. London: Shakespeare Head Press, 1932.

This is one of the classic collections of opinion and evidence, prepared by an unreliable scholar and businessman.

C316   Wood, Butler. "Connection of Charlotte Brontë with the Lake District." *BST*, 5 (1915), 13-24.

Butler Wood helps to fill in the family history.

C317   Curtis, Myra. "The 'Profile' Portrait." *BST*, 13 (1959), 342.

In examining the question of the identity of the sitter in the "profile portrait": is it of Emily or Anne? This author says, Anne.

C318   Edgerley, C. Mabel. "Anne Brontë." *BST*, 9 (1938), 173. Reprinted as "The Youngest Sister" in *The Brontës Then and Now*. Shipley: Outhwaite Brothers, 1947.

Called "gentle and affectionate," Anne is here presented as a real human being. Facts about her life and writing help to bring this lesser sister to life.

C319   Gérin, Winifred. *Anne Brontë, a Biography*. London: Nelson and Sons, 1959.

This well-known Brontë biographer uses material from Anne's novels and poems to support the very few facts known about her life. Gérin's kindly praise of *The Tenant of Wildfell Hall* includes the sentence: "The characters develop; they grow, they deteriorate; they age; they do not remain untouched by experience."

C320   Hale, Will T. *Anne Brontë, Her Life and Writing*. Indiana University Studies, No. 83. Bloomington: Indiana University Press, 1929. Reissued, New York: Folcroft, 1974.

First issued as an academic publication, this was one of the early works to take seriously the writings of the third sister.

C321   Hervey-Bathurst, Pamela. *The Brief Life of Anne Brontë*. Stanbury, Yorkshire: Brontë Booklets, 1971.

A local publication giving facts about Anne Brontë's life, appropriate for visitors to Haworth and the Brontë Parsonage.

C322   Raymond, Ernest. "Exiled and Harassed Anne." *BST,* 11 (1949), 225-236.

A particularly sympathetic study of Anne Brontë.

C323   Schofield, Guy. "The Gentle Anne." *BST,* 16:1 (1971), 1-10.

The biographer credits the earlier work of Winifred Gérin, Phyllis Bentley, Margaret Lane, Ada Harrison and Derek Stanford. Schofield says he always believed that of the Brontës, "Anne was the one with the most appealing human qualities."

C324   Stone, Phillipa. *The Captive Dove: Anne Brontë of Thorpe Green Hall.* London: Robert Hale, 1968.

Recounting the experience of Anne and Branwell with the Robinsons, this biography treats the most turbulent period in her life. Based partly on fact, partly on conjecture, the book balances nicely between imagination and reality.

C325   Trust, Estelle. *Anne Brontë.* Dallas, Texas: The Story Book Press, 1954.

A simplified biography of Anne Brontë.

Biography
Branwell Brontë

C326   Curtis, Dame Myra and Dr. Phyllis Bentley, Miss J. M. S. Tompkins, M. Hope Dodds, Dr. Mildred G. Christian, Daphne du Maurier. "Further Thoughts on Branwell Brontë's Story." *BST,* 14 (1962), 3-16.

Six women who have studied the Brontës answer the question raised by Daphne du Maurier's *Infernal World* (C327) and Winifred Gérin's *Branwell Brontë* (C328): What caused Branwell Brontë's abrupt dismissal in July 1845 from the Robinson's employment? The conflict is not resolved, merely opened for discussion.

C327   du Maurier, Daphne. *The Infernal World of Branwell Brontë.* Garden City, New York: Doubleday, 1960.

"The pendulum of his spirits swung between high and low," this imaginative biographer says at one point. Surely this is the summary of Branwell's life. Miss du Maurier speaks with the authority of a novelist combined with that of a biographer who has gone beyond any other in research and sleuthing on the subject of the Brontë brother. The biography reads like a novel in which the author has become transfixed by the personality of the protagonist.

C328   Gérin, Winifred. *Branwell Brontë.* London: T. Nelson and Sons, 1961.

The biography is based on a selection of facts from available evidence and shows less perception than her later work, the biography of Charlotte Brontë (A388). But it does show, like her other Brontë scholarship, a true feeling for the ambiance and for the Brontës as real people. Vol. also listed as C212.

C329   Gosse, Edmund. *Silhouettes.* London: William Heinemann, 1925.

A chapter, "The Brother of the Brontës," gives serious consideration to Branwell Brontë, his problems and his creative expression. This appeared earlier as an article in *The Sunday Times.*

C330   Grundy, F. H. *Pictures of the Past: Memories of Men I Have Met and Places I Have Seen.* London: Griffith and Farran, 1879.

A loyal defense of Branwell written years after the events and experiences he and Branwell shared. The letters written to Grundy by Branwell give no hint that he was aware of any of the literary activity going on at the parsonage.

C331   Hervey-Bathurst, Pamela. *The Tragedy of Patrick Branwell Brontë.* Stanbury, Yorkshire: Brontë Booklets, 1971.

A local publication giving facts about Patrick Branwell Brontë's life. This is part of a series of booklets designed to aid the Haworth visitor.

C332   Kinsley, Edith Ellsworth. *Pattern for Genius: A Story of Branwell Brontë and his Three Sisters, Charlotte, Emily and Anne, Largely Told in their Own Words.* New York: E. P. Dutton, 1939.

In an effort to show Branwell's influence on his sisters, the author has violently corrupted art and turned it to biography. The biographer uses words, phrases, and sentences from the novels to prove her point, and has renamed the characters Charlotte, Emily, and Anne, to fit her need.

C333   Leyland, Francis. *The Brontë Family, With Special Reference to Patrick Branwell Brontë.* London: Hurst and Blackett, 1886.

The brother of Branwell's friend offers yet another defense of Branwell, this one long and personally concerned.

C334   Olsen, Thomas. "The Weary Are at Rest: A Reconsideration of Branwell Brontë." *BST,* 10 (1945), 284-285.

A sympathetic evaluation of Branwell as a person.

C335   Wall, Francis. "Notes on the Art and Life of Patrick Branwell Brontë." *BST,* 10 (1941).

True facts about Branwell remain difficult to find. Here Wall offers an opinion based on what evidence there is.

Biography
The Reverend Patrick Brontë

C336   Branch, James W. "Concerning the Last of the Brontës." *Books Abroad,* 41 (Summer 1967), 286-288.

A review and discussion of the book by Lock and Dixon (C340), which continues with pertinent observation about the Reverend Brontë.

C337   Colloms, Brenda. *Victorian Country Parsons.* Lincoln: University of Nebraska Press, 1977.

This discussion of various clergymen includes the Reverend Brontë, "the parson with literary connections."

C338   Hook, Ruth. "The Father of the Family." *BST*, 17 (1977), 95-104.

This talk, given at a Brontë Society meeting, offers a thorough study of the Reverend Brontë, emphasizing his value to his family and the parish.

C339   Hopkins, Annette B. *The Father of the Brontës*. Baltimore: Johns Hopkins Press, 1958.

A scholarly and sympathetic treatment of the life and problems of the Reverend Brontë. The book includes a full bibliography.

C340   Lock, John and Canon W. T. Dixon. *Man of Sorrow: The Life, Letters, and Times of the Reverend Patrick Brontë, 1777-1861*. London: Thomas Nelson and Sons, 1965.

When John Lock (and his wife Winifred Gérin) moved to Haworth for research on the Brontës, he collaborated with the former Canon of the Haworth church (1947-1958) to write this study of the Reverend Brontë. The tone of the book is sympathetic and the information is based partially on supposition. Of interest, though, is their account of Evangelism and its effect on the Brontës.

C341   O'Bryne, Cathal. "The Gaelic Source of the Brontë Genius." *The Columbia*, 10 (July 1931), 12-13, 36. Reprinted, *The Gaelic Sources of the Brontë Genius*. Edinburgh and London: Sands, 1933.

The biographer identifies the Irish traits of the Brontës. Their grandfather, Hugh Prunty, was famous as a story-teller, or "shanachie." The article also discusses Catholicism in the family.

C342   Prunty, Maura. "Father of the Brontë Sisters." *Irish Digest*, 73 (Dec. 1961), 52-54.

This character sketch of the Reverend Brontë emphasizes the importance of his Irish ancestry. The article also suggests that the Brontës used facts from their father's stories in their writings.

C343   Reilly, A. J. "Celtic Elements in the Brontë Genius." *Ave Maria*, 38 (Sept. 23-30, 1933), 393-396.

Reilly traces the Brontë ancestry to the famous Gaelic poet, Padraic O'Prunta. He is able to discern certain elements from their Celtic heritage in the Brontës' writing: a use of duality — aggression and subtlety, order and imagination — and an expression of their love of nature. He feels that Emily Brontë's poetry follows the Irish mode.

C344   Senior, James. *Patrick Brontë*. Boston: Stratford, 1921.

An American biography of the father of the Brontës. Noted but not inspected.

C345   Wright, William. *The Brontës in Ireland*. London: Hodder and Stoughton, 1893.

A well-known early study of the background of the Reverend Brontë.

C346   Yates, W. W. "The Brontës at Dewsbury." *BST*, 1 (1895), 8-13.

This is a report given at the first annual meeting of the Brontë Society. The list of those attending includes such Brontë enthusiasts as Butler Wood, Briggs, Cockshut, Dobie, Sugden, and J. Horsfall Turner. The article gives an account of the Reverend and Mrs. Brontë at Dewsbury where Charlotte, Branwell, Emily, and Anne were born. It also mentions Charlotte's godparents, who sent her to Miss Wooler's school but who broke with her over *Jane Eyre*, feeling that the novel was too critical of the clergy.

C347   Yates, W. W. *The Father of the Brontës: His Life and Work at Dewsbury and Hartshead*. Leeds: Fred R. Spark, 1897.

Another early work on the Reverend Brontë which gives a view of the home life in Haworth as well as his earlier career before he arrived there.

Biography of Mrs. Maria Brontë

C348   Rowe, Joseph Hambley. *The Maternal Relatives of the Brontës.* Shipley: Outhwaite Brothers, 1923.

This biography of the family of Maria Branwell Brontë was first given as an address to the Bradford Historical and Antiquarian Society, April 28, 1911.

Fictional Biography

C349   Amster, Jane. *Dream Keepers: The Young Brontës: A Psycho-biographical Novella.* New York: The William-Frederick Press, 1973.

Juvenile historical fiction.

C350   Banks, Lynne Reid. *Dark Quartet: The Story of the Brontës.* London: Weidenfeld and Nicolson, 1976.

The author of *The L-Shaped Room* presents a fictional biography using quotations from letters as though they were words spoken by the characters. The story covers the years from 1821 to 1849.

C351   Banks, Lynne Reid. *Path to the Silent Country: Charlotte Brontë's Years of Fame.* London: Weidenfeld and Nicolson, 1977.

The years 1849-1855 are covered in this sequel to *Dark Quartet* (C350). Again the author uses direct quotations from letters as the spoken words of Charlotte Brontë.

C352   Clarke, Pauline. *The Twelve and the Genii.* London: Faber and Faber, 1962. Reprinted, Puffin, 1977.

Juvenile fiction about a child who finds the soldiers which the Brontë children played with.

C353   Cook, E. Thornton. *They Lived.* New York: Charles Scribner's Sons, 1935.

C354   Cornish, Dorothy H. *These Were the Brontës.* New York: Macmillan, 1940.

C355   Jarden, Mary Louise. *The Young Brontës: Charlotte and Emily, Branwell and Anne.* New York: Viking Press, 1938.

C356   Moss, H. "Instant Lives: The Brontës." *Vogue,* 163 (May 1974), 420.

          Attempted humor in an imaginary conversation between Emily and Charlotte.

C357   Rauth, Heidemarie. "A Survey of Brontë Plays." Doctoral dissertation, University of Innsbruck, 1971. Reprinted in *BST,* 16:4 (1974), 288-290.

          A chronological listing of plays produced and published between 1927 and 1971. Plays are also listed in Yablon and Turner, D25.

C358   Vipont, Elfrida. *Weaver of Dreams: the Girlhood of Charlotte Brontë.* New York: Walck; London: Hamish Hamilton, 1966.

          A fictionalized biography about the years from 1820 to 1835.

C359   Wallace, Kathleen. *Immortal Wheat.* London: Heinemann, 1951.

          Popular novelist tells how it might have been. Another fictionalized biography.

D. BIBLIOGRAPHIES

D1   Abernathy, Peter L., Christian J. W. Kloesel, and Jeffrey R. Smitten, eds. *English Novel Explication,* Supplement I. Hampden, Conn.: The Shoe String Press, 1976.

Includes a four-page bibliography of Brontë material.

D2   Anderson, John Parker. "Bibliography" in *Life of Charlotte Brontë* by Augustine Birrell. London, 1887. Reissued, Ann Arbor, Michigan: Finch Press, 1972.

D3   Anon. "Brontë Society Publications." *BST,* 14 (1965), 100-106.

List of all major articles published 1895-1964.

D4   Arnold, Helen H. "Americans and the Brontës." *The Brontës Then and Now.* Shipley: Outhwaite Brothers, 1947. Reprinted from *BST,* 10 (1940), 12.

D5   Barclay, Janet. *Emily Brontë Criticism 1900-1968: An Annotated Check List.* New York: Public Library, 1974.

A most thorough bibliography which covers the works on Emily Brontë from the turn of the century to the date of writing. The helpful annotations are a guide to the importance of the work.

D6   Blondel, Jacques. "Cent ans de critique autour d'Emily Brontë." *Les Langues Modernes,* 42 (1948), A51-A56.

A review of major texts, summarizing 100 years of criticism, moving chronologically and at the same time grouping the items according to the major trends in critical approaches. Comments are terse and sensible, for while Blondel remarks on the distinguishing features of some 37 critics, he concludes: "la question est de savoir si la critique, en cherchant toujour plus de vérité, ce qui est son devoir, a su . . . retrouver tout en le respectant le mystère qui baigne l'oeuvre d'Emily Brontë."

D7   Byers, David Milner. "An Annotated Bibliography of the Criticism on Emily Brontë's *Wuthering Heights*, 1847-1947." Unpublished doctoral dissertation, University of Minnesota, 1973. *DAI*, 34:2611.

This "bibliography contains accounts of all criticism of *Wuthering Heights* found in all published listings (and one unpublished listing), excepting only newspaper accounts and letters."

D8   Christian, Mildred G. "The Brontës" in "A Guide to Research Materials on the Major Victorians" (Part III). *Victorian Newsletter,* 13 (Spring 1958), 19.

A summary of where material is to be found.

D9   Christian, Mildred G. "The Brontës" in *Victorian Fiction: A Guide to Research.* Ed. Lionel Stevenson. Cambridge, Massachusetts: Harvard University Press, 1964.

The most informative bibliography of the Brontë criticism up to date of publication. Christian notes that "the contradictory judgments on *Wuthering Heights* are the most striking fact in its critical history."

D10   Cross, B. Gilbert. "A Brontë Reading List." *BST,* 15 (1970), 424-426; 16 (1971), 52-54; 16 (1972), 146-150; 16 (1973), 228-231; 16 (1974), 299-302; 16 (1975), 402-405; and 17 (1977), 141-144.

D11   Dalziel, Margaret. *Popular Fiction a Hundred Years Ago: An Unexplored Tract of Literary History.* London: Cohen and West, 1957.

This study shows the general interest of the reading public in the 1850's, indicating the books which were appearing in the same general period as the Brontë novels.

D12   Devers, James. "A Brontë Reading List, 1976." *BST,* 17:1 (1976), 62-65.

D13 Downey, Marian J. *Studies in Charlotte Brontë.* Unpublished doctoral dissertation, University of Illinois at Urbana-Champaign, 1938. *DAI,* W1938, p. 90.

The works are only listed, not annotated.

D14 Dugas, Joseph Henry. "The Literary Reputation of the Brontës, 1846-1951." Unpublished doctoral dissertation, University of Illinois, 1951. *DAI,* 12:61.

This bibliographic study covers the reactions to the Brontës' writings from the appearance of their first book of poetry to the criticism of 1951. *Jane Eyre* was more popular in 1850's, *Wuthering Heights* in 1950's.

D15 Foster, Amy G. *Analytical Index of the Contents of the Brontë Society Transactions Vol. I (1895) - Vol. 15 (1967).* Keighley: Keighley Printers, 1968.

A very helpful booklet which lists by subject and by author the major articles which have appeared in *BST* from the beginning.

D16 Leclair, Lucien. *A General Analytical Bibliography of the Regional Novelists of the British Isles, 1800-1850.* Clemont-Ferrand: G. de Bussac, 1954.

D17 Parkison, Jami. "Charlotte Brontë: A Bibliography of the 19th Century Criticism." *Bulletin of Bibliography,* 35 (1978),72-83.

A thorough investigation of early criticism.

D18 Passel, Anne. "Charlotte Brontë: A Bibliography of the Criticism of Her Novels." *Bulletin of Bibliography.* Part I: 26 (1969), 118-120; Part II: 27 (1970), 13-20.

Annotated list of criticism covering the years 1848-1967.

D19 Peters, Margot. "Charlotte Brontë: A Critico-Bibliographic Survey 1945-1974." *British Studies Monitor.* Part I: 6 (Summer 1976), 10-36; Part II: 7 (Winter 1977), 57-70.

One of the most complete listings of major critical works for this thirty-year period.

D20   Pollin, Burton R. "The Brontës in the American Periodical Press of Their Day: One Hundred and Ninety-three Reviews and Comments Annotated." *BST,* 16:5 (1975), 383-399.

Offered as "a kind of posthumous reparation for Charlotte's distress over the reviewers," this article gives a clear factual presentation of American reaction to the Brontës, alphabetically arranged according to periodical name.

D21   Reilly, Joseph J. "Some Victorian Reputations." *Catholic World,* 145 (April 1937), 16-23.

A modern view of Victorian writers given in an overview of criticism from 1850 to 1925.

D22   Rosengarten, Herbert J. "The Brontës." Ed. George H. Ford. *Victorian Fiction: A Second Guide to Research.* New York: Modern Language Association, 1978.

A valuable contribution to Brontë scholarship, this bibliographic study is included with those of sixteen other major Victorian writers and an article on research, "General Materials," by Richard D. Altick.

D23   Schreiner, Wilhelmina R. "The Criticism of Emily Brontë." Unpublished master's thesis, University of Pittsburgh, 1937. *Bulletin of MA Theses,* 34:422.

An overview of criticism from 1847 to 1937, in which the author shows the shift with times and critics.

D24   Watson, Melvin R. "*Wuthering Heights* and the Critics." *Trollopian,* 3 (March 1949), 243-263.

A look at 100 years of criticism which shows the change after 1920 to more rational approaches. The worst schools are thought to be (1) parallel studies, (2) autobiographical readings, and (3)

Freudian interpretations. Watson cites J. A. MacKereth (B231) and David Cecil (C58) as offering the best interpretations.

D25 Yablon, G. Anthony and John R. Turner. *A Brontë Bibliography.* London: Ian Hodgkins; Westport, Conn.: Meckler Books, 1978.

An important resource for collectors, librarians, and students. A beautifully designed and carefully researched listing presents more than 600 books on the Brontës, including many hard-to-find early works.

D26 Zandvoort, M. "Recent Literature on the Brontës." *English Studies* (Amsterdam), 24 (Dec. 1943), 177-192.

Bibliographies and Catalogues of Brontë Writings

D27 Christian, Mildred G. (compiler). "Catalogue of the General Collection of Manuscripts, Drawings, Paintings, and Manuscript Association Material in the Brontë Museum." Unpublished compilation in the hands of the Brontë Council and Museum, Haworth, Yorkshire, 1958.

D28 Christian, Mildred G. (compiler). "A Census of Brontë Manuscripts in the United States," in five parts. *The Trollopian,* 2 (Dec. 1947), 177-199, and 3 (Dec. 1948), 215-233.

This comprehensive presentation appears in five parts in the journal. It is supplemented by Leslie A. Marchand's "An Addition to the Census of Brontë Manuscripts" (D36).

D29 Doubleday, William Elliot, ed. *Catalogue of the Brontë Books and Manuscripts, Hampstead Public Libraries.* Hampstead: Central Public Library, 1931.

D30 Field, W. T. "Catalogue of the Objects in the Museum of the Brontë Society." *BST,* 4 (June 1908), 43-72.

The first "official" catalogue.

D31   Galloway, F. C. "Descriptive Catalogue of Objects (including manuscripts) in the Brontë Museum." Privately printed, 1896.

The earliest, unofficial listing of the materials gathered in the museum in the Haworth Parsonage.

D32   Green, John Albert. *Brontë Collection: List of Additions, 1907-1916.* Manchester: Moss Side, 1905.

Additions to the catalogue D33.

D33   Green, John Albert. "A Catalogue of the Gleave Brontë Collection at the Moss Side Free Library, Manchester." Manchester: Moss Side, 1905.

The listing of the material in the Gleave Brontë Collection in Manchester. Originally prepared in 1905, this catalogue was revised often until 1916, possibly later.

D34   Hatfield, C. W. (compiler). "Catalogue of the Bonnell Collection in the Brontë Parsonage Museum." Privately printed, 1932.

This accurate catalogue of the material in the Brontë Museum in the Haworth Parsonage was the gift to the Brontë Museum by Mrs. Henry H. Bonnell in memory of her husband, the chief American Brontë collector.

D35   Hatfield, C. W. "The Early Manuscripts of Charlotte Brontë: A Bibliography" in three parts. *BST,* 6 (1922), 97-111; 6 (1923), 153-165; 6 (1924), 220-235.

D36   Marchand, Leslie A. "An Addition to the Census of Brontë Manuscripts." *Nineteenth Century Fiction,* 4 (June 1949), 81-84.

Branwell Brontë's manuscripts and some of Charlotte Brontë's letters were added to the Symington Collection of Rutgers University.

D37   Symington, J. Alex (compiler). "Catalogue of the Brontë Museum and Library." Privately printed, 1927.

D38   Wise, Thomas J. *The Ashley Library: A Catalogue of Printed Books, Manuscripts and Autograph Letters.* Edinburgh: Dunedin Press, 1922.

A descriptive catalogue of Emily Brontë's holograph poems, editions of *Wuthering Heights*, and *Poems* edited by Clement Shorter (see B11).

D39   Wise, Thomas J. *A Bibliography of the Writing in Prose and Verse of the Members of the Brontë Family.* London: Richard Clay and Sons, 1917.

D40   Wise, Thomas J. *A Brontë Library. A Catalogue of Printed Books, Manuscripts and Autograph Letters by the Members of the Brontë Family.* Privately printed, 1929.

D41   Wise, Thomas J. *A Reference Catalogue of British and Foreign Autographs and Manuscripts,* Part I. Privately printed for the Society of Archivists, 1893.

D42   Wood, Butler. "A Bibliography of the Works of the Brontë Family." *Transactions and Other Publications of the Brontë Society,* 1 (1895), 3-34.

The bibliographic secretary of the Brontë Society compiled this listing of the writings which were then known of all the members of the Brontë family. This is part one of the first volume of what is now *Brontë Society Transactions.*

D43   Wood, Butler. "Some Bibliographical Notes on the Brontë Literature." *BST,* 4 (1911), 189-198.

This later addition adds to the earlier articles. It contains notes on biography and events connected with the publication of the Brontë novels.

D44   Wood, Butler. "Supplement" (to the bibliography, D42). *BST,* 1 (1897), 3-19.

D45   Altick, Richard D. and William R. Matthews (compilers). *Guide to Doctoral Dissertations in Victorian Literature 1886-1958.* Urbana: University of Illinois Press, 1960.

D46   Altick, Richard D. and Andrew Wright. *Selective Bibliography for the Study of English and American Literature.* New York: Macmillan, 5th edition, 1974.

D47   Altick, Richard D. *Victorian Studies in Scarlet.* New York: Norton, 1970.

D48   Anon. "Annotated Checklist." *Victorian Studies,* yearly supplement.

D49   Anon. *Index to American Doctoral Dissertations.* Compiled for the Association of Research Libraries. Ann Arbor, Michigan: University Microfilms, 1958-1963.

D50   Anon. *MLA International Bibliography of Books and Articles on the Modern Languages and Literature.* New York: University Press, 1964-

D51   Bate, Walter Jackson, ed. *Criticism: The Major Texts.* New York: Harcourt, Brace, 1952.

D52   Bateson, F. W. (ed.). *The Cambridge Bibliography of English Literature.* Vol. III. Cambridge: Cambridge University Press, 1941.

D53   Bateson, F. W. *A Guide to English Literature.* Chicago: Aldine Publishing Company, 1965.

     The guide lists the major critics and the acknowledged approaches.

D54   Bell, Inglis F. and Donald Baird. *The English Novel, 1578-1956: A Checklist of Twentieth-Century Criticism.* Denver: Alan Swallow, 1958.

D55   Block, Andrew. *The English Novel, 1740-1850: A Catalogue*. London: Grafton, 1939; revised edition, 1961.

D56   Bowers, Fredson (ed.). *Studies in Bibliography*. Papers of the Bibliographical Society of the University of Virginia. Vol. 19. Charlottesville, Virginia: The University Press of Virginia, 1966.

D57   Dyson, A. E., ed. *The English Novel: Select Bibliographical Guides*. London: Oxford University Press, 1974.

      Includes a bibliography of the Brontës prepared by Miriam Allott.

D58   Dyson, A. E., ed. *English Poetry: Select Bibliographical Guides*. London: Oxford University Press, 1971.

D59   Houghton, Walter E., ed. *The Wellesley Index to Victorian Periodicals, 1824-1900*. Toronto: University of Toronto Press, 1966-

D60   Limrick, Zada, ed. *Readers' Guide to Periodical Literature*. New York: H. W. Wilson Company, 1900-

D61   Pingree, Elizabeth, ed. *Humanities Index*. New York: H. W. Wilson, 1975-

      Formerly *International Index*, 1907-1965; *Social Sciences and Humanities Index*, 1965-1974.

D62   Poole, William Frederick. *Poole's Index to Periodical Literature*. Gloucester, Massachusetts: Peter Smith, 1958.

D63   Slack, Robert C., ed. *Bibliographies of Studies in Victorian Literature for the Ten Years, 1955-1964*. Urbana: University of Illinois Press, 1967.

D64   Templeman, William D. *Bibliographies of Studies in Victorian Literature for the Thirteen Years, 1932-1944*. Urbana: University of Illinois Press, 1945.

D65   Watson, George, ed. *New Cambridge Bibliography of English Literature.* Vol. 3, 1800-1900. Cambridge (England): Cambridge University Press, 1969.

D66   Wright, Austin. *Bibliographies of Studies in Victorian Literature for the Ten Years, 1945-1954.* Compiled by William Frost *et al.* Urbana: University of Illinois Press, 1956.

INDEXES

INDEX OF AUTHORS AND EDITORS
OF SECONDARY MATERIAL

Numbers Refer to Items, Not Pages

A Indicates Material on Charlotte Brontë
B Indicates Material on Emily Brontë
C Indicates Material on Brontë Family
D Indicates Bibliographies

Bennett, J. T. C150
Benson, A. C. A263, A363, B350
Benson, E. F. A364, B80, C235
Bentley, P. A34, A38, A195,
    A226, A264, B16, B81, C8,
    C9, C55, C151, C152, C236,
    C237, C238, C239, C240,
    C241, C242, C243, C244,
    C326
Benvenuto, R. A97
Beversluis, J. B82
Birrell, A. A365
Bjork, H. A265
Black, M. B83
Blackburn, R. M. A98, C245
Blayac, A. B84
Bleikasten, A. B85
Block, A. D55
Blom, M. A. A99, A245, A266,
    A267
Blondel, J. B86, B87, B88, B112,
    B426, B351, B352, D6
Bloomer, N. H. B427
Bloomfield, P. B89
Bluestone, G. B90
Bonnell, H. H. A268
Booth, W. C. B91
Bosco, R. B92
Bostridge, M. A366
Bowen, E. C56
Bowers, F. D56
Bowlin, K. J. B93
Bracco, E. J. B411
Bradby, G. F. A367, B428, C246
Bradner, L. B94
Braithwaite, W. S. C247
Brammer, M. M. A240, A241
Branch, J. W. C336
Brash, W. B. A368, B482

Brayfield, P. L. A269
Brendon, J. A. A369
Brick, A. R. B95, B96
Bridges, R. B353
Briet, S. A222
Briggs, A. A196
Briggs, C. F. B41
Bromley, L. A. A270
Bronstein, E. B174
Brontë, C. A10, A42, B2, B49,
    C15
Brown, E. K. B97
Brown, H. B14, B354, B355,
    B356, B429
Brown, T. J. C248
Buchen, I. H. B98, B430
Buckler, W. E. B99
Buckley, J. H. A100
Buckley, V. B100
Bullock, F. A. B431
Burkhart, C. A101, A223, A224,
    A225, A271
Burkhart, R. E. B101
Burns, W. A102, B102, B103
Bushnell, N. S. A103
Butler, W. A. A45, B26, C26
Butterfield, H. C249
Butterfield, M. B104, C250
Byers, D. M. D7
Byron, M. A370

Caine, J. B105
Capetanakis, D. A272
Carr, D. R. W. B357
Carrère, F. B106
Carson, J. B107
Carus-Wilson, W. A371
Cazamian, L. A197, C57
Cecil, D. C58, C59, C60

298

302

Nelson, J. G. C45
Neufeldt, V. A. B261, B456
Newton, A. E. A31, C285
Newton-de Molina, D. A79
Nicholson, N. B262
Nicolai, R. B263
Nicoll, W. R. A14, A15, B502, C176
Nissl, N. A152
Nixon, I. B264
Nussey, E. A409, A410

O'Bryne, C. C341
Ocampo, V. B457
Odom, K. C. C177
Odumu, O. B265
Offor, R. A411
Ohmann, C. B458
Oldfield, J. A153, C106
Oliphant, M. A318
Olsen, T. C334
O'Neill, J. C107
Oram, E. B459, C286
Osborne, M. M. A154

P., W. P. C40
Paden, W. D. A155, B415
Parkinson, E. M. C108
Parkison, J. D17
Parrish, M. L. B477, C178
Parrot, T. M. C109
Partington, W. C217
Pascal, R. A237
Passel, A. W. A156, A210, A319, D18
Patterson, C., Jr. B266
Paul, D. C110
Pearsall, R. B. B267
Pearson, F. R. A412
Peck, W. G. B43

Pell, N. A157
Peters, Margot M. A320, A321, A413, D19
Peters, Maureen C287
Peterson, M. J. A158
Peterson, W. S. A159
Petit, J-P. B268, B269, B460, B461, C111
Petyt, K. M. B270, B271, B272
Phelps, W. L. B273
Pingree, E. D61
Pinion, F. B. C179, C288
Pittock, M. B274
Plath, S. B275
Platt, C. V. A238, C180
Pollard, A. A322, A414, C156
Pollin, B. R. A415, B62, C46, D20
Poole, W. F. D62
Porter, D. O. A160
Power, S. A. B276
Powys, J. C. B462
Praz, M. A323
Prescott, J. A161
Preston, B. A416
Pritchett, V. S. B277, B278
Prunty, M. C342
Putzell, S. M. A324

Quennell, P. B279, C289
Quertermous, H. M. C181

Raine, K. M. B389
Rainwater, M. J. C196
Ralli, A. J. A325, B503
Rancy, J. B280
Ratchford, F. E. A30, A254, A417, B22, B390, B391, B392, B393, B416, B463, C182, C183, C184
Rauth, H. C357

305

SUBJECT MATTER INDEX

A listing of some of the major works which supply information on various topics

Catholicism and Anti-Catholicism
A225, A227, A262, A333,
C190
Celtic Elements (*see also* Irish
Background) A349, B79,
B227, B334, B442, B481,
C239, C242, C341
Chekov C271
Children A104, A175, B319,
B430, B454
Christian and Anti-Christian
Elements A64, A99, A267
Consuelo A240
"The Cout of Keeldar" A193
Cowan Bridge School (*see also* W.
Carus Wilson) A98, A187,
A371, A376, A377, A386,
A422, A437, C269

David Copperfield A313
Day-Lewis, C. B361
Demonism (*see also* Wuthering
Heights) C173
Diary Papers B22, B383, B474,
B502
Dickens, Charles A110, A270,
A313, B66
Dickinson, Emily B351, B357,
B371, B404, B408, C196
Drawings by the Brontës C315,
D27
Dreiser, T. B194
Durrell, L. B491
Dutch, Criticism in B405

Education (*see also* Governesses,
Cowan Bridge School, *and*
Heger Pensionnat) A227,
A313, C112, C236, C269,
C302

Eliot, George A61, A224, A256,
A268, A282, A283, A318,
A324, A383
Elsie Dinsmore A189
Emma by Jane Austen B163, C128
"Emma" by Charlotte Brontë (*see
also* "The Moores" *and* "Willie
Ellin") A4, A11, A15, A33,
A251, A432
Environment (*see also* Brussels,
Haworth, Heger Pensionnat,
Moors, Parsonage, *and*
Yorkshire) A388, B434,
B442, B444, B481, C112,
C224, C236, C252, C256,
C274
Essays A18, A24, A35, A36, A38,
B23, B24, C11
European Influence A352, B353,
C133

Fairy tales A146, B171, C47
"Farewell to Angria" A30, A34
Faulkner, William B194
Feminism A60, A83, A84, A85,
A86, A95, A108, A109,
A157, A163, A172, A174,
A180, A182, A188, A192,
A205, A206, A209, A210,
A217, A218, A236, A238,
A258, A261, A262, A263,
A265, A266, A267, A269,
A270, A271, A285, A297,
A299, A304, A305, A307,
A312, A314, A327, A332,
A333, A335, A336, A345,
A355, A413 B55, B59, B185,
B253, B265, B309, B318,
B338, B339, B340, B423,
B451, B454, B458, C35, C51,

312

Gothicism (*see also* Jane Eyre *and* Wuthering Heights) A103, A164, A291, A308, B147, B148, B223, B225, B260, C49
Governesses (*see also* Education) A96, A158, A190, A227, A283, A347, C166, C189, C231, C269, C302
Greek criticism A272
"The Green Dwarf" (*see also* Angria *and* Juvenilia) A30, A202
Grimshaw, W. B482
Gulliver's Travels A276
Guy Mannering A110

Hamlet (*see also* Shakespeare) B135, B165
Hardy, Thomas B271, B364
Harte, Bret A123
Haworth (*see also* Yorkshire, Moors, *and* Parsonage) A435, B284, B443, B507, B510, B512, C224, C232, C236, C242, C259, C276, C285, C301, C304
Hawthorne, N. B194
Health (*see* Medical History)
The Heart of Mid-Lothian A110
Heger, M. (*see also* Brussels) A16, A247, A364, A380, A407, A408, A426, B123, B238, B484, C112, C179, C241, C290
Heger Pensionnat (*see also* Brussels) A377, A407, B417
Heredity (*see also* Celtic Elements *and* Irish Background) B442, C112, C236, C256
History A348

Hoffmann B56, B94, B162, B231

Initiation B171
"An Interesting Passage in the Lives of Some Eminent Men of the Present Time" A41, A246
Irish Background (*see also* Celtic Elements) B162, B299, C239, C341
Irish Tales (*see also* "The Bridegroom of Barma") B94, B162, B231
"The Iron Shroud" B186
Italian, Criticism in A273, B398, B464
Ivanhoe A202

James, Henry A112, A159, A185, B66, B462, C227
Jane Eyre A1, A5
I. The book
authorship A60, A84, A149
criticism A51, A56, A64, A111, A112, A140, A278, C52, D14; psychological criticism A102, A106, A113, A168, A176, A182, A327, A357, A378, C110, C280; sociological criticism A157, A159, A227, A357; negative criticism A61, A64, A149, A155, A159, C80
people and places (real) A392, A415, A441
place in literature A56, A125, A287, A349, C52, C78, C113, C129, D13, D14
publication A128, C222
reader A145, A150, A346
sources A110, A179; fairy tales, folklore, myth A146, A173, A182, A327, C47, C118

315

318

Victorianism A102, A158, A217,
A231, A270, A324, A333,
A433, B154, B161, B289,
B298, B306, B339, B409,
B448, C88, C89, C117, C136,
C178, C189, C308
Villette A3, A6
characters A233, A236, A270,
A317, C134; Lucy A91,
A227, A228, A236, A238,
A239; Dr. John A224, A236
criticism A224, A228, A240,
A349, C68; negative criticism
A88, A232, A269;
psychological criticism A225,
A227, A231, A233, A266,
A327, A357; feminist
criticism A236, A238, A263,
A307, A345
incidents A220, C54, C158
language A199, A239, A303,
A320, A333, C68; image
A223, A230, A240, A260,
A303, A306, A334, C68
morality A220, A270, A285
narrator A289, A301, A331
people and places (real) A226,
A228, A232, A235, A237,
A441
setting A343
social statement A236, A270,
A281, A283, A310, A357
structure A220, A229, A233,
A234, A239, A240, A285,
A319; duality A229, A233
supernatural A225, A234, C168
symbols A153, A223, A225,
A230, A292, A325; dreams
A291

themes A29, A86, A221, A227,
A229, A233, A236, A271,
A285, A311, A327, A331,
C239
tone A86, A87, A220, A222,
A227, A229, A230, A239,
A262, A308; Gothic A291,
A353; myth A327

Warboise, E. J. (*see also* Cowan
Bridge School *and* W. C.
Wilson) A98
Waverley A110
Weightman, W. B486, B509, C310
Wesleyanism (*see also* Calvinism
and Religion) C190
West Riding A204, A205
Westminster Review A224, C44
Wide Sargasso Sea A160, A162,
A184
"Willie Ellin" (*see also* "Emma"
and "The Moores") A33,
A251
Wilson, W. Carus (*see also* Cowan
Bridge School) A98, A187,
A371, A391, A422
Winkworth, C. A73, A165, A419
Wise, Thomas J. (*see also* author
index) A385, A439, B347,
B475, C217, C221
Women Writers (*see* Feminism)
Woolf, V. A327
Woolcott, A. B420
Wordsworth, W. B410, B433
Wuthering Heights
I. The book: B65, B88, B114,
B118, B244
authorship A54, A309, A364,
B41, B44, B48, B52, B57,

321

Wuthering Heights
Craftsmanship
  content (continued)
    B116, B180, B285, B294,
    B316, B378; religion B149,
    B177, B235, B313, B502,
    B503, C137, C162; self B266,
    B278, B295, B312, B469; self
    in society B82, B92, B99,
    B174, B219, B248, B272,
    B295, B298, B320, B326,
    B337, C76, C138
  evil B257, B417, C140; sadism
    and demons B38, B45, B92,
    B252, B266, B288, B310,
    B322, B326, B437, C62,
    C131, C173; incest B252,
    B303, C60, C119; sexuality
    B77, B164, B255, B339; death
    B77, B102, B121, B160,
    B252, B269
  folklore B177, C119
  incidents B86, B121, B167,
    B228, B259, C54, C158
  language B43, B64, B69, B115,
    B267, B284, B292, B325,
    C68; dialect B113, B127,
    B203, B240, B270, B271,
    B272, B299, B333; imagery
    B87, B110, B129, B166, B293
  law, knowledge of B38, B116,
    B290, B305
  poetic B264, B308, B441, C135,
    C146; special passages C264;
    special chapters B99, B182,
    B234; relation to Gondal
    poetry B94, B117, B122,
    B133, B363, B445, B465,
    C101
  setting B73, B87, B91, B104,
    B161, B171, B181, B188,

    B191, B230, B241, B279,
    B284, B307, B315, B324,
    B443, B510, C105, C144
  structure B69, B96, B99, B101,
    B158, B182, B187, B254,
    B257, B264, B283, B293,
    B295, B326, B335, B431,
    C48, C50, C69, C88, C90,
    C127, C168; duality A79,
    B87, B101, B124, B144,
    B158, B189, B237, B251,
    B277, B283, B287, B294,
    B295, B312, B315, B316,
    B320, B340, C47, C81, C105,
    C123
  style B41, B140, B192, B340,
    B453, C54, C58, C68, C72
  symbolism B69, B233, B302,
    B325, B326, C123; dreams
    B63, B78, B150, B191, B235,
    B297, C168; ghosts B191,
    B192, B317, C67, C168
  theme B219, B229, B235, B335,
    B454
  time B109, B117, B122, B158,
    B166, B183, B187, B276,
    B290, B365, C48, C82
  tone: Gothicism B147, B148,
    B194, B253, B260;
    Romanticism B75, B82, B83,
    B97, B140, B199, B256,
    B285, B296, B311, B334,
    B337, B427, B428, B429,
    B430, C123, C128, D6; reality
    B183, B293, B296, B332,
    B456, C128; prophecy,
    mystery, vision B160, B281,
    B306, B446

Yorkshire (*see also* Haworth *and*
  the Moors)   A204, A205,

323

TITLES OF PRIMARY AND SECONDARY ITEMS

Numbers Refer to Items, Not Pages

334

337

357